Lethal Tides

ALSO BY CATHERINE MUSEMECHE

Small: Life and Death on the Front Lines of Pediatric Surgery

Hurt: The Inspiring, Untold Story of Trauma Care

MARY SEARS AND THE MARINE SCIENTISTS WHO HELPED WIN WORLD WAR II

Lethal Tides

Catherine Musemeche

WM
WILLIAM MORROW
An Imprint of HarperCollins*Publishers*

HarperCollins books may be purchased for educational, business, or sales promotional use. For information, please email the Special Markets Department at SPsales@harpercollins.com.

FIRST EDITION

Designed by Elina Cohen
Title art photo by US Navy/FPG/Getty Images
Part opener art courtesy of Shutterstock / Ann679
Map by Nick Springer, copyright © 2022 Springer Cartographics LLC

Library of Congress Cataloging-in-Publication Data has been applied for.

ISBN 978-0-06-299169-0

22 23 24 25 26 LSC 10 9 8 7 6 5 4 3 2 1

The ocean would serve neither side in the war. It would merely treat more kindly those who knew it best.

—*Columbus O'Donnell Iselin, director,*
Woods Hole Oceanographic Institution during World War II

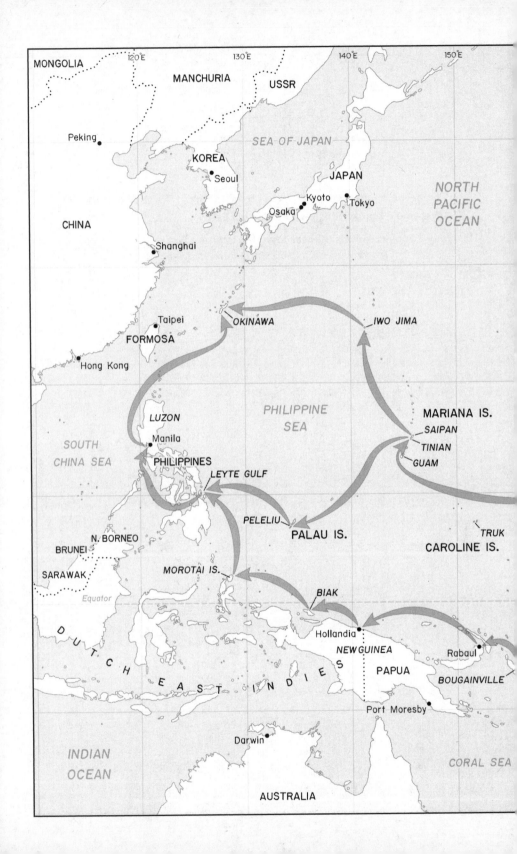

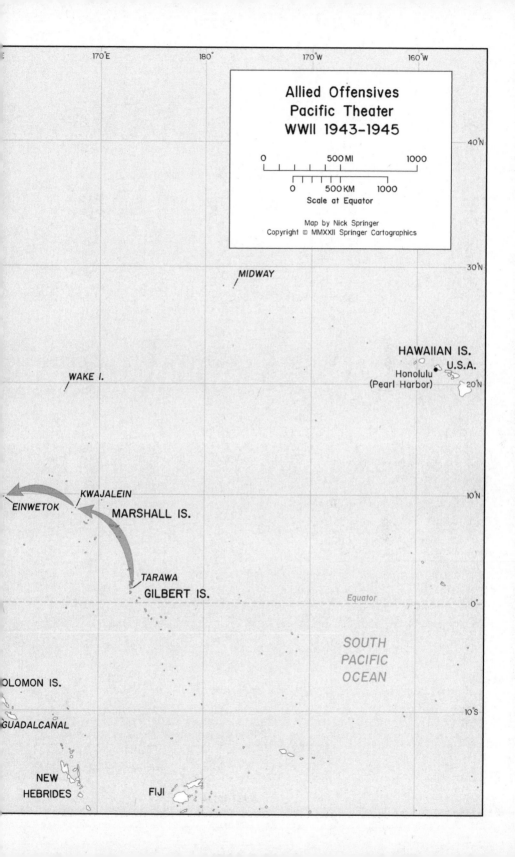

Allied Offensives
Pacific Theater
WWII 1943–1945

0   500 MI   1000

0   500 KM   1000
Scale at Equator

Map by Nick Springer
Copyright © MMXXII Springer Cartographics

40°N

30°N

MIDWAY

HAWAIIAN IS.
U.S.A.
Honolulu
(Pearl Harbor)
20°N

WAKE I.

10°N

KWAJALEIN
EINWETOK   MARSHALL IS.

TARAWA
GILBERT IS.

Equator   0°

SOUTH
PACIFIC
OCEAN

SOLOMON IS.

10°S

GUADALCANAL

NEW
HEBRIDES   FIJI

170°E   180°   170°W   160°W

Contents

Part 2: The Mission Begins

Prologue

When the United Nations deemed 1998 the International Year of the Ocean, the United States Navy sponsored a contest that would, for the first time, allow schoolchildren to propose names for a new oceanographic survey ship. They hoped it would motivate students to learn about the ocean while gaining experience with the newly popular Internet.

Second graders in Fort Worth, Texas, came up with the USNS *Blue Marble*, "because the sea is blue." A team of fifth graders in Indiana proposed the USNS *Rachel Carson*, in honor of the marine biologist and author of *Silent Spring*, who raised awareness of the dangers of chemical pesticides. A tenth-grade honors class in central Florida chose the USNS *Odysseus* as a fitting moniker in light of the Greek king's mythical seafaring adventures.

Students at Zion-Benton Township High School in Zion, Illinois, submitted the USNS *Mary Sears*. They had scoured online articles and discovered this unsung hero whose wartime reports were "critical to the survivability of U.S. submarines in World War II." Their entry made the list of ten finalists.

After evaluating sixteen hundred entries, the navy picked the USNS *Bruce Heezen*, in honor of an oceanographer who mapped ocean floors, but the Zion students' selection of the USNS *Mary Sears* stuck with

Richard Danzig, the incoming secretary of the navy. A year later, he announced that the USNS *Mary Sears* would become the navy's next oceanographic survey ship, the first survey ship named after a woman.

Up until that point, Sears's numerous contributions had been almost completely lost in the annals of war, a history that often overlooked the roles of women who served behind the scenes. One person who was not surprised to hear of the honor was Sears's half-sister, Leila Sears, who served as a WAVE in the navy's code decryption department in World War II. Leila remembered a day during the war when she delivered a stack of decrypted dispatches to Admiral Chester W. Nimitz's naval office in the Pentagon for his review and signature. While signing the reports Nimitz noticed the name tag SEARS on the young courier's uniform and asked if she was related to Lt. Mary Sears. Upon informing Nimitz that Mary was indeed her older sister, the naval commander rose from his chair, took both of her hands in his, and said, "Someday the country will learn how much it owes to your sister, Mary."

That day came on October 19, 2000, three years after Mary Sears's death, when Leila gathered with family members and friends of the naval oceanographer at Halter Marine shipyard in Pascagoula, Mississippi, to christen the USNS *Mary Sears*.

Mary Sears overcame gender, age, and rejection by the navy only to find herself in the middle of a global two-ocean war making lifesaving predictions on the eve of major battles. But this story is bigger than one woman's meritorious service to her country. It is also the story of how the nascent field of oceanography came of age and refocused its efforts to provide tools and intelligence to help win the war and how fledgling amphibious forces grew into a premier assault team. In the end, Sears, oceanography, and the navy all became intimately intertwined as they joined their efforts to forge a path to victory in the Pacific Campaign.

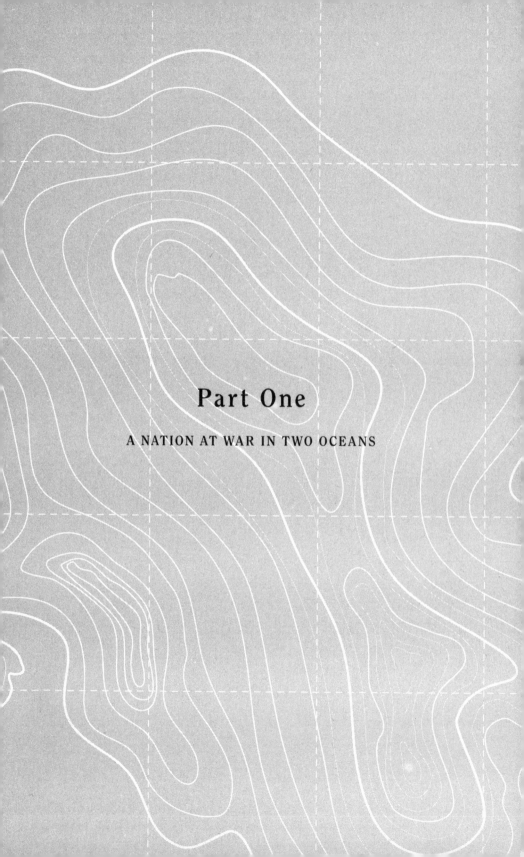

Part One

A NATION AT WAR IN TWO OCEANS

CHAPTER 1

Chasing Plankton on the Eve of the War

— Peru, 1941 —

On December 7, 1941, marine biologist Mary Sears, working in the warm waters off the western coast of South America in Pisco Bay, unfurled her plankton net from the back of the trawler *Don Jaime* and tossed it back into the swirl of an open sea. She watched as the net billowed off the stern of the boat and filled with salt water, collecting only the tiniest of organisms she had come to Peru to study. She reeled her catch back in again and carefully emptied the samples into glass jars, then marked the date and location on each one, completely immersed in the research that had brought her to this foreign land on the eve of war.

Sears had chosen a dangerous time to travel overseas. In August of 1941, when she had embarked on her voyage from Boston, Massachusetts, the United States was not yet at war, but it was close. Germany had already overpowered France and Yugoslavia; Greece had just surrendered, and the British were barely hanging on after the Battle of Britain. German U-boats had already attacked and sunk hundreds of merchant ships in the Atlantic. But even with the lurking Nazi threat, Sears wasn't about to pass up the excursion.

La Compañía Administradora del Guano of the Peruvian government had requested her expertise to solve a problem that threatened the country's guano industry, the bedrock of their economy. The supply of Peruvian guano, a lucrative resource for the country and considered some of the finest fertilizer worldwide, was under threat. Sears was one of the few people who could help save it.

When Peruvians first mined the natural fertilizer from coastal islands in the 1800s, the rich deposits were two hundred feet deep and considered so valuable that two wars broke out over who owned the islands, with Spain, Bolivia, and Chile all trying to claim them. Because of the intense extraction efforts, the guano deposits had since melted away and Peru now depended on the annual renewal of the crop.

During a normal season, the guano birds of Peru—guanay cormorants, Peruvian pelicans, and boobies—gathered by the millions to feast on anchovies produced in abundance in a narrow band of cold water along the coast. Their primary nesting grounds were the Chincha Islands, three small granite-covered islands, thirteen miles off the coast of Pisco that reeked of bitter ammonia. Native Quechuan-speaking laborers swept up the guano using shovels and large brushes and packed it into sacks for processing.

In 1939, American ornithologist William Vogt had traveled to Peru at the request of the guano company to study ways to increase production. While Vogt was working in Peru the El Niño of 1941 had hit, causing a warming of waters where the birds fed. Hundreds of thousands of birds died, crippling the guano industry. Suddenly, Vogt's mission changed. His new focus became preventing the death and possible extinction of the guano birds.

Early in the crisis Vogt deduced that the birds were dying of starvation because their primary food source, the anchovies, were disappearing from the seas with the influx of the warmer water currents. He knew that anchovies fed off of plankton, an indicator species that served as a measure of the health of marine life. He wondered if the El Niño could be affecting the lower chain of the ocean food supply and if so, what could be done about it? Vogt's area of expertise was birds, not marine life. If he was going to save the guano birds, he would have to find a marine biologist who could help explain this strange phenomenon.

Vogt's search had led him to Sears, one of the leading planktonologists in the country, at Woods Hole Oceanographic Institution in Woods Hole, Massachusetts. As someone who had already helped catalog numerous plankton collections and published extensively on the topic, Sears was exceptionally qualified to assist in analyzing the conundrum. At first Vogt collected plankton samples and shipped them to Sears in Woods Hole, but with the birds dying in greater numbers, he requested that Sears travel to Peru. If she could perform field research in Pisco Bay, collecting and analyzing anchovy and plankton specimens on-site, she might be able to expedite a possible solution.

There was an irony in Vogt's invitation to Sears. While she was an undisputed authority on plankton, she had managed to achieve this status without ever once going on an overnight seafaring expedition. At Woods Hole in Massachusetts, where Sears had trained as one of the first ten research fellows at the institution and had been a member of the staff ever since, women were not allowed to sail on the institution's research vessel *Atlantis*.

After nearly a decade as a research scientist, Sears had checked all the boxes on the way to making her mark on American oceanography except for this one, and she knew it was hurting her career. All the great oceanographers that preceded her in the field had established their reputations by going out on expeditions. They had gone for the adventure, for the thrill of exploration, but they had also gone to collect their own specimens. Being on the ship, accurately recording the location, weather, ocean temperature, and depth mattered to a scientist and affected the analysis of the data. Sailing around the world, roughing it at sea, was how the best made their marks. Being a woman had thus far kept Sears far from the action, apart from the most important activity of her career.

Relegated to shore, she had to depend on male colleagues to bring back specimens from their expeditions for her. Sears would anxiously await the return of *Atlantis* at the Woods Hole dock along with the wives welcoming back their husbands and coworkers, cheering as the men sailed triumphantly into harbor, swinging from the mast.

She would collect the crate of fresh specimens and rush back to her lab, her hope of new discoveries soaring. She would drip a few drops of seawater onto a glass slide and place it carefully under the lens of a microscope, focusing and refocusing while she looked through the eyepieces. And what she would see, or rather fail to see, would send her expectations crashing back down to earth. She would scan the slide a second time, a third time, as many times as it took to be sure, moving it back and forth across the stage. But in the end she would find only bits and pieces, fragments of a once living thing but nothing intact that she could identify and describe. The men had failed to preserve, to label, to pay attention to detail, fundamental mistakes that rendered the vast majority of the catch utterly useless. The men had failed her again.

There was no way for her to know if the carelessness was spawned by ignorance, indifference, or if the men were actively trying to sabotage her research. They might have relegated the task to some rookie grad student who didn't have a clue about how to collect marine specimens—a rookie, who, as demeaning as it was to contemplate, superseded Sears when it came to boating privileges by virtue of gender alone.

The seeker in her, that undaunted spirt that believed if you just tried hard enough you could achieve anything in this world, would work her way through each jar, hunting for some life-form that might make the exercise worthwhile. But instead of finding plankton or protozoa, she found only frustration. Thoughts of what might have been swirled in her head. *What if she were on an equal footing with the men? What if she had been able to collect for herself and apply the same exacting standards that she brought to every aspect of her studies?*

By being confined to shore, not only was Sears missing out on having acceptable material to study but she was also deprived of the stimulation of being at sea, with the waves crashing across the bow and the sea air filling her lungs. She missed the chance to help reel in the catch and the comradery that emerged from the shared tasks onboard.

Sears knew that had she been able to go to sea, her research would have been more fruitful, she too could have earned a reputation as one of oceanography's great explorers. But, as she well understood, "it was not done in my day," and as time passed the reality sunk in deeper, a scar on her psyche and soul that was etched deeper over time. She would never be able to reach the career heights that the men in her field did, even though she was at least as smart, twice as capable, and industrious beyond measure. Sears was trapped in an immutable time warp that cruelly capped her potential as a scientist.

She later admitted that the exclusion policy was "strange" and that it "ruined a lot of good ideas," but she chose to skirt the issue rather than to openly oppose it during her time at Woods Hole. Opportunities for women scientists in the 1930s were so limited that Sears had been fortunate to land any job at all. The fact that she had chosen a field where there was no demand for women made her position all the more precarious.

The prohibition on women sailing on oceanographic vessels grew out of ancient taboos that originated in myths and legends, like Homer's *Odyssey*, where, after the Trojan war, Odysseus sails home with his all-male crew. Although he encounters numerous female characters during his stops along the way, nary a one dares to set foot on his ship. Ships are where men exercise their manly skills like war mongering and fending off monsters while simultaneously battling storms and rogue waves. Allowing women on board would only distract the crew from their duties and incite the wrath of an angry sea, leading to certain misfortune. For hundreds of years sailors clung to these beliefs and preserved the all-male domain at sea even while perpetrating the striking paradox that a female body carved into the bow of a ship would bring good luck on a voyage.

But not every woman was willing to adhere to this nonsensical restriction. In the 1600s, botanist Jeanne Baret went to sea disguised as a man on a French ship slated to circumnavigate the globe. Clothed in loose-fitting pants and oversize long-sleeved shirts, the female adventurer readily adapted to her duties on board, her own shipmates never once suspecting that a woman was sharing their bathrooms and bunks. But, during a stopover in Tahiti, the local natives picked up on the fact that Baret was in fact a female and disclosed her gender. The captain could have thrown Baret off the ship but, noting that she was extremely modest, hardworking, and not particularly attractive, he allowed her to complete the voyage.

Even in modern times, long after rampant myths had been debunked, ship captains and expedition leaders in the United States adhered to the tradition of excluding females. On rare occasion, exceptions were made for the wives of expedition leaders, but certainly no unmarried women were ever permitted to sail. Illogical excuses continued to be made to justify the irrational custom. At Woods Hole, the lack of separate bathrooms for women on the research vessel, *Atlantis*, was cited to justify the discriminatory policy while, in reality, there was no actual reason why the two sexes could not share the same toilet. The separate stalls and showers aboard *Atlantis* were a luxury compared to the primitive facilities Sears was forced to use aboard the fishing boats in Peru. And as she was quick to point out, separate bathrooms or not, there was always a pail.

This unwritten policy would exist for at least another three decades in spite of an embarrassing episode in Woods Hole history in 1956 when Roberta Eike, a twenty-three-year-old graduate student from Radcliffe, "stowed away" on a five-day research cruise. When she was discovered in the bilge of the R/V (research vessel) *Caryn* the captain locked her in a cabin, turned the ship around, and returned early to port. Because her mere presence had created a crisis aboard that her professional colleagues could not conceive of managing, Eike had to pay the price.

In an article in the *Falmouth Enterprise*, the forward-thinking Eike argued in her defense that "a scientist is a scientist first and sex should have nothing to do with whether or not she qualifies for a marine expedition." Despite her sound argument and stated desire to merely collect her own specimens on the expedition, the director dismissed Eike and canceled her fellowship.

Not everyone at Woods Hole agreed with the director's actions. A group of senior scientists wrote a letter defending the young graduate student.

"It has been somewhat amusing to observe that there have been cases of men who did not want to go to sea and intentionally 'stayed away' from oceanographic cruises but here we have a woman who sincerely wanted to go to sea but had to 'stowaway' as the last resort," the letter read.

"We're in the Dark Ages about it around here. If they are competent to do the work and have a reason to go there's no reason in the sun why women can't go to sea," added oceanographer Fritz Fuglister.

"The advantages to be gained in the long run by the Institution in enabling women to go to sea greatly outweigh the disadvantages, which as usually expressed arise almost entirely from prejudice," wrote meteorologist Alfred Woodcock.

Despite the strong internal support, the policy stayed, and Eike was not reinstated.

A similar policy was in place at Scripps Institution of Oceanography in San Diego, when, at the height of the cold war in 1963, Russia was invited by the State Department to send two oceanographers on a Scripps research expedition aboard the R/V *Argo*. The Russians, who had long allowed women to perform research at sea, assigned geophysicist Elena Lubinova to make the trip. The Scripps administration was dismayed to learn that a woman had been chosen but they were in no position to incite an international incident by objecting to the Russian delegation so they allowed the female scientist to participate.

At the start of the expedition, the American crew was somewhat suspicious of the Russians, especially the female of the two, but Lubinova remained focused on her work. She diligently collaborated with her American colleagues and they eventually warmed to her presence and grew to respect her contributions.

"Notwithstanding the presence of a woman on board, we encountered no major storms . . . we hit no iceberg . . . we were not assaulted by pirates . . . the ship did not sink. . . . At Scripps, they realized that women oceanographers were not a threat," Italian oceanographer Enrico Bonatti, one of her shipmates, later wrote.

It took a visiting Russian scientist, an outsider, to break the taboo. Scripps's policy gradually gave way within the next few years.

At Woods Hole the sexist restrictions had finally been forced into extinction in 1959 when oceanographer Betty Bunce was awarded funding for an expedition for which she was to be the chief scientist. The mission faced cancellation if Bunce was not allowed to lead it, so Woods Hole, with a valued mission at risk, allowed her aboard *Atlantis*. Bunce's crew had no difficulties managing the presence of a woman and easily worked out a way to share the facilities onboard.

Once the door had opened, Bunce achieved one remarkable feat after another. She would lead expeditions all over the world, including for a portion of the National Science Foundation–sponsored International Indian Ocean Expedition. She was the first woman to dive in the *Alvin*, a deep-ocean research submarine developed at Woods Hole and the first female chief scientist in the Deep Sea Drilling Project where she mapped some of the deepest parts of the Atlantic Ocean floor.

Though the two women scientists overlapped at Woods Hole, Bunce noted that Sears was quite shy and could not be rushed into friendships. On one occasion, she stopped by Sears's office to pick up a reference book she needed to prepare for an expedition. Out of nowhere Sears broached the topic of the restrictions that her male superiors had placed on her career.

"I am so jealous of you," Sears said. "I spent all my years here wanting desperately to take my data at sea, and nobody, nobody would let me."

Conspicuously absent from the correspondence about the Eike incident is any mention of Sears, who was still on staff and a senior member of the Woods Hole Corporation. Year after year, photos of the Woods Hole trustees displayed men standing proudly in suits and ties with Sears, the sole female, standing in the middle in her dress and heels, clutching her purse.

By this time in her career, Sears had established herself as a major figure in American oceanography, but something had been lacking all those years. Her career had been held back because of her gender and the sting of being treated differently had not dissipated. For three decades, she had declined to voice her frustration in any official capacity, but she was willing to confide her feelings to a trusted female colleague, one who had overcome an obstacle that Sears could not.

• • •

The long-standing tradition of excluding women from ships had weighed on Sears as she made her decision about whether to go to Peru. With the United States on the brink of a world war it was risky to travel through the Atlantic. If her ship was attacked, she might be exposing herself to the possibility of injury or drowning. Working off the coast of Peru for six months posed hazards also. If the United States entered the war, she might be captured by enemy forces sailing those same waters, but there was another side to the coin. If she chose to play it safe and passed up this expedition, she might never get a shot at another one, at least not in the United States.

In the end, Sears told Vogt she would come to Peru to see what she could do to help. She booked her passage to Lima, packed the clothes, notebooks, nets, and jars she would need and prepared to leave. She took a steamship from New York, through hazardous waters, down the Atlantic coast, through the Panama Canal and into the Pacific, a 3,627-mile, fifteen-day journey, to Pisco Bay, Peru, the U-boats be damned.

This is how Sears found herself on board the Peruvian trawler *Don Jaime* with an all-male crew during the waning months of 1941, scooping plankton out of Pisco Bay, harvesting anchovies and performing autopsies on 3,500 fish to assess their stomach contents.

Since her arrival in Peru, Sears had been facing her own challenges aboard the guano boat, not the least of which had been finding a place to use the bathroom. On her first trip out to sea, she "suffered all day long," caught off guard by the fact that the boat used for day trips was not outfitted with a "head," the mariner's term for a toilet. When the boat returned to shore she asked Vogt how and where she was supposed to relieve herself on day trips with an all-male crew and no bathroom. Vogt made sure that in the future, Sears would have a private moment with a pail on the stern of the boat while the men shuffled up to the bow and looked the other way. On overnight trips, the crew went out on a larger boat, one equipped with a toilet housed in an electrician's closet, which Sears shared with the men without complaint from either side.

The only woman aboard quickly adapted to the austere living conditions on the guano boat. When she found out her quarters could only be reached through the men's, she resolutely climbed over sleeping deckhands to get out of her bedbug-infested bunk in the morning. She learned to sidestep the accumulated "skim," of meals prepared by a cook who used his one, grimy rag to "blow his nose, wipe down the table, and clean the dishes." She never ate down to the bottom of the plate because she knew it wasn't clean, and she drank only from the left side of the communal cup that was passed around at mealtime. Sears, who spoke several languages, even conversed in Spanish with the crew when she discovered that William Reed, the translator hired to interpret for her, spoke very little English.

The patrician New Englander, far away from the white tablecloths at the dining hall in Woods Hole, was roughing it, her accommodations in no way tailored for comfort, but, whatever the hardships, she was willing to put up with them. Though Sears had scarcely imagined just how primitive conditions would be, she hadn't come to Peru expecting a luxury cruise. She had made the journey seeking acceptance and opportunity, both of which the Peruvians offered in abundance, a distinctly receptive attitude in marked contrast to that of her male peers in the United States.

During her time at sea, Sears collected plankton samples for later study, assessed ocean transparency with a Secchi disk and recorded the water temperature and depth. She measured hundreds of anchovies from snout to tail fin and the ovaries of the female, which she found slender and immature. She slit open the stomachs of tuna, bonito, and other fish to see what they had been feeding on and recorded her findings in her cruise book. She scribbled descriptions of whales, sharks, swordfish, tuna, pelicans, gray gulls, and guanays and got on and off of at least four boats. She even kept an eye on the birds that the guano industry depended on, noting on October 24, 1941, "Birds coming in from the North about 7:30 a.m. Does this foreshadow warm water from the North?"

Approximately two months into her excursion she apparently craved a drink, noting, "Unfortunately only alcohol for preservation!" She tolerated heavy winds and rough seas, observing on one occasion, "Quite a sea by the time we came to this station." One harrowing night, as the *Pacific Queen* was returning to Chincha Norte, it veered off course, finally landing at midnight at a port seventy-eight miles south of the intended destination. The ship righted its course but did not dock at its home pier until 8:00 a.m. the next morning.

Through it all, Sears proved herself quite capable of performing the rigors of field research, including bringing along her own winch to haul in the nets she used to collect plankton. On one occasion a towline attached to her net—one of only two she had brought—broke. Rather than lose her precious net, Sears demonstrated her grit by jumping overboard to retrieve it, her action alarming the men on board who thought she had fallen over by accident. But Sears knew exactly what she was doing. As a seasoned swimmer, she figured she was the best person to rescue the valuable equipment. She also knew that most of the men on board couldn't swim and she wouldn't dream of asking them to do anything that would put them in harm's way.

While Sears combed the waters off the coast of Peru on December 7, 1941, President Franklin D. Roosevelt sorted stamps for his collection in his private study at the White House, savoring a few moments of calm in what had otherwise been a hectic week. Six days earlier the president had learned through an intercepted diplomatic communication, that the Japanese were moving massive numbers of troops to Indochina. This same week, Japanese diplomats were expected in Washington, D.C., for ongoing talks about their expansion into China, a move the United States, along with the British and the Dutch, viewed as a hostile invasion and countered with an oil embargo. Roosevelt had asked Secretary of State Cordell Hull to request that the Japanese "inquire at once" of their government exactly what their intentions were in the region.

He was still waiting for an answer when the phone rang. It was the secretary of the navy, Frank Knox, telling Roosevelt that Pearl Harbor was under attack.

"No!" Roosevelt yelled into the phone.

In the midst of ongoing negotiations, the president had been duped at the expense of thousands of lives and the viability of the Pacific Fleet. Roosevelt knew the Japanese had been amassing warships for weeks to invade a target somewhere in the Pacific. He feared it might be in the Philippines, Burma, or Malaya but he had no clue that Hawaii would be the target or that the Japanese were even capable of pulling off an attack from four thousand miles away.

W. J. Holmes, assigned to the Fourteenth Naval District's Combat Intelligence Unit at Pearl Harbor, was even closer to the action, but he too was fooled. Holmes was at home in bed when the bombs began to drop on the morning of December 7, 1941. He didn't know the attack was coming either. When his commanding officer summoned Holmes to return to the base, he thought it was for a practice drill, but, as he drove to work, a pillar of black smoke rising above the cane fields in the distance changed his mind, then came a trickle of cars leaving Pearl Harbor carrying blood-spattered passengers, victims of strafing by Japanese fighter planes.

Holmes arrived at the Navy Yard at 9:00 a.m., where he was met by a torrent of bullets and bombs. He immediately hurried to the safety of the basement of the Administration Building where he worked. Holmes's intelligence unit covered the Pacific area, interpreting radio dispatches intercepted from the Japanese and reviewing aerial reconnaissance photos to plot their ship movements. There had been a marked increase in both radio and ship traffic during November, movements that suggested that the Japanese Navy was gathering in the Marshall Islands and planning to attack either the Dutch East Indies or the Philippines but no one suspected an attack on Pearl Harbor was imminent.

The intelligence the unit had gathered was accurate, but the conclusions they reached were not. Their focus on the Marshall Island operation had diverted them from detecting a second task force being amassed in the Kuril Islands, supplied by six Japanese aircraft carriers from which 353 enemy aircraft would take off and head toward Pearl Harbor. Even Holmes's intelligence unit, located at Pearl Harbor, tasked with supporting Pacific naval operations and protecting the fleet docked there, had failed to predict the bombing of Pearl Harbor.

Holmes huddled with the other intelligence officers, listening to the carnage taking place right outside their door. When the attack abated, he finally left the basement at around noon and got his first look at the decimated harbor.

"It was dense with smoke, obscuring details, but the extent of disaster was apparent. The *Oklahoma*'s bottom bulged obscenely above the oily water. The *Arizona*'s masts were cocked at a crazy angle above a pall of smoke. The *West Virginia* was burning furiously. The *Nevada* was aground at Hospital Point. For the moment, no guns were firing," Holmes later wrote.

The bodies of 1,102 sailors who were aboard the *Arizona* when it exploded and sank would soon rest at the bottom of Pearl Harbor.

As the news of Pearl Harbor spread across the country—the killing of 2,403 Americans, the wounding of 1,178 more, and the destruction of a swath of the Pacific Fleet along with a bevy of American fighter planes—word of more attacks started coming in. Over the next seven hours, in a series of simultaneous attacks, Japanese aircraft flew across the Pacific Ocean, bombed American bases in the Philippines and attacked Thailand, Singapore, and Malaya. A nation the size of California had not only kicked the United States in the teeth but also had launched an imperialist quest to control all of Southeast Asia and was well on its way to doing so.

Roosevelt addressed the nation and Congress the next day, decrying the unwarranted aggression that left no choice but to declare war on Japan twenty-seven hours after the first bombs had fallen in Hawaii. A stunned American military, with half of its navy at the bottom of the ocean and the other half reeling from the devastation, was left with no option but to deploy its depleted resources to multiple battlefronts around the globe.

The Japanese had forced the Americans to act, but, as Roosevelt would admit only to his wife, Eleanor, he really didn't know how the navy would go about fighting across two oceans with such a severe shortage of ships.

He could only hope to stave off disaster while waiting for American ship-builders to produce more.

Half a world away, Sears would not hear the news of Pearl Harbor until two days later when a supply boat came out from the mainland to the guano boat. She missed the urgent news bulletins that interrupted the regular Sunday afternoon programming and jolted the American public into the stark new reality of a nation at war. She did not hear the president's address to Congress the next day that reached sixty million people, the largest audience in the history of radio.

She escaped the desperate hoarding of household goods, the clearing of shelves at the grocery stores, and the sight of young men swarming into military recruitment centers, their queues spilling out onto side-walks and wrapping around the block. She did not feel the fear that gripped Americans during those first few days, wondering where the next attack would hit. *Would the Japanese bomb the nation's capital? Would they send planes to the West Coast? Now that they were in this war, how bad were things going to get before they got better?* Questions about the future abounded, but no one could answer them.

When the news finally reached Sears on the boat three hundred miles offshore, it unnerved her. Her initial fears reemerged. She started to have second thoughts. Trawling around the Pacific Ocean with her country now at war might actually be too risky, no matter the gains to be had. Enemy submarines could very well be patrolling Pacific waters nearby. Their boat could be torpedoed. She couldn't help but wonder if it would be prudent to leave early to get back to the safe shores of the United States. As she pondered the possibility of these new invisible dangers, she urged the crew to fly the Peruvian flag, especially at night, lest the boat be mis-taken for an American vessel and blown to bits.

Despite the inherent danger of being offshore overseas, Sears decided to finish her research project. Her younger brothers had vision problems and would be exempt from military service. There was no need to rush back to the United States to send them off. Nor was she worried about seeing her sisters off to war, because in 1941, women weren't allowed to serve. She probably wasn't needed at Woods Hole either. Columbus Iselin, the director, had been recruiting male scientists to head up all the wartime research projects since before the war began. Sears wasn't sure what position she would fill even when she did return.

She stayed another three months and finished what she'd started.

When the "last American tourist to Machu Picchu," as Sears dubbed herself, finally boarded a plane back to the United States, she couldn't help but feel a sense of pride in what she'd accomplished in her six months at sea. She had measured anchovy gonads, autopsied fish, collected plankton specimens, and filled her notebook with observations. The only conclusion she could reach early on was that the spawning period for the anchovies had been interrupted during the "crash" period. Any further determinations would have to wait until she had studied her plankton specimens.

More importantly to Sears though was what she had proven to herself and to anyone else who dared to question her skills. A woman could hold her own on a multiday expedition, even one that took place entirely in another country during wartime, alongside a crew with whom she shared a bathroom but not a common language. She had found a way to get her fieldwork done and withstood the primitive conditions aboard ship.

She had carefully packed and crated her plankton specimens for shipment, intending to spend many hours at the microscope studying them, describing their distinct colors and unique anatomical details, and then she would write up her findings for publication. As Sears completed the last entries in her cruise book in early 1942, she could not have known that by the time the crates arrived at Woods Hole, the world and her position in it would have changed dramatically. The unpacking of her jars would wait a very long time, until she had finished playing her role in fighting a world war.

CHAPTER 2

Choosing an Unlikely Path

— Wayland, Massachusetts, 1905 —

Mary Sears was born in Wayland, Massachusetts, with the expectation that she would blossom into a debutante, not a scientist, but fate redrew that original blueprint time and again, first by tragedy, later by education, and, quite unexpectedly, by the life-changing impact of a world war. Wayland, formerly East Sudbury, is located about eighteen miles west of Boston. Established in the 1600s as a communal farm system, the town grew out of an initial settlement of five square miles of verdant pastures nourished by a nearby river. Settlers contributed to the thriving community by farming, raising dairy cows, and providing services such as smithing or milling. In the latter half of the nineteenth century, the acres of communal farmlands evolved into havens for wealthy businessmen and manufacturers from Boston who established estates to escape the city.

The expanding population brought Sears's great-grandfather, Edmund Hamilton Sears, a poet and preacher, to Wayland in 1839. The Harvard Divinity School graduate came to take over the ministry of First Parish, a Unitarian church. A staunch abolitionist, he supported the Underground Railroad to aid runaway slaves. He also believed in the equality of men and women, a subject he returned to often in his Sunday sermons.

The Reverend Sears also wrote hymns—500 of them. Inspired by the end of the Mexican-American War in 1849 he wrote one of his most famous hymns, "It Came Upon the Midnight Clear." Initially sung at a First Parish Sunday school celebration, the hymn was later recast as a Christmas carol that would come to be known all across America. Because of this lineage, the Sears name was well known throughout the area for several generations preceding Mary Sears's birth.

Sears's maternal ancestors came to Wayland a little later when her grandfather, Edwin Buckingham, remodeled a one hundred fifty-year-old farmhouse as a birthday present for his wife, the former Mary E. Cutting. It became a summer home for the Boston family and would come to be known as "the famous old Buckingham place."

As described in a gossip column in the *Boston Globe* in 1905, the "splendidly preserved," three-story house was "shaded by very large and shapely elm trees, among the finest in the state" and overlooked a "beautiful sheet of water covering eighty acres surrounded by oak, maple and birch tree groves." Sears's mother Leslie and her aunt, Marian, became accomplished equestrians who rode throughout the countryside. During their Wayland summers they attended concerts and the theater and lived the carefree life enjoyed by debutantes of the day.

The girls' blissful existence was derailed in 1896 when they lost both parents within a year. Their father succumbed first to typhoid, and their grieving mother perished three months later from pneumonia. Thirteen-year-old Leslie and seventeen-year-old Marian were taken in by their uncle, Alfred Wayland Cutting, who also lived in Wayland. Cutting was an accomplished nature photographer and local historian, who documented the pastoral surroundings and wildlife of Wayland. His photos and writings are now housed at the Wayland Historical Society.

Several years after the death of their parents, the "Mistresses Buckingham," as they were referred to in the Boston society pages, traveled to Europe with a chaperone, where they spent over two years touring the Continent. Upon returning to the United States, they met two handsome brothers from Boston, Francis and Edmund Sears. Leslie married first, to the dashing Harvard graduate Edmund, a blueblood businessman listed on the *Social Register* of Boston. He thrived in the manufacturing business and later cofounded the American Felt and Belting Company of Boston.

Their storybook wedding took place at First Parish in Wayland, where Edmund's grandfather and namesake had once been the pastor. A cadre of "society people" traveled from Boston for the special occasion in reserved passenger cars that had been added to the train, underscoring the significance of the event. Edmund and Leslie exited the reception in dramatic fashion by riding off into the sunset on horseback.

They enjoyed a luxurious three-month honeymoon in Europe, including a tour of Greece on horseback. When the couple returned, they split their time between "the old Buckingham place" and their home in Boston. A year after their marriage, Leslie's sister, Marian, married Edmund's brother, Francis Sears. The two couples shared the Buckingham summer house in Wayland until their expanding households outgrew the space. Francis and Marian Sears then moved into a home of their own in Wayland.

Mary, the firstborn, arrived on July 18, 1905. She was christened without a middle name, with the expectation that she would follow her mother's path and marry and her maiden name would become her middle name. Her brother, Edmund (Ned), arrived two years later and sister, Katherine (Kit), two years after that.

The setting of the childhood home was ideal in many ways. The Wayland farm had a large barn that allowed the family to keep two ponies and Edmund's prize herd of Guernsey cows. The children had a horse-drawn carriage that they took out on nearby country roads. Their property abutted lush Heard Pond, allowing Sears the opportunity to spend summer days swimming and exploring. She collected plants for her terrarium in the bogs nearby and naturally found a good many creatures too, turtles being her favorites. Like many naturalists of the day, her long hours spent outdoors as a child no doubt planted the seed for her later interest in studying zoology and collecting marine specimens.

In an unfortunate repeat of history, Sears's idyllic upbringing was also interrupted by tragedy. In 1911 her mother, Leslie, at just twenty-eight years old suddenly took ill with an aggressive case of anterior poliomyelitis. The resulting paralysis rapidly overwhelmed her respiratory system, and within a week she was dead, leaving behind the six-year-old Mary, four-year-old Ned, and two-year-old Kit. To make matters worse, Sears's father became "despondent" after the abrupt loss of his true love, and "for a while traveled a great deal" in Europe in the aftermath.

The historical record is unclear on exactly how old Sears was when her father left or how much time Edmund spent out of the country during Mary's childhood. During his absence the children were left in the care of a patchwork ensemble of domestic help, part-time nannies, relatives, and family friends. On at least one trip, he returned to the United States from Italy in 1915 when she was nine, though he left again a year later to travel to England on business. Edmund provided for the family from a distance during this unsettled time but left it to others to take care of their daily needs.

It is difficult to imagine how Sears, the oldest, dealt with her father's absence, though she clearly felt it, saying more than once, "Father forgot to send us to school." From this statement alone one gleans that life had not carried on in any normal fashion while he was away. Even though she was quite young, the sudden parental void forced Sears to grow up in a hurry. Showing a glimmer of the qualities that would later ensure her success in life, she took her new responsibilities to heart and helped look after her brother and sister to the best of her precocious ability.

Thankfully, a silver lining to the domestic upheaval emerged in the presence of Miss Sophie Bennett who had grown up in Wayland and be-friended Sears's mother. Bennett became one of the cadre who looked after the children while Edmund was in Europe. Fortuitously, Bennett, a graduate of Radcliffe College and Columbia University's Teachers College, taught full-time at the Winsor School, one of only two private schools for girls in Boston.

Mary Picard Winsor had opened her first neighborhood school in 1886 for grades five through twelve, with the goal of preparing girls to become self-supporting women. She truly believed in this radical concept, as her own mother had lost both parents early, forcing her to find employment as a schoolteacher. Winsor sought to create a personalized, nurturing environment, first in a drafty house in Boston's Back Bay neighborhood and later in the larger "new school" outfitted with state-of-the-art science laboratories, music and art rooms. The prestigious Winsor School developed a reputation for academic excellence and the ability to instill "the competence and confidence necessary to be lifelong learners and strong, courageous women."

In 1915, the ten-year-old Mary Sears enrolled in the Winsor School, where Bennett was her fifth-grade homeroom teacher. The shy little girl from the rural environs of Wayland rode the morning train into Boston, where she rubbed elbows with the cultured elite of Boston. She had some catching up to do at the highly competitive Winsor and put in extra hours to manage the broad but rigorous curriculum. In the eighth grade, for example, Sears studied grammar, composition, literature, history, French, Latin, algebra, cooking, drawing, singing, and gym.

The Winsor School opened up a whole new world for Sears, one in which women were encouraged to attend college. She met alumnae who had eschewed the marriage track and sought careers in male-dominated professions like law and medicine. The Winsor curriculum ventured beyond the basics to include course offerings that prepared young ladies for college, with the expectation that many would apply.

Sears attended the new state-of-the-art campus built in the Lockwood area in 1910, an embodiment of Winsor's motto "sound mind in sound body." The three-story building included a gymnasium and an indoor pool with abundant surrounding fields for team sports. Sears joined the hockey, baseball, and basketball teams, thriving on the opportunities to play with children her own age and launching what would become a life-long obsession with fitness.

Sears's years at Winsor from fifth grade through high school, 1915 to 1923, were times of great societal change. During World War I, fifty-eight Winsor graduates served overseas in Red Cross hospitals helping to care for the wounded. One even drove an ambulance to the war front in France. When the women returned home, they published *The Overseas War Record on the Winsor School, 1914–1919*, describing the dates and locations of their service. Sears and the other Winsor students who were collecting clothing and funds for war relief were fully aware that women had begun to take on new roles by seizing the initiative to provide overseas war relief.

During those formative eight years, the young Sears saw women advance in other major ways. She was fifteen when the Nineteenth Amendment passed in 1920, granting women the right to vote. Though Winsor took no official position, Sears was exposed to teachers and alumnae who supported the suffrage movement. With women gaining fundamental rights and the plethora of driven role models close at hand, all things seemed possible to Sears as she looked to the future.

When Edmund Sears returned from Europe in 1915, he must have noticed Bennett's devotion to his children. He began "to court" Bennett, as Sears later recalled, and invited her to the family home in Wayland to spend time with the children and picnic on Heard Pond. Two years later her father and Bennett entrusted Sears first with the "secret" that they planned to marry, as she was especially close to her future stepmother. Bennett certainly had different aspirations for herself and her adopted family than Sears's mother had, but Sears adored her and could not have wished for a more ideal substitute.

While her grades were consistently average at Winsor, Sears held her own, performing best in the study of Greek, a subject she loved. Nothing in her course selection indicated an interest or aptitude for science. "Mary Sears is a fine girl, upright, responsible and loyal. She is a steady, industrious student who is constantly developing more intellectual power as she grows older," wrote Headmistress Katharine Ford for Sears's application to Radcliffe. Even at a young age, what Sears lacked in academic achievement she more than made up for in character. With the death of her mother and absence of her father, Sears had been thrust into the role of the hero child, maintaining a steady presence for her younger siblings.

The 1923 edition of the student yearbook, *The Lantern*, recognized Sears as "the future leader of the farm bloc in Congress." Evidently, her rural upbringing along with her father's herd of cows had cast her as a knowledgeable future farmer. She was also slotted as "the most conscientious girl in class," because she took her knitting to basketball practice so as not to waste time while she sat the bench. Between her need to study long hours to catch up at school, her commitment to team sports, and her responsibilities at home, there was little time to goof off or daydream.

She was also described as "reserved," a trait she would be known for the rest of her life. The yearbook duly noted that "her family depend on her a great deal to look after her brothers and sisters," duties that grew as the family expanded with the birth of three half-siblings—John, Leila, and Elisabeth.

By all accounts the blended family was a happy one that enjoyed indulging in the arts. Bennett, a concert violinist, would join with Edmund on the piano to play tunes for the children. Eventually both of Sears's brothers also began to play the piano with her youngest brother, John, maturing into an accomplished musician. Bennett also had a strong interest in the works of Shakespeare and started a Shakespeare club, inviting friends over to read the plays aloud.

Edmund Sears enjoyed considerable success in the wool business however during World War I, Willett, Sears and Company suffered severe financial losses. Willett ultimately sued his bankers, a case that would take years to resolve. In the meantime, updates were widely published in the newspapers. Although Edmund had left the company earlier, the publicity was a source of embarrassment for someone of his social standing.

In a move reminiscent of his departure after his first wife's death, Edmund decided once again to decamp to Europe, but this time he invited Mary to join him for a grand tour of England, France, Italy, and Belgium. In her passport photo, the sixteen-year-old Sears, bearing a strong resemblance to her mother, looks into the camera, serious and unsmiling, her eyes set within a smooth round face framed by dark hair.

Sears enjoyed the months-long tour and saw a great many sights, but the reason the trip had come about was inescapable. Even though her father was not at fault, he had been dragged into a financial scandal that threatened his livelihood. She might not have openly discussed this misfortune, but the lesson was driven home once again. The only person she could truly rely on in this world was herself. When they returned,

Edmund became a director at a textile company and Sears returned to Winsor, a bit wiser and more worldly than when she had left.

When the time came for Sears to choose a college, Bennett steered her stepdaughter toward her alma mater, Radcliffe. A long line of Sears men had attended Harvard, from Sears's great-grandfather to her father. While she could not enjoy the same male privilege of attending the most prestigious university in the nation, she could be proud of having been accepted to "the Harvard Annex." Radcliffe women had to be smart, not only to gain admission but also to survive the rigors of what was, essentially, a Harvard education under the Radcliffe name. They took the same entrance exams as their male counterparts and were allowed to enroll in many of the same courses as the men, although they were taught separately by Harvard professors who walked over to the Radcliffe campus.

Sears attended Radcliffe College from 1923 to 1929, a time when the general public viewed the collegiate woman as a societal oddity at best and at worst as a threat to the American family. This was especially true of women attending one of the Seven Sisters colleges in the Northeast, which were labeled "spinster factories." Stereotypes abounded for the women-only schools—Wellesley enrolled debutantes; Mount Holyoke attracted the prim and proper; Radcliffe students were unattractive with big brains. The stigma of the bookish, socially awkward female with stringy hair and thick glasses would hover over Radcliffe for decades and invite critiques from a host of commentators.

In a 1926 issue of *Harper's Monthly*, R. Le Clerc Phillips openly contemplated whether women were "encouraged to go to college because they are ugly . . . or whether they become plain and unattractive as a result of hard study." Students were blamed for not paying more attention to their appearances while the faculty were cited as poor role models in these "Adamless Edens."

Worried that the negative portrayal of students at women's colleges threatened both enrollments and endowments, the Radcliffe administration devised a plan to combat the negative press. The Radcliffe Publicity

Department formed a press board to place articles in Boston newspapers that would craft a more positive image of the "Cliffies." In 1929, articles appeared that shined a spotlight on the "pretty girls" at Radcliffe who wore stylish yet practical attire. Articles on the fashion sense of Radcliffe women appeared so often that within a couple of years, the Radcliffe imprimatur was being used to market sweaters, skirts, and saddle shoes.

That a publicity campaign had to be launched to broadcast the message that women could be both attractive and smart is telling for the times in which Sears attended. It wasn't enough that she had been able to get into an academically superior college; she still wasn't treated with the same respect as her male counterparts. It wouldn't be enough that she excelled in her studies and earned a doctorate. Because she was a woman, Sears would have to endure an added layer of scrutiny her entire career no matter what her accomplishments.

Sears did not have access to the superior libraries at Harvard, the museums, the Harvard pool or gym, or even the best dormitories. Because she was barred from attending classes with the men, she missed out on some course offerings. She was discovering there was a wider world beyond the boundaries of the Radcliffe campus, one ruled by the patriarchy where Sears would always be an "other."

Sears was fortunate that her undergraduate years overlapped with the arrival of Ada Comstock from Smith College in 1923 as the incoming president of Radcliffe. Comstock was a strong advocate for the higher education of women, a person who "radiated strength and decisiveness," and served as a source of inspiration for her students. Even though at the time of Comstock's arrival, Harvard's male faculty would still walk across the courtyard to repeat their lectures to the women, she would eventually change this policy. It took her another twenty years, long after Sears finished her doctorate, but Comstock finally secured the joint instruction of students and expanded women's access to the full Harvard course catalog. Other restrictions on Harvard resources would continue well into the 1960s.

When Sears expressed her intention to major in Greek, as her father had at Harvard, her stepmother urged Sears to consider other options.

She suggested that Sears choose her classes not by subject but by the quality of the professor and to challenge herself with courses outside the traditional liberal arts path favored by women.

The prominent zoologist George Howard Parker, who specialized in the anatomy of fish and the sense organs of crustacea, had a reputation as an excellent lecturer, so Sears enrolled in his class. "I was hooked," Sears later wrote about her first biology course with Parker. After her first year, Sears dove headlong into the sciences, taking four botany courses, four zoology courses, Greek, and German over the next two years.

During a summer break from Radcliffe Sears traveled to Bermuda, a popular destination for American tourists, with her father and step-mother. Sears had enrolled in a Harvard-sponsored program at the Bermuda Biological Station, which welcomed female scholars. With its many islands, Bermuda was an ideal site for studying marine biology and the surrounding coral reefs. Sears returned to Radcliffe armed with the knowledge that there was at least one place that welcomed women inter-ested in the sciences and if there was one there had to be more.

She grew into a strong, broad-shouldered young woman who made time for the intramural hockey team, where she enjoyed competing amid the comradery of female teammates. She also made lifelong friends, in-cluding Alice Beale, who would later become her roommate in graduate school. By her senior year she was taking almost all zoology courses, making straight A's, and spending most of her time studying or in the laboratory. Despite her middling performance at Winsor, when she had turned her path toward science she had found her calling and excelled.

Sears was sure she wanted to keep studying zoology after she gradu-ated. She would apply to graduate school and go as far as she could go in the field. She wasn't sure what shape that would take, but she didn't need to know. Life had already taught the budding scientist that those who made plans would likely have them interrupted by tragedy or misfortune. She would learn all she could about the science of animals and let the future find her.

CHAPTER 3

Finding a Mentor Fosters a Career

— Boston, 1926 —

I was a victim of happenstance," Sears wrote in later years "Nothing in my life was ever planned."

The "happenstance" that definitively mapped the trajectory of Sears's career was crossing paths with Dr. Henry Bryant Bigelow in 1926 on the fifth floor of Harvard's Museum of Comparative Zoology when she was a junior at Radcliffe. As a female, Sears was relegated to the Radcliffe Room, a converted storage room at the museum. Elizabeth Cary Agassiz, the first president of Radcliffe, had negotiated the use of this space for her female students in 1894 when Harvard's libraries and museums were restricted to men only. As a naturalist herself, and the widow of Harvard professor and explorer Louis Agassiz, who had founded the museum, Elizabeth well knew how important it was for the women to have at least some sliver of access to the vaunted collection.

Thirty years after Elizabeth Cary Agassiz claimed the storage room for her female students, the environment at the museum remained less than welcoming. To get to the closest bathrooms for women, Sears had to either walk down four flights of stairs and back up two flights to galleries open to the public or finagle a lock one floor below that opened the door to the cleaning ladies' facility. The women's cramped, poorly lit space, tucked under the building's eaves and sandwiched in between storage areas, was hardly ideal when a full class gathered for a lab or lecture. Still, the arrangement allowed the women access to the world-class collection of zoological specimens and the expensive microscopes needed to examine them.

The tiny room had a window that provided a view to how the male students spent their days. Sears could see them, laughing and slapping one another on the backs, going in and out of a much larger, well-lit room with huge oak desks that allowed them to spread out their specimen jars and notebooks. She also had a clear view of a bathroom located conveniently across the hall; the door neatly stenciled with the word MEN.

Sears could also see into a room across from hers where a bespectacled, white-haired man "hidden away among the miles of specimen cabinets," worked. Henry Bryant Bigelow spent hours alone, bent over "a very primitive optical set-up," squinting at the contents of what looked like jars of curdled tomato soup. But the telltale smell of formalin fumes wafting through the air suggested that it was not lunch he was peering at but zoologic specimens.

Years later Sears would realize that the "soup" Bigelow was so intently examining "must have been just a good catch of planktonic copepods," microscopic sea animals that float in the sea, waiting to be gobbled up by fish higher up the food chain. Bigelow had been checking his specimens one last time as he corrected his final proof of *Plankton of the Offshore Waters of the Gulf of Maine*, a 509-page tome, published by the United States Fishery Bureau in 1926. Bigelow and his team had performed 10,116 net hauls to sample marine life in the Gulf of Maine from 1912 to 1924 and set one thousand drift bottles afloat to measure the currents. No other body of water had ever been so thoroughly studied. Bigelow's orchestration of the feat established him as one of three preeminent oceanographers in the United States and, according to Sears, the only one versed in the full spectrum of physical and biological oceanography.

Bigelow had found his way to oceanography at a time when the field had yet to be formally recognized or named. Born in Boston in 1879, he had spent summers at Cohasset on Massachusetts Bay sailing, rowing, and fishing. He'd even monetized his love of the sea when his father, a banker, urged his sons to earn their own pocket money. Bigelow and his older brother started taking out a seventeen-foot sailboat to trap lobsters to sell to the local fish market.

"There was a great deal of labor involved," Bigelow later wrote. "The 'Shrimp' was propelled by sails when there was a breeze, or by a long sculling oar over the stern when it was calm. We also had to haul our pots by hand."

Bigelow continued to hone his outdoor skills, fishing for trout in Scotland, shooting plover on Prince Edward Island, and camping on the shores of Spednic Lake, New Brunswick, with a member of the Passamaquoddy tribe, where he shot ducks, hunted deer, and trapped muskrats. As he continued to engage in these traditionally masculine pursuits, Bigelow also picked up skills along the way that would serve him well in his future endeavors on the water.

After Bigelow graduated from Milton Academy early, he enrolled for a semester at the Boston Natural History Museum. Studying under the noted paleontologist Alpheus Hyatt, Bigelow was excited to learn that he could merge his passion for the outdoors with science and become a naturalist. With his career path starting to take shape, Bigelow enrolled at Harvard the next year, excited to begin his study of natural history in earnest.

During his junior year, he was invited to join an expedition in 1900 led by two Harvard professors to study the Labrador region in Newfoundland. His first scientific expedition yielded a publication on the birds of the northeastern coast of Labrador and the burning desire to go on another. The next chance came during his senior year when he heard that Harvard zoologist Alexander Agassiz, son of the famous naturalist Louis Agassiz, was planning an expedition to the Maldives Islands, an archipelago a thousand miles southwest of India in the Indian Ocean. Through their expeditions, Agassiz and his father, equal parts explorers and scientists, had laid the groundwork for the future field of oceanography that concentrated on the characteristics of the oceans and their inhabitants.

Agassiz agreed to take Bigelow along, and showed him a side of science that he had never before experienced.

"We had a water-glass with us, and what we saw through it was a revelation to me which I have never forgotten. Through the glass the bottom at six fathoms looked hardly that many feet below us, and we could see the outlines and the colors of the corals perfectly distinctly. Schools of brilliant red, blue, green, yellow and golden fishes swarmed among the branches of the corals or hung, motionless, beside the latter."

Agassiz trained Bigelow to be a field researcher and schooled him in the exacting nature of taxonomy as they collected and cataloged jellyfish. Thus began a friendship that would endure until Agassiz's death a decade later. The close association would not only shape Bigelow's career but also all of American oceanography. Bigelow had found his vocation—a life spent studying the sea.

While Sears was spying on Bigelow from her perch in the Radcliffe Room, he must have noticed her too. With her straight, chin-length hair, wire-framed glasses, and a distinct preference for tailored blouses and skirts over dresses, Sears looked the part of the studious female. One day Bigelow greeted her on the stairs and asked if she would be interested in a job as his research assistant. He needed help identifying plankton specimens he had collected the previous summer in Monterey Bay off the coast of California. She needn't worry if she knew nothing about the species. They would work side by side and he would teach her everything she needed to know about marine biology.

Bigelow's offer caught Sears by surprise but flattered her beyond her wildest dreams. She had never imagined that a Harvard professor would seek her out to be his research assistant, particularly one as prominent as Bigelow. As much as she wanted to leap at the opportunity, she had to be honest with him. Much of her time was already committed to finishing her thesis for her undergraduate degree in zoology, making a full-time job unrealistic for the rest of the year. The only way she could accept the opportunity was if he allowed her to share the job with her study partner, Alice Beale. Bigelow readily agreed to the condition.

"We learned a lot that winter," Sears recalled. They sat motionless for hours at a stretch staring into the twin eyepieces of a microscope, sketching, identifying, labeling, and cataloging specimens. Working one-on-one with Bigelow afforded the young biologist access to "an education not otherwise to be had at Radcliffe—or even at Harvard." It was as if she had her own private tutor in oceanography from "the only person who was *ever* competent to write about all aspects of oceanography . . . not only from the United States but also from Europe."

And Bigelow had found the perfect person—a detail-oriented assistant who could be trusted to do the job the right way even when he wasn't there.

Bigelow needed an assistant because he was busy preparing a report at the behest of zoologist Frank R. Lillie, the chairman of the National Academy of Sciences Committee on Oceanography. Lillie, the former director of the Marine Biological Laboratory, was trying to procure funding for a major oceanographic center on the East Coast that would be on par with the best around the world.

Even though the Marine Biological Laboratory and the United States Bureau of Fisheries were already located at Woods Hole, neither was in the business of building a formal program to explore all branches of oceanography. Lillie wanted Bigelow, the biggest name in oceanography, to write the proposal detailing all the ways oceanography could benefit the country. Bigelow agreed to spend a year compiling the report with input from scientists across the country and from around the world, but he needed Sears to free him up to work on it.

"We could hear Dr. Bigelow dictating his report and we could hear his conferences with the other occupants of the room: William C. Schroeder of the then U.S. Fish Commission was helping Dr. Bigelow revise the volume, *Fishes of the Gulf of Maine* and the Ice Observation [officers] of the U.S. Coast Guard were working on a report of ice conditions off the east coast from Labrador to Georges Bank," Sears recounted. "Too, over the years that I worked in that room there was a procession of distinguished European oceanographers—Professor Johan Hjort, a fisheries scientist, Professor Bjorn Helland-Hansen, a Norwegian oceanographer, Dr. Edouard Le Danoise, a French marine zoologist, Professor H. H. Gran, a Norwegian planktonologist, and many others."

Watching Bigelow interact with a veritable parade of the "Who's Who of International Oceanography," and listening in on his discussions with these learned men one can easily see how Sears concluded, "In short, he was a one-man task force in oceanography operating off our east coast." This experience would leave an indelible mark on her career, teaching her the value of international collaboration and how to foster her own world-wide network of colleagues.

Sears finished her degree in zoology in 1927, graduating *magna cum laude* and was elected to Phi Beta Kappa. She entered the graduate school of zoology, intent on specializing in frogs and salamanders and continued her association with Bigelow. Sears must have known it would be difficult to carve out a niche as a woman in oceanography but Bigelow's passion for plankton—the tiny colorful undersea creatures that the marine food chain depended on—had spilled over to Sears too.

As a grad student, her days were full of science, attending classes at Radcliffe in the mornings and working with Bigelow at the Museum of Comparative Zoology in the afternoons. When Bigelow decamped to the Marine Biological Laboratory (MBL) to spend the summers in Woods Hole, Sears went with him, occasionally accompanied by Alice Beale, her friend from Radcliffe, who would tag along. She roomed at an apartment house across the street from the laboratory and ate at the MBL mess, where meals were served on linen tablecloths by waiters in white jackets.

Having chosen to pursue a career in science in the 1930s, Sears had no expectation of marrying and raising a family. "You had to choose between the two," Sears later explained. "You could have a career or you could have a family but you couldn't have both."

Potential employers viewed married women like temporary employees, expecting them to pick up and leave any day to follow their husband's careers or to have a baby. They were not promoted. They were not paid well. They were not taken seriously. Sears knew this and made a choice early on to invest her time and energy in her career instead of a family.

Two of her three sisters did the same. Her sister Katherine attended Smith College, taught at the Chapin School in New York, and become an administrator in the history department of Wellesley. Her half sister Leila would follow in Sears's footsteps, graduating from Radcliffe and joining the WAVES during World War II. She would later attend law school on the G.I. Bill and serve as town clerk of Wayland for twenty years. Only Elisabeth, the youngest sister, chose marriage over career, enrolling in college after raising her children. Her brothers did not have to make the Hobson's choice of career over marriage. Both married. Edmund joined an investment firm while John fulfilled his dream of becoming an accomplished pianist.

As a result of Bigelow's report, the Rockefeller Foundation donated two million dollars to fund the Woods Hole Oceanographic Institution in 1930. A year later the cutting-edge facility moved from a blueprint on the page to a four-story red brick building on the Woods Hole waterfront with Bigelow as the first director.

Woods Hole, the only full-service oceanographic institution on the East Coast, boasted a room where constant temperature could be maintained for marine specimens and laboratories that were piped with salt water for aquariums and experiments. Fifteen research laboratories lined the lower hallways, with specialized rooms upstairs for photography equipment, drafting tables, and nautical charts. The institution, an oceanographer's dream come true, attracted the best talent from leading universities in the United States and visiting professors from overseas.

Equally important to the development of the Woods Hole Oceanographic Institution was its state-of-the-art research vessel, *Atlantis*. Bigelow had commissioned the construction of the first American ship built specifically for marine research from shipbuilders in Denmark. The 142-foot steel-hulled vessel was outfitted with two laboratories, two winches, and quarters for six scientists and seventeen crew members. But Bigelow, never intending for women to join expeditions, failed to include separate quarters or a bathroom for them.

The anticipation and excitement of the opening of the laboratory and the arrival of *Atlantis* was tempered by tragedy when Bigelow's son, Henry, Jr., was killed by a large rock while mountain climbing in the White Mountains in New Hampshire in 1931. A circle of friends and colleagues, including Sears, closed ranks around Bigelow and his wife during this dark time. She would be there again in 1934 when Bigelow's daughter was killed when a horse reared back, striking a fatal blow.

Although he had two other children, Bigelow must have looked to Sears, his young protégée, as a surrogate daughter. He teased her, once telling her to "pull in her big, fat derriere," when he was passing her chair in the library. He could share his private opinions about various scientists with Sears. She could even read his mind when he couldn't find the words to finish a sentence, often writing "M.S. fill in here," on draft manuscripts.

Sears's thesis for her Ph.D. from Radcliffe in 1933, "Responses of Deep-seated Melanophores in Fishes and Amphibians," explored how pigmented cells in the connective tissue of frogs and small fish expanded and contracted in response to changes in the environment. It was a work that demonstrated not only her interest in marine biology but also her aptitude for scientific research.

Professor George H. Parker, the eminent biologist who first sparked Sears's interest in biology, was on the committee that administered her doctoral exams. "Miss Mary Sears is an unusually able and clear-headed student of Biology. Her examination for the doctor's degree was the best I have attended in a long time," he wrote in a letter of recommendation. This enthusiastic endorsement from one of the best-known zoologists of the day confirmed that Sears was an up-and-coming talent.

With her doctorate in hand, Sears settled into a routine working for

Bigelow year-round. She spent the fall and spring semesters at the Museum of Comparative Zoology in Cambridge and the summers at Woods Hole, staying wherever she could get a room.

Even with the strength of Bigelow's mentorship, Sears took nothing for granted. She obsessively collected and studied specimens, particularly when she was in Woods Hole. In the summers she would bring specimens home from her dissections in the lab and line them up across her kitchen shelves. One summer day her stepmother, Sophie, and younger half sister, Leila, visited Sears at Woods Hole to take her to lunch. Upon entering Sears's sparse apartment, Mrs. Sears noticed the unusual display of mason jars on a shelf in the kitchen and asked about them. Sears explained that they held the contents of fish stomachs, each one having come from a different part of the ocean, which accounted for the large number of jars. She had failed to realize that others might find the display distasteful, particularly in the kitchen.

Sears then asked her family to sit and wait until precisely twelve noon before she could visit with them, even though they had driven from Wayland, over seventy miles away, to see her. Instead of happily spending as much time as their travel schedule would allow, Sears demonstrated how serious she was about her work and adhered to a regimented schedule. She limited her lunch break to a strict forty-five minutes, including the fifteen minutes it took to walk to the café. She timed the visit to the minute.

While Sears's dedication to her studies was admirable, the failure to spend even an hour with her family hints at how narrow her life had become. As she pursued her studies with a singular focus, Sears had little room for a social life and spent most of her time alone or with her much older, introverted mentor.

Along with her scientific abilities, Sears had a gift for collecting and organizing data developed during the summers that she worked for Bigelow. At that early stage no one suspected that her ability to compile data would someday evolve to the level of a superhero's special power, which she would use to help win a war. Though she had accomplished much in the intervening years, Sears was still the steady, dependable, reserved person she had been at Winsor who employed a no-nonsense approach to work. As Sears's association with Bigelow stretched over months and years, each found something valuable—for Bigelow a reliable, top-notch assistant who would grow to become a valued colleague, and for Sears an inspiring mentor and a life's work.

When the lab first opened, Woods Hole was a small, homey place where everyone knew each other. There was one secretary in Bigelow's office and one phone line with an upstairs extension. She would shout down the hall to the scientists working in their labs if they got a call. There wasn't a lot to do in the evenings in the early days in Woods Hole. Sears would frequently join colleagues who were also working late in a kitchenette off the library for coffee to listen to sea tales told by Captain McMurray of *Atlantis*.

Bigelow was a hands-on director, insisting that everyone working in the lab keep their doors open so he could walk in anytime and see what they were working on. Yet administration, the people side of the job, came second to his true passion, marine research. Bigelow always preferred to be in the lab studying specimens rather than sitting in meetings and presiding over the operations of a world-famous oceanographic institution.

When he did make time for visitors, he made sure his young associate met preeminent scientists from across the country and around the world when they came to confer with him at Harvard or Woods Hole. Sears made connections that she would maintain her entire career as she sought her place among the network of oceanographic experts.

As long as Bigelow was at Woods Hole, Sears was working by his side, helping to catalog thousands of specimens. In addition to his famous Monterey Bay collection, they would study plankton species distributed across the continental shelf from Cape Cod to Chesapeake Bay and describe jellyfish collected off the coast of Bermuda. When asked once how long she worked for him she answered quite simply, "Forever."

Because Woods Hole was a summer research institution before World War II, most staff members had faculty appointments at universities on the East Coast. When Sears was offered a position as an instructor in the Department of Zoology and Physiology at Wellesley, Bigelow encouraged her to take it.

"He pushed me out because he said if I remained his assistant I'd be an assistant forever," Sears later said.

Sears held the faculty appointment at Wellesley from 1938 to 1943 and lived in Cambridge during the school year. On the days she wasn't teaching she still worked at the Museum of Comparative Zoology with Bigelow. She thought of herself as a "lousy teacher." Even though her teaching career was short-lived, it was Wellesley that awarded her a faculty fellowship that helped fund her trip to Peru and provided her with the opportunity for a life-changing adventure.

In one sense, Sears had found the perfect spot at Woods Hole, working for Bigelow, a famous oceanographer who helped launch her research career, coauthoring papers with Sears and recommending her for faculty appointments. Opportunities in the obscure scientific field of oceanography were sparse, even for men. The job market for women scientists was even more limited because society stereotyped them as oddities: "as scientists they were atypical women; as women they were unusual scientists."

Women were able to study the sciences and get their doctorates, particularly at women's colleges. Once they finished their studies, however, they were subjected to a system of segregated employment—shunted into positions as research assistants or instructors, rather than encouraged to pursue postdoctoral fellowships that might have furthered their careers. Given the sexist attitudes of the day, women scientists were lucky to land any position at all.

While Bigelow had mentored Sears, he was also holding her back with his policy that prohibited women from going to sea. Performing fieldwork was considered so important to career advancement as an oceanographer that Bigelow had insisted that all *male* scientists at Woods Hole make at least one voyage each year on *Atlantis*.

If Bigelow were going to make an exception for any woman, he should have made it for Sears. Unlike some of the men who ducked out on voyages whenever possible, Sears had sailed extensively both at home and abroad and loved the sea. A sturdy five-foot-four and 130 pounds, she could more than hold her own physically with the men aboard ship. Though she occasionally enjoyed a whiskey with her male colleagues at the fisherman's bar across the street after work, she was not the type to turn men's heads or create a fuss. She did what it took to fit in, assimilating as seamlessly as possible into the male-dominated culture of oceanography.

Even though Sears had risen to the level of an accomplished protégée, Bigelow would not yield on the men-only expedition policy. Instead, he perpetrated a system that marginalized women scientists, thus denying Sears the opportunity to gain valuable experience. In Sears's own words he was "an old-fashioned man who never expected women to do everything." Bigelow was not going to change.

If Sears decided to leave Woods Hole, there was no guarantee anyone else would hire her. She would not find greener grass no matter where she went. She stayed at Woods Hole where, even if she wasn't treated as an equal, the quality of her work was respected, knowing that when her time to take a leading role finally came along, she would be ready.

CHAPTER 4

Smoke Screens and Submarines

— Woods Hole, 1942 —

After six months of getting on and off fishing boats and living in the guano company's quarters in between, Sears was anxious to return to the serenity of Woods Hole in March 1942. The S.S. *Lucia* she had taken south in peacetime had ceased running in the dangerous Atlantic waters, where U-boats hunted down commercial ships with abandon. She had to take a plane to get back to the United States.

Sears was glad to be back home in the quaint seaside village located at the extreme southwestern edge of Cape Cod. She could once again sleep in her own bed in her modest, thousand-square-foot clapboard house, built on a small wooded lot, on Glendon Road in Woods Hole. Single women rarely built their own homes in 1939, but that didn't stop Sears. In her staunchly independent way, she headed over to Wood Lumber in Falmouth to choose the house plans and hire the crew to build it. Having her own place turned out to be a very good thing when she came back because housing was all but impossible to find. The boardinghouses and garage apartments she once called home had been taken over by an influx of construction workers, sailors, and scientists coming to town to prepare for war.

Woods Hole had once been a hub of the whaling industry in the 1800s and had since evolved into a hub of marine science starting with the arrival of the U.S. Commission of Fish and Fisheries in 1871, followed by the Marine Biologic Laboratory in 1888, and continuing with the establishment of the Woods Hole Oceanographic Institution in 1930. This powerhouse lineup had literally put Woods Hole on the map, drawing in the nation's most accomplished marine biologists from universities along the East Coast every summer. They probed its harbors teeming with marine life, filled its boardinghouses and dormitories, and packed the local bars, but now a new change was underway, a wartime transformation that had already begun even before Sears had left for Peru.

One of the first changes to come to the southwestern corner of Cape Cod as the possibility of war approached had been the sight of tents springing up on two thousand acres in nearby Falmouth in 1940, home of the future Camp Edwards and Otis Field. Both were part of a network of camps and bases built to house and train new draftees after Congress enacted the Selective Training and Service Act of 1940 requiring men between the ages of twenty-one and forty-five to register for the draft. The federal government had contracted with local builders to erect barracks to house a staggering thirty thousand men within a seventy-five-day deadline. The contractors, desperate for help, put out calls for 5,000 carpenters to start right away. At the height of construction there were 18,343 employees working three shifts, seven days a week, putting up an average of thirty buildings a day.

Inevitably, the influx of workers created a housing shortage in Falmouth and surrounding areas. One local resident reported that although she had "no need or desire to take in roomers," when two men showed up at her door with no place to go, she allowed them to rent out her maid's quarters just to do her part for the war effort. The quick-paced construction launched an orchestra of hammers across the wide-open fifteen thousand acres of future housing and converged into a background hum "like the pervading song of the seventeen-year locusts" that could be heard for miles across the upper Cape. Traffic between Falmouth and

Sagamore backed up for months as men and lumber were ferried across Buzzards Bay in a procession of trucks. By January 1941, army nurses started arriving to tend to the medical needs of the incoming troops.

Camp Edwards, adjacent to nearby islands like Martha's Vineyard, had been deemed an ideal location to train troops in amphibious landing tactics. Soon the Amphibious Training Command arrived to begin training exercises with landing boats that would be used to assault hostile beaches and transport men and equipment ashore. The citizens of Falmouth and Woods Hole looked on with a mix of curiosity and amazement as oversize DUKWs (six-wheeled amphibious trucks) squeezed through their narrow city streets and out to the beaches. Thousands of army infantrymen destined for the beaches of Normandy and the Pacific islands drilled day after day, their training later culminating in a mock invasion of Martha's Vineyard covered extensively by the *Falmouth Enterprise*.

One of the more unusual installations to arrive, the Navy Pigeon Loft, brought four pigeon fanciers and a flock of pigeons to the harborside. Pigeons had proven to be reliable messengers even in combat when they would return "battered and bruised, sometimes with their legs shot off." The birds found their niche off the coast of Woods Hole on board the fishing vessels the *Cap'n Bill*, *Anna*, and *Priscilla B*. During periods of strict radio silence, the crews used the pigeons to alert the navy to sightings of any strange craft, such as German submarines in the area.

The combination of the submarine threat and the navy's training exercises crowded out colorful fishing boats and replaced them with the dull gray of naval ships. The community even lost two ferries vital to tourism, the *Naushon* and the *New Bedford*, which ran between Woods Hole and Nantucket. First, the navy painted them gray and then they vanished altogether, requisitioned by the war department, the *Naushon* destined to become a hospital ship for the Atlantic theater.

When Sears returned, she learned soon enough about mandatory blackouts and how to comply with them. Blackout wardens wearing steel army helmets from World War I patrolled neighborhoods looking for violators. Jutting out into the edge of the Atlantic Ocean, Woods Hole had become a target for German submarines with the advent of war. Because of these threatened submarine attacks, the residents of Woods Hole had started hanging light-blocking curtains over their windows while city workers wrapped streetlights with black metal shades to direct light scatter downward.

Drivers brave enough to venture out into the pitch-black, deserted streets were required to fasten blackout lids to their headlights and adhere to a strict fifteen-mile-per-hour speed limit. The overall effect of the blackouts, especially in the winter, was to shroud the town in gloom, making the long winter days seem endless.

Blackouts of coastal towns also helped protect convoys of merchant ships. Enemy submarines could detect the silhouettes of ships against the backdrop of a lit-up coast, making them prime targets for attack. Up to sixty merchant ships and their military escorts would congregate in nearby Buzzards Bay under cover of darkness and proceed through the Cape Cod Canal to Boston to join larger convoys bound for Great Britain.

The value of the blackouts was literally brought home on the afternoon of July 3, 1942, when the police arrived and roped off Water Street in the village of Woods Hole. A German U-boat had torpedoed an American merchant ship 150 miles off the East Coast, hitting her port side and setting the ship ablaze. Captain Carl Froisland, who in forty-eight years at sea had never lost a ship, later described the "gauntlet of fire" that swept through the vessel after it was torpedoed. Within thirty minutes of the attack the ship "settled beneath the waves."

Word soon circulated that a ship had been dispatched to rescue survivors and they would need a place to go. The citizens of Woods Hole responded by pouring into the Red Cross to volunteer. The local fire station became a base of operations while the volunteers prepared the Community Hall as a shelter. The townspeople stayed up all night awaiting survivors, their arrival delayed by a heavy fog.

When the rescue ship finally arrived, escorted by the Coast Guard, a physician was ferried out to triage the wounded. Ten crew members were never found. Five of the thirty-one survivors were taken to local hospitals by ambulance. The rest were taken to the Community Hall, where the women of Woods Hole fed them beef stew and passed out clothes and shoes donated by local businesses.

The residents of Woods Hole never questioned the necessity of the sacrifices they made. They observed curfews, crept through darkened streets, opened their homes to servicemen, sewed patches on uniforms, and hosted dinners, dances, and fundraisers. Even after giving up husbands and sons, beachfronts and recreation areas, most of the fishing industry, nights out on the town and a general sense of peace and security, they carried on.

After Sears unpacked she shopped at the local market, hoping to find favorite foods that she had dearly missed while overseas, but such outings were bound to end in disappointment. Most had disappeared, either bought out by hoarders or diverted to the military and replaced by unfamiliar brands and substitutes. Even before rationing had gone into effect, staples like flour, sugar, and butter had jumped off the shelves because of panic shopping. The same thing had happened at gas pumps, where Sears was greeted by long lines. But even with all the changes brought on by a wartime economy, it was better to be home.

She couldn't wait to get back to the familiar surroundings of the Woods Hole Oceanographic Institution (WHOI, pronounced who-ee) and her work colleagues. Sears, one of the first research assistants hired when the institution opened in 1930, knew everyone who had ever worked there. She knew that the war had brought new projects, but when she headed over to WHOI, she found that the harborside laboratory had been cordoned off with barbed wire fencing along with the Marine Fisheries building and the Marine Biologic Laboratory. The aquarium and seal pool on the bustling campus, once popular gathering places for summer crowds, were closed to the public until further notice.

White wooden guard shacks had sprouted up near the lab entrances, further signaling that entry was now limited to those with government-issued IDs on official business. There were no IDs required before Sears left. She had her driver's license and could prove who she was to the helmeted guards, but it was the first time she had needed to introduce herself to get in the door.

This was her first clue that change had descended on WHOI, but when she pushed through the heavy glass-paned double doors of the red brick building, there were many more. Instead of the early morning hush she was used to as one of the first to arrive, she entered hallways crowded with people she'd never seen before—men in uniform laughing, talking, and walking briskly in and out of offices and more in shirtsleeves jammed with pocket protectors and pens gathering in labs. She poked her head into the doorways as she walked by, taking in the new faces, clustered around work benches, squinting at gauges, and jotting down readings in notebooks.

Who were these people and what were they doing at WHOI?

She couldn't help but notice that on the smooth black counters, racks of glass slides, and rows of microscopes had been replaced by large, clunky instruments, like the twenty-pound bathythermograph, which measured the temperature of the ocean at varying depths. An infusion of government funds had enticed university faculty with graduate students in tow to journey to Woods Hole to do "real war work," transforming the sleepy summer research station into a military subcontractor brimming with urgency. It was only March and, already, the place was busier than at the peak of July.

Sears was pretty sure she knew why. Columbus O'Donnell Iselin, the second director of WHOI, who had taken the place of her beloved "HBB," Henry Bryant Bigelow, was responsible for all of this. Before she left for Peru she had heard rumors of the changes that were afoot, but still, the extent of the transformation took her by surprise. When she had left, Woods Hole was a center of marine biology research. Now Iselin had turned it into a center of naval research.

While still trying to absorb the newfound direction of her workplace, Sears found out rather abruptly that her job description had also changed. When she had embarked on her voyage to Peru six months earlier, she had begun to make her mark on the world of marine biology, specializing in the study of plankton. The annual reports for the institution regularly listed her ongoing research projects and highlighted her expedition to Peru.

None of that seemed to matter anymore, now that the country was at war. Government funding shifted priorities from the kind of basic science research that Sears performed to applied oceanography projects that could help ships and submarines navigate more safely in enemy waters. The scientists at Woods Hole were now focused on formulating new materials, techniques, and tools that would provide a strategic advantage to the navy in combat.

More often than not this meant spending time with mechanical devices that the scientists fabricated or tinkered with in the on-site Woods Hole workshop, trying to improve or expand on their existing capabilities. These high-priority missions often required rebuilding instruments from scratch, which meant handling tools that could grind, sand, and weld metal. In other words, it was men's work, particularly men with physics and engineering backgrounds.

Sears had just risked her very safety traveling to Peru on the eve of war to secure the one credential she was lacking as a marine biologist. Now, she wondered if that experience had any value at all in this new environment. As a woman in science, she had wrestled with carving out a role for herself, almost from the moment she'd chosen to enter oceanography. And just when it seemed she was poised to make significant strides with her research and surely advance her career, she was faced with making a course correction once again. This new world order was all a bit overwhelming if not out-and-out discouraging.

What was her place now?

The changes at Woods Hole that Sears observed had not come about by accident. In the summer of 1940, thirty-five-year-old Columbus O'Donnell Iselin had succeeded Henry Bryant Bigelow, becoming only the second director of the Woods Hole Oceanographic Institution, and his fingerprints were all over the bustling military experiments underway.

For almost any other director taking the reins of a not-yet-ten-year-old institution devoted to a fledgling science, news of the impending war might have signaled a crisis, but Iselin saw an opportunity, one that could change the fate of Woods Hole and potentially the entire field of oceanography.

Iselin, the scion of a wealthy New York family, graduated from Harvard in 1926, one year before Sears graduated from Radcliffe. Like Sears, Iselin had crossed paths with Bigelow at the Museum of Comparative Zoology. Bigelow had encouraged him to take up the nascent field of oceanography. For a man, though, that would take on a different meaning.

While Sears spent her graduate school years in the Museum of Comparative Zoology sitting at a microscope next to Bigelow, sketching the organs of minute plankton species, Iselin's path took another trajectory. In Iselin, Bigelow saw not only a replica of his own scientific self, but also a future seafaring explorer, a path that in Bigelow's eyes, Sears could not pursue. Bigelow viewed male scientists and female scientists through a lens distorted by sexism and laid out radically diverging expectations on the basis of gender. He forbade women to go on expeditions while insisting that every male oceanographer go to sea.

Bigelow advised Iselin, an experienced sailor, to take to the sea to map the Labrador Current and the Gulf Stream, missions that Iselin undertook with both zeal and proficiency. While still in graduate school, the tall, dark-haired, square-jawed Iselin designed a seventy-seven-foot schooner, *Chance*, equipped it with a winch for oceanographic work, and then sailed it to the Labradors with an eight-man crew. During the cruise, Iselin showed glimmers of the calm leadership he would come to be known for during his years as director of Woods Hole.

When Bigelow decided to step down as director there was no question that he would nominate Iselin to succeed him. In 1940, the directorship of an oceanographic institution was unquestionably a man's job: no one would accept a woman supervising male scientists. By all objective measures Sears was as qualified, if not more so. Unlike Iselin, she held a doctorate and had published extensively in the oceanographic literature. Yet she had collided with the impenetrable glass ceiling that thwarted the careers of so many women scientists in the 1930s and would for decades to come.

The board of trustees had chosen Iselin to succeed Bigelow just as the United States was teetering on the edge of war. The new director sensed early on that he would be faced with a dilemma that could set the young institute on a collision course. A military draft had already begun, and he worried what it would mean for the "motley mixture of scientists, yachtsmen, fishermen, and amateurs" that he had inherited. Some were already in the reserves, like Iselin himself, and would surely be called up to active duty any day. The rest of the draft-eligible staff could be packing for boot camp within weeks, especially if the United States entered the war. Universities vying for military contracts would be Iselin's competition, scavenging any leftover senior scientists who had aged out of conscription or been rejected for medical reasons.

During the early 1940s, sixty-three of WHOI's employees left for active military service. If Iselin sat back and let everyone leave, the labs would be virtually empty for the duration of the war and WHOI might take years to recover its stature in the scientific world. This would spell the end of his tenure as director. He needed to find a way to keep the institution relevant.

Up until 1930, American oceanography was largely a self-funded science, led by wealthy male adventurers who could afford to underwrite the cost of worldwide expeditions. But with the founding of the Woods Hole Oceanographic Institution on the East Coast, and Scripps in San Diego, ocean science was evolving into a more formalized and distinct science in its own right. Combining an endowment, research labs, and the research vessel, the *Atlantis,* all under one umbrella, had signaled that the leadership of Woods Hole had been astute enough to integrate all the components necessary to lead the field.

With World War II looming, the nation was about to enter a two-ocean war against the Japanese, an island-based enemy, and this meant the military needed to know as much as possible about the marine environment where battles would be waged. Even before the war, university scientists were performing cutting-edge research with potential military applications but a tribal mentality among the military brass blocked their participation in relevant projects, to the detriment of both sides.

"The meaning of the words 'ocean' and 'atmosphere' seemed to be little more than 'water' and 'air,'" Iselin had written, regarding the prevailing pre-war attitude of naval officers.

Iselin knew from experience that there was a divide to be crossed because he had done it once before. In 1936, he had been asked to consult on a problem the navy was having with its first-generation sonar system. They had recently introduced sonar on destroyers to detect enemy submarines but the new tool was notoriously unreliable, working at some times of the day but not at others. A sonar ping deployed straight down from a naval ship would, unpredictably, go off course and fail to detect a submarine that might be idling underneath it, particularly later in the day.

Iselin had sailed south to Guantanamo Bay so that *Atlantis* and the destroyer USS *Semmes* could "ping off each other" while Iselin collected oceanographic data with water bottles and thermometers lowered into the sea. After analyzing the data Iselin deduced that it wasn't the sonar equipment that was the problem; it was the ocean.

Throughout the day, the surface layer of the ocean warmed while underneath, the water stayed cooler and became increasingly colder with depth. The way sound traveled through water layers of different temperatures bent and distorted the sonar beam. Because the distortion was more pronounced later in the day, Iselin called this the "afternoon effect." His analysis provided a major insight into how sonar worked and how it could be applied in submarine warfare.

As World War II approached, Iselin drew on his previous experience with the navy and drafted a memo to the newly formed National Defense Research Committee (NDRC), laying out his case for putting Woods Hole's oceanographic expertise to good use in the upcoming war. He pointed out that, with Germany and Scandinavia leading the way, oceanography had become a "highly developed field of science" over the last decade. He underscored that during the previous five years, German oceanographers had been working intensely on naval issues, including mapping currents in critical battle areas. The United States, on the other hand, was no doubt missing key information in potential war zones like the Pacific Ocean.

Iselin highlighted Woods Hole's existing facilities—ample laboratory space, living quarters for researchers, and one of the best marine science libraries in the world—that provided everything that was needed for an intensive research effort. Woods Hole had all the experts the navy would need to solve just about any technical or research problem, including "geographical, physical, chemical, biological or meteorological" resources. He also offered up Woods Hole as a training site for naval officers in specialized techniques such as the use of sonar in submarine detection before going to sea.

In response to Iselin's persuasive proposal, the NDRC awarded additional research contracts to Woods Hole. The oceanographic institution geared up to take on a wide range of applied oceanographic research on behalf of the navy.

When Sears returned to the labs, she quickly found a project that could make good use of her marine biology expertise, assisting on the bottom fouling project, one of the first contracts that the navy had awarded to WHOI. Marine organisms and vegetation were known to accumulate on ship hulls, a problem known as "bottom fouling." Barnacles and seaweed buildup could slow a ship down and decrease fuel efficiency by 10 percent or more during long cruises. For ships at war, where both speed and fuel were precious commodities, a solution to the bottom fouling problem could pay substantial dividends in the form of efficiency and cost savings.

WHOI had assembled a twenty-person team made up of physical chemists, microbiologists, and marine biologists to study the problem and start to formulate antifouling paints for ship bottoms. As a marine biologist, Sears was well versed in the scientific literature on different species of barnacles. Using her legendary information-finding skills, she researched and cataloged the types of marine life that were likely to attach to ships' hulls, including their geographic locations, and compiled an extensive bibliography.

While Sears spent hours bent over a desk, combing through references on barnacles, seaweed, and other undersea organisms, she couldn't help but notice that the hallways were becoming less congested; the crowd of men was thinning out. In advance of getting drafted, they were leaving to join the navy. She wanted to go too.

Toward the end of 1942, "feeling very full of patriotism," Sears applied to join the newly established women's naval reserve, the WAVES, but she failed the medical exam and was rejected. Two years before, Sears had come down with fever and pain in her finger and consulted Dr. Joseph Denton, a physician in Woods Hole. Denton had diagnosed her with ar- thritis resulting from a streptococcal infection of her wisdom teeth. After he treated her, she had a full recovery, but the mere mention of arthritis in her medical records and the possible long-term complications the di- agnosis implied, disqualified her from taking her valuable expertise to the navy.

This was an example of the military's one-size-fits-all approach to evaluating recruits, overlooking the fact that a scientist, especially a woman, would more likely be sitting at a desk than engaging in any stren- uous activities affected by a history of arthritis. Sears had no current health issues; she exercised regularly and was an excellent candidate for the WAVES. She might have spent the war years stuck at WHOI, helping out wherever she could at the behest of her male colleagues, but for the intervention of Lt. Roger Revelle, an oceanographer from the Scripps Institution of Oceanography in San Diego.

Revelle found his way to Scripps, the West Coast counterpart to Woods Hole, in 1931 as a geologist with an interest in ocean sediments. Scripps was just a basic marine station then with one laboratory building and a small research vessel. Still, Revelle was able to establish connec- tions that led him to join research expeditions. In 1934, he sailed aboard the naval ship the USS *Bushnell* taking water samples from the Aleutian Islands to Pearl Harbor, an experience that prompted him to join the U.S. Navy Reserve. By 1936 he had earned his doctorate from the University of California at Berkeley and went on to study at the Geophysical Institute in Norway, where he networked with some of the same Scandinavian leaders in oceanography that Sears had met through Bigelow.

Called up for active duty in 1941, six months before the attack on Pearl

Harbor, Revelle began to work on sonar and the underwater propagation of sound waves in San Diego. In 1942, the navy reorganized its research program, which led to Revelle being assigned to the Hydrographic Office in Washington, D.C., with added duties at the Bureau of Ships developing a program in oceanographic research.

Revelle's ideal role would be to serve as a liaison between the navy and the field of oceanography. While he was more than pleased to be sent to D.C. to oversee research projects for the Bureau of Ships he had no interest in spending his time at the Hydrographic Office. He described the Hydrographic Office as "a hopeless place . . . entirely a charting outfit—making maps in that same old-fashioned way they'd been doing for a hundred years." There he would merely be editing charts and serving as a gopher to navy brass looking for odd bits of information about the ocean. Instead, he wanted to take on "real work" at sea. Using his foothold at the Underwater Sound Section of the Bureau of Ships Revelle could see more action in the field, but first he had to get out from under Admiral George Bryan at the Hydrographic Office, and to do so he would have to find a replacement. That would be next to impossible, given that most scientists had already found war-related work.

Revelle knew that Iselin had taken over as director of Woods Hole, the site of the largest concentration of oceanographic scientists in the country. He made a point to schedule a trip to meet with the director to see if he could convince him to give up one more of his precious scientists to the navy to serve in his place at the Hydrographic Office.

When they met, Revelle appealed to Iselin's sense of patriotic duty and asked him to name one member of his staff who wasn't vital to the Woods Hole wartime research projects. Iselin pointedly informed Revelle that everyone on his staff was already involved with defense work and each one was "vital" for the war research taking place at WHOI. He couldn't part with a single person. In fact, he wished he had more scientists on staff. With the navy's insatiable appetite for data, reports, and new instruments to measure the sea, more naval contracts were coming in every day.

But Revelle, desperate to be free of the Hydrographic Office assignment, wouldn't back off. There had to be someone who wasn't essential, someone whom he could send over to the Hydrographic Office to sit at a desk and answer questions about the ocean for the navy. Iselin knew that with Revelle's position, he was well situated to award future research contracts to Woods Hole so he offered a concession. There was one scientist he could part with, only one he deemed nonessential to the pressing wartime research taking place in the lab.

"You can have *her*," Iselin said, referring to Sears. He directed Revelle to her office down the hall.

Revelle knew nothing about Sears but he went looking for her that very day. Soon after, Sears looked up from her desk and saw a "tall, broad-shouldered man in naval uniform" filling her doorway. Revelle had wasted no time in tracking down the lone woman scientist at Woods Hole who just happened to be the only oceanographer Iselin was willing to part with.

"I was 'palmed off' on him," Sears later wrote. She knew that to Iselin, she was expendable, that he didn't appreciate how a woman who studied plankton for a living could possibly contribute much to the "war work" he was steeped in with his male colleagues. But, if being Iselin's castoff was what got her into the navy and allowed her to serve her country, so be it.

Revelle, as confident as he was tall, seemed certain he could pull the right strings to get Sears accepted into the navy, despite her medical history. She had no way of knowing if that was true. There was some discussion about whether she could work at the Hydrographic Office as a civilian as many did, but because of the high security clearance she would need to be in charge, she would have to become a commissioned officer in the WAVES.

After Revelle's visit, Sears reapplied for a commission in the Women's Naval Reserve. The prerequisites to be considered for officer training school included high physical and moral standards, an undergraduate degree or at least two years of college, two years of professional experience, and the candidate had to be from twenty to forty years old. Sears's qualifications easily exceeded the requirements. Her only issue had been her medical history, a high hurdle to clear but one that Revelle had assured her would not be a problem.

She filled out forms for a Waiver of Physical Defect for Enlistment and sent in medical records to document her treatment. Her first update from the Naval Procurement Office, on November 16, 1942, informed Sears that her application was still pending but also included general information for the V-9 training class she would be joining if her application was accepted. Enclosed was a set of uniform regulations for the Women's Reserve, including a list of items she would need to bring with her to indoctrination camp.

The navy hadn't yet accepted her, but Sears was encouraged by the response nonetheless. She could almost imagine that she had cleared the last barrier to entry. She could envision the snug, secure fit of the tailored navy-blue blazer, one similar to what Revelle had sported in her office. She could see herself slipping into the shiny black oxfords the navy required all prospective women officers to purchase before arriving at training school. It was almost as if the closer she got to getting into the WAVES, the more impassioned she became. Yet, she knew it was anything but a certainty that her application would make it through the second time around. Even with Revelle's maneuverings, she could still be rejected again. All she could do was wait and hope that the navy wanted her as badly as she wanted them.

CHAPTER 5

Hydro Fights a War

— *Washington, D.C., 1943* —

In the lead-up to World War II, Admiral George S. Bryan found himself in the middle of a perfect storm. Bryan was the officer-in-charge of the Hydrographic Office ("Hydro"), the agency that published nautical charts that mapped the seas and issued sailing directions to ensure the safe navigation of the oceans.

No matter what crisis befell the nation, Hydro had persevered since 1830, when it was known as the Depot of Charts and Instruments. It had withstood the volatility of the Civil War, when its superintendent left to join the Confederate navy. It had kept up with the annexation of new territories as the country expanded its borders. It had scaled back to survive budget cuts during the Depression. But now, with the anticipation of a truly global war, the demand for charts and other publications had begun to rise like an incoming tide, a level of need that climbed with each passing day as the country marched inevitably toward war.

Part of the surge in demand was created by the logistics of how the coming war would be fought compared to past conflicts. During World War I, the army had followed one major sea route across the Atlantic to Europe, but World War II was a different war. The Allies had opened multiple fronts, in Europe, North Africa, Asia, and the Pacific basin, crossing the world's oceans and navigating smaller waterways for the first time. In the Pacific alone, the troops needed hundreds of charts—charts for supply lines that extended thousands of miles from Hawaii to Okinawa, charts that mapped routes to overseas ports, and charts that supported amphibious operations, which formed the core of the strategy to defeat the Japanese.

As Bryan sat in his office reviewing the latest production figures he could see the tsunami coming. There was nothing he could do to stop it. Was there anything he could he do to manage it?

Even as Bryan contemplated the answer, Hydro's mission continued to expand as the war brought new threats to the safety of navigation. When the war in Europe broke out in 1939, the agency was presented with a critical new task. With German submarines in the Atlantic and their Japanese counterparts in the Pacific, Hydro started to prepare "Special Warnings" to American ships, notifying them of threatening submarine movements and the dangers of mines and underwater ordnance. Each day at 10:00 a.m. and 10:00 p.m., the agency broadcast urgent updates by radio that had been sent over from the State Department. These were later published as Daily Memorandums and Weekly Notices.

As the crisis of war deepened overseas, Hydro felt the downstream effects on its stock of charts. For decades the agency had depended on a supply of foreign charts published by other countries, but in the interest of wartime security, these had all dried up. Even the British Admiralty had shut down the supply line to its future ally, the United States.

The sudden loss of foreign charts coupled with the need to produce new charts in areas of strategic importance created an imminent workload crisis. Going into the crisis Hydro had already lacked sufficient personnel, funding, and space to fulfill its mission. The printing presses, the engines of the chart production process, were twenty-five years old and obsolete. Mold fringed the walls of the leaky, drafty building in Washington, D.C.

Bryan was faced with trying to recruit more civilians in what was becoming one of the tightest labor markets in history, hampered by a low government pay scale and stressful working conditions. As the war drew closer, he turned over every rock he could think of to keep the agency staffed with skilled employees. Then a new problem came along. Hydro's civilian employees started enlisting in the armed forces, leaving Bryan with an even bigger labor gap.

Bryan summed up the situation in the Hydrographic Office's Annual Report of 1939, noting that "the lack of personnel and inadequacy of money available made it impossible to keep up-to-date in the production of nautical publications. . . . The Hydrographic Office was in no position to meet possible wartime demands for charts of strategic areas throughout the world." Bryan didn't mince words. Nautical charts and navigation aids were vital to the military's operations, but his wasn't the only governmental entity in need of help. The entire United States military was hustling to catch up and prepare for war.

After the United States entered the war in 1941, Bryan's worst fears came true. Almost overnight, multiple theaters cropped up all across the globe leading to "an unprecedented demand for charts." Just as he had predicted, these new demands strained Hydro's capacity even more. In the face of an all-time-high production demand, employees had started working three shifts around the clock to make full use of the limited supply of presses. Not only did the charts have to be printed, but the serial publications that warned of nautical hazards had to be periodically updated and prepared for shipment and distribution to naval and commercial vessels.

Bryan put the scope of the burden on Hydro in perspective during a 1942 address to the American Geophysical Union. "Our job is a big one," he said, "for it involves the correction and printing of over thirty-nine hundred charts and one hundred thirty publications covering all the navigable waters of the globe. In addition, our air navigation charts today cover a wider field due to the rapidly changing conditions of the theater of war. . . . For many months our Reproduction Plant has been laboring to meet the ever-increasing demands for charts. The *monthly* average of one million copies equals twice the *yearly* average of production of a few years ago, and the Hydrographic Office is now the leading chart producing agency in the world.

"In this emergency, however, we believe that time is the most important factor under consideration. Therefore, the Hydrographic Office is not wasting any of it in the 'pursuit of an impossible perfection.' . . . The information is needed now and those that are fighting this war are not concerned with minute accuracy of detail."

Hydro had long prided itself on producing the most accurate charts, but now speed, not accuracy, became the overriding priority. With an annual workload that had increased from 500,000 to 12,000,000 in chart copies alone, it was easy to understand why. Even though it pained Bryan to admit that standards would have to be lowered, even temporarily, the war left him no choice.

At first, Hydro tried to hew to its tradition of hiring only men. On April 3, 1942, the agency advertised in the *New York Times* that it was looking for "several men with navigating experience and the educational equivalent of two years of college to assist in publishing and keeping current all the sailing directions and notices to mariners and naval air pilots." But by 1942, finding men who were not already committed to the war effort was difficult. Finding men with navigation experience and two years of college was next to impossible.

The labor crunch got so bad that the assistant secretary of the navy authorized Hydro to rehire any civilian employees who had previously been fired for suspicion of committing fraud. When that failed to alleviate the shortage, Hydro was allowed to hire "older persons and the physically handicapped," a move that added a few more men to the workforce. It was still not enough.

The complexity of constructing a nautical chart de novo drove the need for skilled labor at Hydro. It required teams of engineers and technicians working together to produce an accurate reference for military operations. In the case of an entirely new map for an undocumented locale, the first step was planning a surveying expedition and sending out one of Hydro's few survey vessels to the area.

Once the survey had been completed, the data would be transmitted or delivered to Hydro in the form of smooth sheets that had been plotted by field personnel. The survey teams also sent records of where the data had been gathered, and noted ocean depth measurements, coastline features, and other topographic detail.

Technicians would photograph the smooth sheets, reduce them to scale, and fit them together in the shape of the area to be covered. Once the features were added in, the layout was photographed onto glass negatives. The glass negatives were then traced onto a copper plate using a pantograver, an instrument that allowed the engraver to etch the chart features onto the metal plate with a steel point. Additional features such as titles, lettering, and other symbols were added by hand. The completed plate was treated with acid to etch the lines of the engraving to a suitable depth for printing, preparing a mounted original.

The mounted original was then printed lithographically onto zinc plates, a separate plate being made for each different color used to highlight various features such as land, water, lights, and radio aids. The zinc plates were then chemically etched and individually printed with the agency's presses, using a building-up process with successive runs for each color. As many as eighteen successive runs were sometimes necessary to produce certain specialized charts.

Needless to say, this multistep, labor-intensive process required skilled employees who had been trained in the use of specialized equipment. It was no wonder Bryan worried about how to keep the presses running in the face of ongoing losses of men to the war effort.

The entire time that the labor force was stretched at the Hydrographic Office an obvious solution waited in the wings—women. Women had already proven themselves capable of serving in the British Army's Auxiliary Territorial Service, formed on the eve of the war against Nazi Germany. Although women were barred from combat, they served in all theaters of war, manned antiaircraft guns, and performed technical duties like operating radar equipment and ferrying planes. By 1941, sixty-five thousand British women were serving in the armed forces. Unmarried women between the ages of twenty to thirty were even being drafted. Women were also serving in the Russian Army where they had been trained as snipers to help defend Moscow from German attack.

In May 1941, Representative Edith Nourse Rogers had sponsored a congressional bill providing for the formation of the Women's Army Auxiliary Corps (WAAC). After passage, Roosevelt signed it into law a year later. Women were allowed in the army but on an auxiliary basis only, not as part of the regular army. Even though this meant less pay, no benefits, and a different system of determining rank, the program still proved to be enormously popular with American women. In May 1942, at the end of the first day that applications were accepted at a New York recruiting office, fourteen hundred women had shown up to apply.

The next logical step was to provide a similar opportunity for women to serve in the navy but they strenuously resisted any efforts to allow women in their ranks.

"Now if the Navy could possibly have used dogs or ducks or monkeys, certain of the older admirals would probably have greatly preferred them," Dean Virginia Gildersleeve of Barnard College wrote about the prevailing attitudes toward women.

Joy Bright Hancock, a forty-year-old civilian in the navy's Department of Aeronautics, must have wondered what all the fuss was about. She recalled how in 1917 Secretary of the Navy Josephus Daniels ordered the navy to "enroll women in the Naval Reserve as yeomen," to help alleviate a labor shortage during the Great War. The nineteen-year-old Hancock had joined over ten thousand other "Yeomanettes" who served in World War I as secretaries, translators, draftsmen, fingerprint experts, and recruiters. Having already worked for the navy in different capacities over two decades, she was living proof that women were more than capable of filling shore-bound positions.

In the lead-up to World War II, the Department of Aeronautics, which supported admitting women to the navy, sent Hancock to Canada to observe how the Royal Canadian Air Force had integrated women into their ranks. Based on her report the Department of Aeronautics drafted a comprehensive plan to enlist women to work in naval aviation and presented it to the navy. No action was taken.

Edith Nourse Rogers had now turned her full attention to passing a bill to allow women to serve in the navy. She prompted Admiral Chester Nimitz, then of the navy's Bureau of Navigation where he oversaw personnel, to seek the input of commanding officers about how women could be utilized within their departments. The response was less than enthusiastic. During Nimitz's informal survey of numerous naval departments only two expressed an interest in enlisting women—the Bureau of Aeronautics and the code-breaking group, both of which already employed civilian women in technical roles.

Typical responses to Nimitz's query included: "Do not visualize a need" (Bureau of Medicine and Surgery); "No use for the services of Women's Auxiliary is seen at this time" (Judge Advocate General); "Such a corps is unnecessary to assist this bureau in carrying out its functions" (Bureau of Yards and Docks); "It does not appear that the establishment of a Women's Auxiliary Corps would be desirable" (Bureau of Supplies and Accounts); "there are no billets . . . which might be filled by one of the proposed auxiliary reserves" (Admiral Bryan of the Hydrographic Office).

"Their lack of enthusiasm stemmed, I believe, from a fear that a change would take place. It was much simpler to say 'no,' rather than 'yes,' particularly when 'yes' would mean doing a job that could be avoided," Hancock later wrote.

Despite the lukewarm reception, American women continued to demonstrate their eagerness to serve by preparing for military service while awaiting congressional approval of the WAVES bill. They enrolled in night school to learn about radio and electronics. They sought degrees in engineering and mathematics. They took ESMDT (engineering, science, and management defense training) courses sponsored by the United States Office of Education to learn skills essential to national defense.

Women's colleges, including Bryn Mawr, Goucher, Radcliffe, and Wellesley, offered courses that would fulfill a "war minor" to go along with a more traditional major. These new courses included meteorology, geological survey, photogrammetry (the method of extracting information from photographs), the chemistry of powder and explosives, and drafting.

The navy continued to drag its feet, assisted by staunch opposition from the Senate's Committee on Naval Affairs. Senator David I. Walsh of Massachusetts, the chairman of the Senate Naval Affairs Committee, declared that a woman's place was in the home and that to permit women to become members of the armed forces would destroy their femininity and futures as "good mothers."

But President Roosevelt; First Lady Eleanor Roosevelt; Virginia Gildersleeve, the dean of Barnard College; Ada Comstock, Sears's dean at Radcliffe College, and many other prominent academics fully supported allowing women in the navy.

"Are they really going to use women for 'trained personnel'? Yes, they are," Gildersleeve told her students a month after Pearl Harbor. "They have begun to realize that the 'man power' of the country includes also the woman power, and that the government and industry will be forced to use women for nearly every kind of work except the front-line military and naval fighting."

"Life in the armed services is hard and uncomfortable, but I think women can stand up under that type of living just as well as men," Eleanor Roosevelt wrote in her "My Day" newspaper column.

When there were delays in getting the WAVES legislation signed because of interference by Congress, supporters sought the first lady's help. "I showed your letter about the organization of the Women's Reserve of the Navy to the President," Eleanor wrote back, lending her assurance to the cause.

Congress finally passed the long-awaited bill on July 30, 1942, accepting women into the Naval Reserve and Roosevelt quickly signed it into law. The navy wanted the women folded into the existing Naval Reserve for security reasons. There would be restrictions on their service because the men in charge could not live with women being granted equal footing in a branch of the military. The women would be paid the same as the men, rank for rank, but WAVES officers would not supervise men. They would be shore-bound and banned from serving overseas, although exceptions were later made for service in Hawaii and nurses serving overseas. They would serve only for the duration of the war plus six months and after discharge they would not receive retirement benefits. At first, promotions for women officers were capped at lieutenant commander, and only 35 percent of the remaining officers were allowed to hold the rank of lieutenant (junior grade). As the war wore on and more women were admitted, these caps gradually fell away.

Initial estimates provided for approximately 10,000 WAVES but when the Bureau of Aeronautics alone requested 20,000, those estimates were revised upward to 75,000 enlisted women and 12,000 officers. What quickly became apparent was that not only were women competent to fill clerical positions, the roles envisioned for them early on, but they would also be needed to fill expanding roles in technical areas.

Nowhere was this more obvious than in the Bureau of Aeronautics, where women were welcomed for their technical and mechanical expertise. Joy Bright Hancock, a trained pilot, advocated for women to train as airplane mechanics. Over one third of all WAVES were assigned to Aeronautics, where many served in technical jobs including as aerographer's mates, parachute riggers, radio operators, machinist's mates, and metalsmiths. WAVES even instructed male pilots in instrument flying and worked as air traffic controllers.

By the close of 1942, the labor crunch deepened at the "for-men-only" Hydrographic Office. Between the loss of civilian employees to the war, the crush of an ever-increasing demand, and the dwindling supply of charts from foreign sources, Hydro was falling further and further behind.

"The establishment of theatres of war all over the globe has led to an unprecedented demand for charts, and for the description of charts, port facilities, and navigational aids (for both ships and aircraft). . . . The major reason for increased chart production was the necessity of covering areas in normal times of little importance but now vital to the war, areas of strategic rather than commercial importance," Admiral Bryan explained.

Hydro was supplying materials that were just as important to the war effort as bullets, tanks, and ships. Without nautical charts, the navy couldn't find its targets and wouldn't know where to land if it did. Aeronautical charts were just as crucial to pilots flying over the oceans. Bryan was savvy enough to realize that he had to keep Hydro's production going lest all branches of the United States military be placed at a huge strategic disadvantage.

Hydro had doubled its workforce by requesting an emergency dispatch of "blue-jackets," navy sailors who could be deployed temporarily to handle some of the workload. But the need for charts kept rising from a prewar level of a half million copies per year to almost fourteen million by 1942. Bryan realized it was time. He had no choice but to requisition WAVES.

The first cohort, which reported in December 1942, comprised seven officers and ten enlisted WAVES. Three officers were sent to the secret LORAN project, a long-range navigation system using radio, in the Division of Research. Three began work in the Division of Air Navigation and one officer joined the Division of Maritime Security as a communications officer assigned to the Teletype machine. The ten enlisted WAVES joined the Project on Geographic Names. Within six months Bryan requested another sixty WAVES. The following year a contingent of about a hundred WAVES draftsmen came aboard.

Eventually, women integrated into most sections of the Hydrographic Office, undergoing intensive training in the full spectrum of chart construction tasks. They extracted information from aerial photographs to provide key details for charts. They used specialized equipment to copy charts onto plates for printing. They learned how to sight a transit level, a telescope used in surveying and chart making to locate the relative position of objects and correlation points. The women proved themselves capable of performing almost all tasks involved in printing and distributing charts with the exception of the operation of the heavy printing presses, a task relegated to men. By the end of 1944 the total labor force at Hydro had ballooned to 1,624 (from the original 330 mostly civilian employees), including 786 naval personnel of which 300 were WAVES.

It turned out that WAVES were particularly adept at chart making once they had the opportunity to learn and practice the craft. Lucy Berkey was a twenty-two-year-old college graduate and public school art teacher in Columbus, Indiana, with two brothers already in the service and a third soon to enlist. In 1942 she was feeling the crunch of a teacher shortage and finding it increasingly difficult to keep up with an unmanageable workload and enormous class sizes. The idea of becoming a WAVE first occurred to her on long bus rides where she saw vivid recruiting posters for the first time. "Don't Miss Your Great Opportunity—The Navy Needs You in the WAVES," "Save His Life and Find Your Own," "I'd Rather Be with Them Than Waiting," they proclaimed.

One day she and her roommate walked downtown to see the "Navy Cruiser," a WAVE recruitment trailer, complete with a welcoming striped canopy. She ventured inside, where she watched newsreels and spoke with a sharply dressed WAVE lieutenant in a navy-blue blazer with light blue braid. Berkey knew what she wanted to do. The next day she sent her principal a letter of resignation.

After completing Naval Training School at Hunter College in the Bronx, she started at Hydro in October 1943 as a lithographic draftsman. With her artistic background, Berkey was a natural at inscribing the tiny, intricate hand lettering on zinc plates used in printing charts for the military. She spent long hours bent over a table, using a magnifying glass to match her pen to the correct location, while keeping in mind how important it was to avoid mistakes. American soldiers and sailors, just like her three brothers, were relying on the information she transcribed. Berkey regularly received news from home about young men she had gone to high school with who had been killed or seriously wounded in the war. She was well aware that the quality of her work mattered in a very personal way.

After a while her efforts to improve started to pay off. Her lettering was so good that the men would call others over to admire it. Her supervisors noticed and started giving her high-priority jobs. She was elated when she was promoted to Specialist (X)(3), engineering draftsman. As Berkey and the WAVES showed their bosses what they were capable of, their numbers in the lithographic section expanded from two to sixty-five over an eighteen-month period from early 1943 to mid-1944.

On top of trying to keep the Hydrographic Office staffed, Bryan needed a full-time oceanographer to assist with an increasing demand for maritime intelligence for numerous upcoming military operations, particularly in the Pacific. The only oceanographer he had on board when the war started was Lt. Roger Revelle, who was hell-bent on getting out of his part-time assignment at Hydro so he could spend all his time at the Bureau of Ships. In January 1943, Revelle's selection of Sears hit Bryan's desk with a request for him to write a memo in support of the medical waiver she needed.

Bryan hadn't been happy with Revelle's behind-the-scenes machinations to leave Hydro, but when he learned that Sears was willing to serve in Revelle's place he could not have been more pleased. Bryan knew exactly who Mary Sears was and not just because Revelle had been bending his ear about her. Bryan had been a member of the board of trustees at the Woods Hole Oceanographic Institution for years and regularly took the train to Woods Hole for meetings. Waiting at the station to pick him up would be Sears who, she later said, "had ferried the Hydrographer from the train to WHOI, from the beginning of time." It was Bryan's familiarity with Sears that probably led him to defer to her judgment regarding oceanographic matters and the basis for him giving her "a free rein" throughout the war.

Bryan knew that Bigelow, the most accomplished oceanographer in the country, had trusted Sears to work up his most valuable specimens with precision. There was no higher praise than a stamp of approval from "HBB." It was just about the best credential any oceanographer could carry. An oceanographer of Sears's caliber could step in and make an impact right away in so many different areas at the Hydrographic Office.

Bryan was more than willing to do whatever it took to get Sears into the WAVES and assigned to Hydro.

Because Sears had already been turned down once by the navy, Bryan would have to compose a thoughtful and persuasive letter. At age thirty-eight, Sears was already outside the standard WAVE enlistment age limit of thirty-five years old. She could only be admitted as a commissioned officer, which had an upper age limit of forty. She would also need a commission to step seamlessly into Revelle's position, a role that required an officer's classification clearance.

Bryan called his secretary into his office and began dictating a letter to the chief of Naval Personnel requesting that Sears be considered for a commission in the WAVES and assigned for duty in the Hydrographic Office "in connection with oceanographic investigation being carried on here." He explained that he had even bigger plans for Sears—an appointment to the Joint Chiefs Subcommittee on Oceanography organized under the Joint Meteorological Committee, a position that only officers could hold.

It was Bryan's hope that Sears would be a full-time presence in Washington, D.C., so she could serve as permanent secretary of the subcommittee. In addition, Sears's expertise was needed for the navy's bathythermograph program, a top-secret project related to submarine warfare in which Hydro was "playing an increasingly active part." Having come from Woods Hole, where the bathythermograph was being refined for immediate wartime use, Sears understood the key elements of the program and their applications.

"Miss Sears is a professional oceanographer who is qualified both by experience and training to carry out the duties for which it is requested that she be assigned" Bryan wrote. In other words, Sears was not only available to fill a critical need but she was also the best fit.

At the end of his letter, Bryan acknowledged that Sears's previous application for a commission in the WAVES had been turned down due to a "slight physical disability," and he stressed that he hoped it would be waived, as there was a "definite need for her services as a commissioned officer."

To expedite the process, Bryan copied the director of the Women's Reserve, the secretaries of both the Joint Meteorological Committee and the Subcommittee on Oceanography and "Miss Mary Sears," making it clear to all concerned exactly where Sears was supposed to be assigned once she made it through the indoctrination process, lest she be poached by another agency, given her sterling credentials.

There was another reason why Bryan wanted Sears assigned to Hydro without delay. He knew that the United States was in the midst of planning the heart of its strategy to defeat the Japanese—a string of perilous amphibious landings launched from the Pacific Ocean. Bryan had been at war on a ship before and had been awarded the Navy Cross for commanding a gunboat during World War I. He well understood that in embarking on this new type of warfare, the military would need support from Hydro in analyzing oceanographic conditions for each combat mission. That meant having an experienced oceanographer on board.

It just so happened that the only oceanographer who was not already tied up in war work was a reserved, bookish woman who had spent most of her career studying minute marine life-forms under a microscope. But Sears was more than that, and Bryan knew it. As someone who had surmounted some of life's greatest challenges to get where she was, Sears was imbued with grit. She had a determination about her that virtually ensured she would succeed at any task she undertook. As Bryan put his signature to the page, he kept his fingers crossed. He was looking forward to the day Mary Sears crossed the threshold of the Hydrographic Office, when at least one of his many personnel problems would be solved.

For ten months, Sears had been back at Woods Hole trying to make herself as useful as possible in a war effort that was just over a year old. Day after day, as she had watched her coworkers leave to join the military, she had twisted over the uncertainty of her future. Healthy, energetic, "full of patriotism," and at least as qualified as any of the men who were going off to serve, she still had those strikes against her. She was a woman. She was older and she had been classified as an arthritic. But she clung to the belief that if she got her chance, she could do anything the navy asked of her. No one would outwork her and no one would be more dedicated to the task.

And then the letter came. On January 21, 1943, Sears opened an envelope from the navy that would change her life. Inside she found a medical waiver listing the findings of a "history of acute infectious arthritis, left ankle, and 4th finger right hand, 1940, with apparent recovery after removal of focal infection." She was instructed to bring the waiver with her to present to the medical officer who would be conducting her physical exam prior to starting indoctrination camp. Through some combination of Revelle's persistence, Bryan's persuasiveness, and sheer magic, she was going to get her chance.

Less than a month later Sears was reporting to indoctrination camp at Mount Holyoke in South Hadley, Massachusetts, one of only two locations for women to attend Naval Midshipmen's School and train to be naval officers. She moved into Rockefeller Hall, aka "the SS *Rocky*," a dormitory where roughly 350 officer candidates lived while undergoing eight weeks of intensive training.

Many of her colleagues, accustomed to keeping their own schedules on more leisurely terms, might have found the 6:15 a.m. fire alarm jarring, but Sears was an early riser and it didn't bother her at all. Before heading to a 7:00 a.m. breakfast, the recruits had to prepare their rooms for inspection. This meant making up their beds with "hospital corners," the sheets folded tight enough to bounce a quarter off of them. The procedure for "stowing a locker," storing clothing according to WAVES procedure, entailed hanging skirts, jackets, and raincoats in order and folding shirts in a neat stack with gloves and purse on the same shelf. All other articles of clothing, such as slips, underwear, and stockings, were also folded, stacked, and neatly spaced.

At 9:00 the students marched to classes that lasted until noon, when they reported to the mess hall for lunch. The afternoon was taken up with more classes, drilling and study time, followed by a 5:00 p.m. leisure hour and the evening mess from 6:00 to 7:00 p.m. The navy managed to squeeze in one more dose of classwork from 7:00 to 9:00 p.m., before lights out at 10:00 p.m. and taps. Needless to say, the strict schedule wore everyone out, including Sears, who would fall into bed exhausted after her fifteen-hour day.

Sears was there to learn as much as she could about how the navy worked in eight weeks, with a classroom schedule modeled after the Naval Academy, albeit one that was compacted and abbreviated. She learned the hierarchy of command by studying naval organization charts and became familiar with personnel groupings, naval ranks and ratings, and officers' administrative duties, such as how to manage subordinates. She learned that a work shift was a "watch," a floor was a "deck," and that to assemble was to "muster." Having been at sea in Peru she already knew that the bathroom was "the head," if the ship were so equipped.

She learned the traditions and customs of the navy and the underpinnings of World War II in her Naval History and Strategy course. She memorized the architecture of the navy's fleet so she could tell a battleship from a destroyer. She studied the many operations aboard an aircraft carrier, how a troop transport was loaded, and the types of planes naval aviators flew. She learned the importance of confidentiality, security clearances, and the basics of military discipline and punishment. Sears also got a good dose of physical education to help develop "good posture, trim figures, grace and stamina," an activity the fitness buff readily embraced. There were reams of information to absorb in this intensive immersion in military culture, but the most important goal for the navy was to build military character and sharpen leadership qualities in every officer candidate.

The new recruits also took a course in "uniforming," a particular point of pride for the WAVES, since their uniform had been designed by the American-born Main Rousseau Bocher. Known as "Mainbocher," he was a Chicago-born designer and former editor of *Vogue* who had established a fashion house in Paris before the Nazi invasion of France forced him to relocate to New York City. His many famous clients included Gloria Vanderbilt, Mary Martin, and Wallis Simpson, the Duchess of Windsor, for whom Mainbocher designed an iconic wedding dress to wear at her wedding to Prince Edward, the Duke of Windsor. The unadorned, tailored dress made of "Wallis blue" silk, a hue that matched Simpson's eyes, was later donated to the Metropolitan Museum of Art.

Josephine Forrestal, a former writer for *Vogue* and the wife of James Forrestal, the then undersecretary of the navy, had also been a client of Mainbocher. It was through this connection that one of the leading fashion designers in the world came to design the WAVES uniform.

Decades ahead of his time in designing tailored ensembles for professional women, the talented Mainbocher later disclosed the thought process behind the popular WAVES attire. "Suitability in clothes has long been a formula of mine, but this time I thought of the dignity and tradition of the navy as well. I thought of comfort, freedom and, of course, the lines of a woman's body."

Mainbocher's vision did not include downsizing a man's uniform and replacing the pants with a skirt, as the Army had done. He, instead, came up with something entirely new for the military's newest recruits—a stylish uniform that would be both workmanlike and womanly.

"These women, all American women, are going to do a fine intelligent job but they do not have to look like men," he said.

The hallmark of the Mainbocher navy-blue woolen jacket was a collar with "soft" rounded ends overlying peaked lapels, accented with the WAVES emblem—a fouled anchor (entangled by a chain) superimposed on a three-bladed propeller. Reserve Blue stripes, indicating rank, ringed the lower sleeve instead of the gold of the male officers' jackets. A six-paneled A-line skirt with two inset pockets complemented the fitted jacket adorned with a four-button front; gold buttons for officers and navy-blue plastic buttons for enlisted women.

The appeal of the WAVES uniform, imbued with the Mainbocher cachet, was such that it served as a de facto recruiting tool to draw women into the navy. Once a potential recruit caught a glimpse of a sharply dressed WAVE recruiter in the "snazzy" blue uniform, she too wanted to wear one. It didn't hurt that navy blue was a much more appealing color to women like World War II veteran Eileen Horner Blakely. "I knew I would never have designer clothes, so there was my opportunity. So when someone says, 'Why did you join the navy?' I say, 'Well, number one, blue is my color.' I don't look that great in khaki or green," she said.

Virginia Gilmore, who had also proudly worn the uniform, later remembered, "A famous designer designed them for us and it fit beautifully. . . . It was probably the most expensive thing any of us ever had. Well made. Beautiful material. And besides, it had two pockets just inside where you could put Kleenex."

Blakely and Gilmore were not anomalies in the sentiments they held about the designer uniform even long after the war had ended. Almost every woman later interviewed about serving in the WAVES during World War II raved about her attire. The same cannot be said of the men.

WAVES could also wear the undergarments of their choice instead of the standard-issue olive-drab panties and bras mandated for women in the army. This policy too was a huge draw, as it turned out that women really wanted to choose their own undergarments.

Mainbocher designed a raincoat, overcoat, purse, shoes, hats, and gloves to go with the ensemble. His collection also included a lightweight summer uniform of seersucker material, patterned in a gray-and-white pinstripe. When Mainbocher introduced the new look it was very much appreciated by the many women like Sears who endured the steamy summers of Washington, D.C., with sweat dripping down her back under her woolen uniform jacket.

Knowing what outfit to wear and when was just the beginning for Sears. She had put in long hours at Radcliffe studying plankton and jellyfish but she never expected to be memorizing pages of rules and regulations about how to wear a uniform. Whenever she was outdoors, she would be required to wear a hat, along with white gloves unless it was excessively hot. The back of her hair could touch, but never cover, her collar. She would have to do without hair ornaments and most jewelry, other than her watch and an "inconspicuous" ring.

Whenever she donned a jacket or coat she was to keep it completely buttoned. She would wear a regulation white rayon "victory" blouse under her navy jacket with a short, black tie, knotted squarely and tucked under the tips of her shirt collar. As silk stockings were next to impossible to find during the war, she would be forced most days to wear the cotton (lisle) substitutes. And she would finally get to slip on a pair of black laced oxford shoes with two-inch heels, spit polished to a glossy shine.

In the navy's eyes, a professional appearance went beyond how the uniform was worn. WAVES were also expected to conduct themselves in a manner that was "as military as possible" and a credit to the uniform. This translated into wearing the uniform as instructed, never chewing gum or wearing earrings, keeping shoes shined, and avoiding any public displays of affection, including hanging on an escort's arm. The navy took nothing for granted, even instructing trainees in how to clean the uniform, remove stains, and repair tears so they wouldn't be noticed.

As graduation neared, Sears sat for a series of classification interviews along with the rest of her classmates to determine where she would be assigned to serve. During the interview she calmly informed her commanding officer that she already knew where she was going. She had been selected in advance of her admission to the WAVES to work at the Hydrographic Office as an oceanographer. Initially, her superiors refused to accept that Sears had been recruited to such a high position and that it was being held open for her. She got used to pulling out her copy of Admiral Bryan's letter from an official navy envelope to substantiate her claim. She was the rare recruit who had been selected for a special purpose and she was going to make sure she fulfilled it.

During her final weeks at Mount Holyoke, Sears studied for exams and was fitted for a new dress uniform for the graduation ceremony with the Reserve Blue stripes and gold buttons that she had earned. The esteemed marine biologist had willingly left behind a blossoming career in science, her friends in Woods Hole, and a home she loved to answer the nation's call. It was a call that had come only after intense congressional opposition to the WAVES and resistance from the navy and, for Sears, the agony of waiting for a medical waiver she might never receive.

On graduation day, April 7, 1943, Sears proudly wore her crisp, clean hat, embossed with the same crossed anchors, spread eagle, and silver shield worn by all officers in the United States Navy and received her sailing orders from Lt. Elizabeth B. Crandall officer-in-charge of midshipmen. She marched in formation with her fellow officers in front of local dignitaries and military brass, their heads held high and hearts beating rapidly in anticipation of the adventures ahead.

Sears had surmounted gender, age, and a problematic medical history to walk through the doors of the Hydrographic Office in April 1943. Like many of the women trained to be naval officers, she was a little older than the average recruit, but to the navy, her age signaled maturity, expertise, and administrative skills that could all be put to good use. In the end, her ticket to admission had been her scientific expertise, sorely lacking in the navy, which she had worked so hard to achieve.

On the day she finally sat down at her assigned desk in the Pilot Chart Section of the Maritime Security Division, she took in the bustle of activity swirling throughout the busy office. Sears wasn't quite sure what would be asked of her in this new role as naval oceanographer. All she had to go by was a copy of Bryan's letter, which hinted at her job description, and Roger Revelle's opinion that the Hydrographic Office was a dull place to work. Whatever it turned out to be, after months of preparation, she had arrived, and she couldn't wait to get started.

CHAPTER 6

The War Beneath the Sea

— Woods Hole, 1941 —

Admiral Bryan's motivations in trying to insure that Sears would join the Hydrographic Office had run deeper than just securing a report-generating substitute for Roger Revelle. With each passing day more people he knew went off to war—men he had served with in World War I, men he had worked alongside at the Hydrographic Office, and his own son serving in the navy. The admiral no longer fought on the front lines himself but he could supply the very best data possible that might give the navy an edge in waging this never-ending war. That's why he wanted Sears. He knew she could help win the war.

As a member of the Woods Hole scientific community, Sears knew as much about oceanography as anyone who had ever graced the halls of Hydro. She was also well versed in the wide range of war-related research projects taking place in the nation's foremost oceanographic institution. One such project, the development of the bathythermograph had been foremost in Bryan's mind as he considered the wide-ranging tasks Sears could take on at Hydro.

Even before the war broke out, scientists at Woods Hole had begun working on a promising undertaking, reengineering a primitive version of an instrument that could, if the redesign was successful, help protect navy and merchant vessels from deadly submarine attacks. Bryan may not have known the details of this new top-secret innovation but, as a career navy man who had fended off German attacks during World War I, he well understood just how important the bathythermograph could be to the navy's submarine warfare strategy. He needed someone to translate this new and unfamiliar data into accessible reports that naval skippers could readily understand and apply to their maneuvers at sea. He envisioned Sears, serving as the bridge between the Hydrographic Office and Woods Hole, as the perfect person to oversee a project that would have far-reaching effects in the war beneath the sea.

Germany's large-scale introduction of submarine warfare in World War I upended a century of seafaring dogma that dictated that the stronger battle fleet commanded the oceans. The Nazi U-boat campaign had been so successful in World War I that it had threatened to paralyze British lines of communications and interrupt the shipment of food and supplies from overseas. The Royal Navy only narrowly averted a crisis by organizing convoys to protect merchant shipping. Still, German U-boats had come dangerously close to dooming the British fleet and winning the war.

As World War II loomed, the United States Navy suspected that the Germans would launch a new generation of U-boats, and that these would be more precise and deadlier than ever. Even though the Treaty of Versailles had forced Germany to surrender its submarines, in between the wars the Germans secretly began to redesign an upgraded version with improved optics, navigation, radio equipment, speed, range, and underwater sound gear. With Karl Donitz, a veteran of the World War I U-boat program, in charge of the new command, German U-boat commanders rehearsed and refined tactics, including the night surface attack and the use of wolfpacks, groups of submarines that worked together to extend a search area and maximize strikes.

During the Battle of the Atlantic, the German submarine campaign against British shipping during World War II, U-boat attacks once again threatened to choke off Britain's imports of food, steel, and other essential supplies. At one point the British were losing two to three times the number of ships that they could build. Knowing they could be facing that same threat, the United States Navy had become determined to develop reliable antisubmarine weapons like sonar detection.

Iselin had earlier helped the navy shore up their antisubmarine capability when he used his oceanographic expertise to troubleshoot sonar systems before the war. As war approached the navy wondered if Iselin's discovery of "the afternoon effect," and how different layers in the ocean affected sound transmission, could be used to their strategic advantage.

The navy had asked Iselin if there were worldwide charts that recorded the temperature of the ocean water at varying depths at different times of the year. This data would help them pinpoint thermoclines, the layers with the greatest temperature differential, so as to gain an advantage in defending against an enemy submarine or in attacking one.

Unfortunately, Iselin couldn't offer much in the way of specific data because it didn't exist. What he could offer was the next best thing: a possible way for the navy to gather the data. With his insider's knowledge of oceanographic research, Iselin recalled an instrument that could provide exactly the type of data the navy sought.

The instrument had first been developed in 1934 by Swedish meteorologist Carl-Gustav Rossby who was spending the summer at Woods Hole studying jet streams. In an attempt to measure the changes in water temperature at varying depths in the ocean he had designed a "great box-like contraption" he called an oceanograph. While Rossby's concept of combining a pressure element with a thermometer was promising, his initial prototype was "bulky and cantankerous" and recorded shaky tracings on a piece of smoked foil, a somewhat unreliable method of recording data. In 1936 he handed the project off to his former graduate student, Athelstan Spilhaus, who set out to produce a smaller, more manageable instrument that could be raised and lowered rapidly in the ocean.

Spilhaus first eliminated the linkages that got fouled with seaweed. He then made the instrument smaller and more rugged and substituted a smoked-glass microscope slide in place of the foil to create a more permanent record of the traces. He found that the etching would wash off in seawater so he started greasing the slides before smoking. Spilhouse initially used skunk oil because Woods Hole had a plentiful supply used for lubricating valves. He also redesigned the instrument, adding a needle tip that rose and fell with changes in temperature and etched a more precise tracing on the slide. The body of Spilhaus's version, a long metal cylinder surrounded by a cage, was still unwieldy, but his device, now known as a bathythermograph (BT), could take reliable measurements from an anchored ship.

In August 1937, Spilhaus took his newly-designed two-foot-long device to Woods Hole and carried it on board *Atlantis* where he and Iselin conducted tests, accompanied by a navy scientist. While the destroyer *Semmes* played hide-and-seek with a submarine, Spilhaus was able to locate thermoclines and confirm that they were responsible for bending sound waves and causing the sonar to miss hitting the target. Even though there were still kinks to work out, the navy scientist recognized the instrument's potential and expressed an interest in procuring bathythermographs for naval use.

Iselin still believed, however, that the instrument could be further improved by the right engineer. Allyn Vine, a trained physicist with a knack for engineering, arrived at Woods Hole in 1939 and took on the task of retooling the bathythermograph yet again to decrease variability and improve resiliency in the field, or as Vine himself put it, "to make it so that it was ten times more usable."

Vine reshaped the instrument into a projectile, making it more hydrodynamic. He added a ten-pound brass weight at the tip and fins at the tail to help propel it downward through the water. The end result was a streamlined device that could be lowered off ships at convoy speeds and one that reached greater depths. Because of the urgency to get these into the field, Vine's team built the first seventy-five BTs of this design in the WHOI machine shop. Near this same time, the original patent of the bathythermograph issued by the U.S. Patent Office became the subject of a secrecy order. The BT had become very important to the navy and it did not want the valuable tool to fall into enemy hands.

The development of the bathythermograph as an antisubmarine warfare tool remained the highest priority at WHOI. Iselin advocated equipping as many ships as possible with it, not just naval vessels but also coast guard and merchant ships. But putting the bathythermograph on a ship was useless if the personnel on board didn't understand how to operate it. Iselin himself trained the first groups of naval officers who would deploy the instrument, secure the readings, and send the data back to Woods Hole for analysis.

Carl Andrew Weiant was one of the first to deploy the bathythermograph for the United States Navy. A native Ohioan who graduated cum laude from Kenyon College in 1937, he went to work at his father's ten-acre greenhouse growing vegetables. As war crept closer, though, Weiant, like many of his fellow graduates, chose to enlist in the service rather than wait to be drafted. He enrolled in a program at the U.S. Navy Reserve School to expedite the training of naval officers and emerged as an ensign in June 1941.

In his enlistment photo the clean-shaven Weiant, just under six feet and weighing 148 pounds, looked into his repurposed future with a penetrating gaze, full lips and a chiseled jaw, his shock of brown hair neatly combed and parted on one side. Wearing a gray suit with a white buttondown shirt and polka-dot tie, Weiant looked more like an executive on his way to the office rather than a future sailor.

In August, Ensign Weiant became one of ten men who joined the first class to train in the principles of underwater sound and the technique of deploying the bathythermograph at Woods Hole. Weiant excelled at operating the instrument. After finishing the course, he was sent to the Third Naval District Port Director in New York to await an assignment. On October 2, 1941, he boarded the troop transport the USS *Stratford* to travel from New York to Reykjavik and back to Boston.

To take measurements, Weiant had to stand on deck in wind, rain, and dousing waves, slowly lowering the heavy torpedo-shaped tool into the ocean with a winch, carefully pulling it up, and removing the precious glass slide etched with temperature versus depth tracings. He packed each slide away in a slotted case, replaced it with a fresh one and lowered the instrument again. He performed this exercise hundreds of times while crossing the Atlantic and back. Weiant completed the mission and shipped his slides off to Woods Hole, where the data was analyzed and ultimately reported to the Hydrographic Office. He thereby entered the history books as the first person to perform a complete bathymetric survey of a trans-Atlantic route to Iceland and also the first to complete a round-trip survey.

Weiant began his second mission on January 7, 1942, aboard the SS *Otho*, an American freighter bound for West Africa. With the United States now at war the risk of ocean travel had increased, especially in waters off the coast of the United States where German U-boats routinely patrolled. He had been collecting data for eighty-six days and was on the return trip just a hundred miles off the coast of Virginia when disaster struck.

Weiant was on deck lowering the bathythermograph over the side of the ship, collecting one of his last measurements, when the ship lurched violently. The SS *Otho* had been struck amidships by a torpedo, below the stack, close to where Weiant was working. The impact slammed him up against the bulkhead, causing internal injuries, thigh wounds, and a shattered right lower leg. A fellow officer was immediately killed and two crewmen, thrown overboard, were swallowed up by the sea. The badly injured Weiant and five other crew members managed to pull themselves into a life raft before the *Otho* went down, twelve minutes after impact, one of hundreds of merchant ships lost during the war.

Their raft floated in the Atlantic for twenty-two scorching days. On April 25, 1942, the men were spotted by a Norwegian tanker off the coast of Nova Scotia. The survivors, too weak to move, were carefully loaded aboard. Weiant, emaciated with a full beard, his skin bronzed by the sun, died within hours of being rescued.

Upon being notified of Weiant's death, Columbus Iselin wrote to the young man's navy commander praising his skills and noting that he had returned the first set of records covering an entire ocean route, the most complete records of any of the men Iselin had trained. "When we learned that the late Ensign Weiant was making a trip to Africa, we eagerly looked forward to his return and the receipt of his urgently needed records. It was at this time that we heard of his misfortune," he wrote.

The records, like Carl Andrew Weiant, were another casualty of war.

As data was being returned from the bathythermograph's many runs on naval and merchant ships, it continued to prove its merits, prompting Allyn Vine at Woods Hole to come up with a new idea to help American submarines hide from enemy pursuit. World War II submarines had limited options once submerged. They were not fast and could not elude a pursuer for very long without draining their batteries. To escape detection by a surface ship, the best option was frequently to hide within the thermal layers of the ocean, but finding these layers on the run could be difficult.

If a bathythermograph could be attached to a submarine's hull it might be able to provide instant temperature data to the submarine captain as he dove deeper and help him identify thermoclines. Vine made his dream a reality by reconfiguring the bathythermograph so that the temperature gauge could be mounted on the outer hull of a submarine while inside a mounted stylus etched a smoked slide.

In June 1942, Allyn Vine took his submarine bathythermographs (SBTs) to naval yards, helped install them, and introduced the new technology to submarine crews. The real time identification of thermoclines could help find shadow zones, areas of minimum sound penetration, in which a submarine could hide and hope to elude depth charges plunging down from a destroyer above. If time permitted before launching an attack on a surface ship, a submarine captain would dive to three hundred feet while monitoring the SBT tracing so that he would know where to find the thermocline when the depth charges started to fall.

With the help of the SBT, the commander of the submarine *Scorpion* found a "best escape depth" while eluding an attacking vessel. "The bathythermograph inspires feeling of confidence when in contact with enemy escorts," he wrote to Allyn Vine in May 1943.

These sentiments were echoed by other American submariners, some of whom included messages when they sent back their BT slides.

One officer commented that he was "happy to be able to forward this card because it means we were able to 'walk away,'" after an attack.

"Thank God for Allyn Vine," read another.

These men were grateful to have Vine's BT to aid in the undersea war against the Japanese Navy. They hoped to disable the Japanese merchant marine to effectively blockade the supply of essentials like oil, iron ore, coal, rubber, and food. Without these materials the Japanese machinery of war would slowly grind to a halt. With the help of the bathythermograph readings all of that was starting to look possible.

Weiant's were only the first of over 60,000 bathythermograph slides collected during the war, precious glass treasures that traveled thousands of miles, from the Pacific back to Scripps and from the Atlantic back to Woods Hole. And, when some sense had been made of the etchings of a stylus on a skunk oil slide that had been dropped into the sea and reeled back up again, the data was collated, packed up and sent to Hydro. It would fall to Sears to get it out to the people who needed it the most—the United States Navy and American ships evading German predators.

CHAPTER 7

A Seat at the Table

— *Washington, D.C., 1943* —

The Joint Chiefs Subcommittee on Oceanography was just three months old on April 15, 1943, when Lt. (j.g.) Mary Sears calmly walked into Room 5 of the Combined Chiefs of Staff building in Washington, D.C., crisply saluted the other officers, and took her seat at the conference table. The sunlight streaming through the windows reflected off the gold buttons of her tailored navy-blue jacket. A square-knotted black tie peeked between the collar points of her white blouse. Her white-capped officer's hat affixed with the navy's gold and silver insignia hugged a forehead swept bare of hair. Except for the eight-paneled A-line skirt and Reserve Blue braid on her jacket sleeves, Sears wholly looked the part of a naval oceanographer. She warmed the room with a rare female presence among the military decision-makers.

Sears's seat among the navy's top oceanographic experts—officers who were also scientists and engineers—underscored her credentials. This was the opportunity she had wanted all along, a chance to use her expertise as a scientist. The men had a head start of course, but the attention wasn't on her. It was on the jam-packed agenda and an unsettling feeling that, when it came to oceanography, the navy was seemingly oblivious to just how much it didn't know. If that was going to change in time to impact the war, it was up to the people in this room to fill in some very wide gaps.

The Subcommittee on Oceanography had first come about because the Joint Meteorological Committee of the Joint Chiefs of Staff realized that in addition to needing weather experts to help plan the war, the military needed oceanographers. Without them there was no way to coordinate requests for oceanographic data for military operations.

When the Subcommittee on Oceanography first met in January 1943, in Washington, D.C., the members, made up of career military officers and newly conscripted scientists, felt the pressure of the task at hand. The nation was in a two-ocean war of global proportions, one being waged both above and deep below the surface of the sea, yet there was still much about the oceans that was unknown.

At the first meeting before Sears had arrived, Major Richard Seiwell, an oceanographer who had left Woods Hole to join the Army Air Force's (AAF) Weather Directorate, began by sounding an alarm about the state of oceanography in the military.

"*Speed is essential . . . it is urgent that the matter be expedited,*" he emphasized to the six men gathered around the table.

He went on to describe how difficult it had been to find trained personnel to work in Washington. The only way to get "certain basic information, in a form suitable for military use," had been to contract with the Woods Hole Oceanographic Institution, his former employer.

Seiwell had been besieged by requests for oceanography reports from all directions—the army, the Army Air Force, the navy, military intelligence agencies and government agencies. The military had become a sponge, ready to soak up any bit of data on the ocean that would help win the war. As Seiwell attempted to keep up with the avalanche of requests, he had been struck by the fact that the outsize deficit of basic oceanographic knowledge in the military could very well put the troops in danger and threaten the success of military operations.

While some of the data might be found in Hydrographic Office files, a lot of what the military needed simply didn't exist in any form, anywhere. Unlike countries that had made training oceanographers a priority, like

Japan, Germany, and Russia, the government of the United States had largely neglected the fledgling field and was now lagging far behind. Further complicating matters was the fact that there were only a handful of oceanographers in the United States. This is why Sears's presence in the Hydrographic Office was so crucial. She was the one person who both understood the full range of oceanography and was also available to fill the position of naval oceanographer.

Sears had been in town less than a week, but she had already settled into a one-bedroom apartment in the Suitland Manor neighborhood, seven miles outside of Washington, D.C., where the Hydrographic Office had moved to in 1942. Suitland, Maryland, had been the brainchild of federal planners, desperate to find space for the tsunami of government employees who were descending on Washington to support the war effort. While the population of the capital city had exploded from 487,000 in 1930 to almost 700,000 by the end of 1941, people continued to pour in from all over the country at a rate of 5,000 per month, reaching a peak population of 900,000 in 1943.

The overcrowding was so bad that in 1943 *Life* magazine proclaimed, "If the war lasts much longer, Washington is going to bust right out of its pants." And over the next two years it nearly did. In government agencies such as the Hydrographic Office, desks were assigned in eight-hour shifts, twenty-four hours a day, prompting a chorus of complaints about the cleanliness of prior occupants. Hotels were packed with residents who couldn't find more permanent housing. A "floating hotel," complete with seventy-five rooms and a dining room, docked at a Washington pier. Private homeowners, pressured to rent out rooms, found themselves sharing bathrooms and kitchens with strangers. Dormitory-style housing was quickly put up, where women who moved to town for war jobs slept and stored their clothes in confined cubicles.

Along with the crush of war workers came excessive demands on goods and services. Intercity laundries turned away new customers because of existing backlogs and told them to mail their laundry to their hometowns instead. An overloaded phone company launched a public service campaign to urge residents to cut back on talk time. Arriving families, expecting to enroll their children in public schools, found them at capacity and no longer accepting students.

So many typists moved to town that a typewriter shortage emerged, logically followed by a paper shortage. Impatient consumers waited in lines for everything—buses, trollies, cabs, movies, restaurants, and groceries. Commuters forced to live up to fifty miles away snaked their way back into the city each morning causing horrific traffic jams.

Government bigwigs like J. Edgar Hoover, who wanted to expand the FBI into the National Guard Armory, fought over space with competing agencies and frequently asked President Roosevelt to intervene. The government took over basketball arenas, auditoriums and theaters, rolling back bleachers, pulling up seats, and moving in desks, typewriters, and phones. FDR, who was already busy enough trying to direct a world war, got pulled into debates over price controls, inflation, rationing, and the housing shortage.

The overcrowding became so bad that the Bureau of the Budget urged Roosevelt to decentralize by moving civilian agencies to other cities. Out went the Securities and Exchange Commission to Philadelphia. The Patent Office was shipped off to Richmond, Virginia. Indian Affairs and National Parks got offloaded to Chicago. Eleven agencies in all with a combined 21,401 employees were dispersed outside of D.C., but no matter what was done about overcrowding, it wasn't enough. As soon as space was freed up, it was quickly claimed by new government workers filling jobs in expanding wartime agencies. The next step was to find space farther outside the city in what would become one of the nation's first suburbs.

In 1941, Suitland, Maryland, had been just another small town outside of Washington, D.C. The former owner, Colonel Samuel Taylor Suit, a master whiskey distiller, had the foresight to put in Suitland Road in the late 1800s to connect Suitland to Washington, D.C., literally paving the road to development for the future suburb. In anticipation of wartime expansion, government planners purchased a 437-acre tract of farm and dairy land there and, by 1942, had transformed the rural area—still very much considered "country" living—into a federal office complex. Private developers were brought in to add nearby housing in what became the Suitland Manor neighborhood.

In December 1941, the Census Bureau, with its five thousand workers, was the first to occupy the new Suitland Federal Center, moving into a building that also housed the complex's cafeteria. By the time the Hydrographic Office moved from Washington, D.C., in early 1942, with its eight hundred employees, developers had added a modern shopping center, a fourteen-acre victory garden, and a daycare center, for the convenience of the large numbers of women going off to work for the first time. Even on move-in day, space was already tight for the burgeoning agency, which was constantly adding more people, desks, and equipment as it struggled to fill an ever-increasing demand for nautical charts and navigation guides. It soon spilled over onto a floor of the Census Bureau next door.

The Suitland Manor development, where Sears lived, was directly across Suitland Road from the government complex. It housed a mix of military officers and civilian employees in a cookie-cutter grid of two-story, center entrance, red-brick four-flats that were so close together that their exterior walls touched. They were plain, pitched-roof units with six windows across the top and bottom floors. These cheaply built, drab structures served an urgent need during the war but, troubled by shoddy workmanship and overcrowding, they were destined to become postwar low-income housing.

Amid the crush of newcomers seeking housing, Sears felt lucky to be living in private quarters, but she couldn't help but notice the telltale signs of slapdash construction in her own apartment. The walls in her closets didn't square up at right angles. The furnace kicked in only intermittently, and she could hear her neighbors through tissue-thin walls. One night she came home to find that a section of the floor in the apartment had fallen in. She gave up on getting repairs done when she discovered the building was privately owned by an absentee landlord, who lived in a distant state. At least she had the convenience of living across the street from the office, which became especially important when she became busier at work and began to take on more responsibilities.

Sears might have had reason to envy the "enlisted girls" she worked with who lived in Suitland Hall, a multistory building about a five-minute walk from the Hydrographic Office that offered more comforts than Suitland Manor. Their single rooms came furnished with a blond-wood desk, chair, and bed. They wrote home about the "modern touches," like the flowered drapes, accented pastel walls, and the spacious closets with mirrored sliding doors. Suitland Hall also included shared amenities like the upstairs library and the lobby-level convenience store, which served hot dogs and ice cream and stayed open until 11:00 p.m.

On the rare occasion that Sears's schedule afforded her some leisure time she could drop in at the Suitland Hall recreation space, where dances were held every two weeks, visit the beauty shop for a quick trim, join some friends in the darkroom to take photos of each other to mount on Christmas cards, or try her hand at painting in the hobby corner stocked with art materials. More often than not, however, given the long hours and frequent bus trips to D.C. to attend meetings, Sears spent her evenings at her own apartment, grateful for any downtime she might have before a messenger knocked on her door with an urgent request.

Sears was starting her tenure in the Navy at a critical time in the war. By 1943, the American war machine had ramped up with factories converting from automotive plants into purveyors of military equipment producing forty-seven thousand aircraft and two thousand ships per year in addition to enormous numbers of trucks, tanks, and ammunition. With the fresh supply of troops, armament, and equipment, and with the experience that accumulated with each battle, the Allies began to rack up their own victories at Midway, Guadalcanal, and Tulagi, battles in the Pacific that decisively forced the Japanese into a defensive posture.

The Allies had become the aggressors, bent on not just taking back what the Japanese had ripped away but also on driving their tormentors all the way back to Japan. To do so would require launching amphibious assaults from the sea, each one representing its own set of dangers because of the varying conditions offshore, any one of which might precipitate a disaster.

Amphibious assaults were not unheard of before World War II, but the very mention of them invoked heart-stopping memories of past debacles. In 1915, during World War I, the British Navy under the direction of Winston Churchill, then the First Lord of the Admiralty, had attempted to launch a strike force against the Turks on the Gallipoli peninsula of Turkey. The British had converted an old British cargo ship, the *River Clyde*, into a primitive troop transport by cutting doors into the ship's sides so that troops could disembark from gangplanks affixed to the hull. The ship towed flat-bottomed barges known as lighters alongside that could be deployed as piers for troops to march across the water to shore. Needless to say the configuration of the landing gear rendered the *River Clyde* unwieldy and unstable in the water.

The plan was to attack during daylight, eliminating any hint of surprise, cruising right up to the landing beaches in full view of defenders. But on the day of the invasion, the waves were rough, causing the ship and its attached piers to buck while the men made their way to shore. While attempting to maneuver across the compromised landing bridges, the British troops met intense rifle and machine-gun fire from well-defended shore positions and suffered heavy losses.

The lessons of Gallipoli became forever inscribed in the annals of amphibious lore. Opposed amphibious landings were dangerous and foolhardy, particularly in an era of automatic weaponry where approaching troops would be helplessly exposed to enemy fire.

As hazardous as amphibious attacks could be, Marine Corps Major Earl "Pete" Ellis had anticipated the need for them two decades earlier, after the Treaty of Versailles, the formal agreement that ended World War I, gave Japan control of the German-occupied islands in the Pacific. Ellis worried that the Japanese would someday use these islands to stage an invasion of the United States. If they did, Ellis wanted to be ready with a plan to wrench the islands out of Japanese hands. He drew up Operations Plan 712H that outlined a combat strategy to island hop across the Pacific, launching one amphibious invasion after another, pushing the Japanese back with each victory. Along the way, the Americans would need to set up a system of military bases with airfields to support their advance of nearly four thousand miles to Okinawa, culminating in an attack on Japan.

The marines' early attempts at amphibious landings did little to engender support for Ellis's plan. In 1924 seventeen hundred marines landed on Culebra Island off Puerto Rico in clunky fifty-five-foot wooden landing boats topped with steel covers.

"Chaos reigned," Marine Brigadier General Eli Cole wrote in his after-action report.

The one troop transport employed in the exercise had been loaded without a great deal of thought as to what supplies would be needed first, resulting in delays in food and ammunition reaching the troops. Boat captains were confused about where to go ashore. The boats themselves, insufficient in number and inadequate in design, proved to be death traps if the men needed to disembark quickly.

The marines were learning that there was more to an amphibious landing than simply sending boats ashore. Special landing craft and equipment would need to be designed and tested. Troop transports had to be loaded in the order in which supplies were needed. Communication between ships and troops ashore had to be reliable. Numerous factors impacted the success of an amphibious mission. Each one would need to be carefully analyzed to avoid costly errors in the future.

As Sears took her place at the table at her first meeting, the marines were planning their next series of amphibious landings for the remainder of 1943—Attu and Kiska islands in the Western Aleutians, New Georgia Group in the summer and the central Solomons, Bougainville and Tarawa in the Gilbert Islands in the fall. Even though oceanographic data could be critical, war planners were mapping out operations without complete intelligence. In some cases, they didn't even know what they were lacking or what to ask for and they had no idea how much this deficiency would complicate landings for the troops.

The subcommittee was still defining their nearly impossible but critical mission—how to speed up the process of collecting information for urgent reports for the military. As Sears listened, she recognized that some of the data could be tracked down in scientific journals housed in libraries or in the records of the Hydrographic Office. But she was also aware that data for more remote locales, such as local tides, currents, or beach conditions, had never before been compiled and did not exist in any published form, especially in the Pacific, where the United States had never been to war.

All too often charts and sailing directions, if they could be found at all, were hopelessly out-of-date, in some cases over a hundred years old even for high-priority invasion targets. Some types of data were never going to be easy to obtain because of ongoing hostilities and a lack of manpower to survey the area. Sears was new to her role but she could see that the subcommittee needed someone who could quickly assess the information already available on the shelves of libraries and government agencies and determine what data still needed to be collected.

Sears already had an encyclopedic knowledge of the field that gave her an edge in uncovering data on any topic. She had also networked with members of the international oceanographic community for over a decade, contacts that would prove to be valuable in the months ahead. Sears' selection as a naval oceanographer might have been a move of desperation on Revelle's part, but he had managed to find the one person whose credentials best fit the role.

Revelle informed Sears that she would be assuming the duties of recording secretary, making her the point person for the oceanographic arm of the Joint Chiefs going forward, a rare position of responsibility for a woman in the navy to hold. Revelle also listed priority items for Sears to follow up on, starting with supplying five thousand charts of average sea and swell to the army and navy, for the northwestern Pacific Ocean. She needed to write to the New Zealand Joint Staff Mission requesting oceanographic data on specific locations. Next on her list, was to inform the commander, Amphibious Forces, U.S. Atlantic Fleet of the projects the subcommittee was working on and of the sea and swell charts being prepared by the Hydrographic Office. Sears jotted down Revelle's dictated list and took her notes back to Suitland to her desk, piled high with requests for information that had been backed up awaiting her arrival.

At the group's next meeting a week later Revelle took out several typewritten pages that he passed around. He had prepared a draft outline of oceanographic topics for strategic military surveys prepared in advance of an amphibious invasion.

His outline of thirty-three oceanographic topics included the measurement of landing approaches, dangers to navigation of landing areas, the character of bottom sediment, possible locations of underwater enemy defenses such as mines and nets, beach areas, tides, currents, sea and swell, surf, sea surface temperature and salinity. He also included the transparency and color of water, biologic factors such as phosphorescent life-forms that would illuminate vessels at night, and acoustic conditions that could affect the interpretation of sonar.

Revelle's outline brought home the message that there was a good deal more to military oceanography than simply calculating tides and observing waves. The scope of the data was a wake-up call for everyone on the subcommittee but also for others up the chain of command who reviewed the outline and realized just how much had been lacking in their oceanographic reconnaissance efforts.

Oceanography had been overlooked by the navy but a new urgency was about to propel the field forward. With the country at war at sea, where lives depended on being prepared for rough conditions, oceanography's value to the military was about to have its moment. But the question remained: How would the American military catch up with the oceanographic intelligence it needed when the seas had gone underexamined for decades?

The members found out how the Navy planned to attack this problem at the next meeting of the Subcommittee on Oceanography in May. Revelle announced that the Joint Meteorological Committee had made the decision to centralize oceanographic intelligence in the navy's Hydrographic Office. Seiwell was being deployed to the European theater. He would no longer have any role producing oceanographic intelligence outside of that realm. The Air Force Weather Directorate would no longer be answering questions about the ocean. Though no reason was given for the reorganization, this solution no doubt represented a flare-up of the interservice rivalry between the army and the navy in the form of a territorial dispute.

The impact of the decision permeated the stuffy conference room. With the Army Air Force out of the oceanography business, how were the ongoing needs of the army going to be met and by whom? Most of the estimated one hundred oceanographers in the country had already been claimed for either some branch of the service or in research. Sears's priority was the navy. With Seiwell on his way out, it wasn't at all clear who would take over preparing reports for the AAF Weather Directorate, the many commands in the army, or military intelligence units.

During the five months of its existence, the AAF oceanographic unit had completed an impressive thirty-nine studies for army and navy commanders. A handful of reports were still in progress. The group had also taken the initiative to prepare reports as references, such as the growth and dissipation of waves, methods of forecasting sea swells, and ice in the north Atlantic and Arctic seas and the English Channel. It seemed like there was no end to the number and types of reports about the sea needed by the United States military.

The subcommittee came to the conclusion that the navy should be able to furnish "pertinent oceanographic information" to the army although that meant asking Sears, the one full-time oceanographer at Hydro, to take on a very heavy load. Revelle and Seiwell hoped that some of the AAF personnel could transfer to the navy's Hydrographic Office in the future to help her.

The meeting adjourned without a clear plan for how oceanography would be organized in the future, but before it could be decided, the male members of the subcommittee started deploying to the field. Soon Sears would be the only oceanographer left at the table. If she had any intimations of easing into her role, those had all gone out the window. Only a month into her tenure she was in the thick of things, doing her best to answer the military's many questions with the fiercest battles of the Pacific Campaign on the horizon.

CHAPTER 8

The Vast Pacific Ocean

— Suitland, Maryland, 1943 —

In his first fireside chat after Pearl Harbor, President Roosevelt wanted to make clear to the American people where battles were being fought around the globe so they could understand the challenge ahead. In doing so, FDR would have to "speak about strange places that many of them had never heard of . . . places that are now the battleground for civilization." To help his audience picture these far-flung locales, he asked them to follow along on maps. All across the country, citizens who knew nothing about geography rushed out to purchase large maps of the world. They put them up on their walls and spread them across their dining room tables in preparation for Roosevelt's radio broadcast, ready to do anything the president asked if it would help win the war.

FDR told the American people that things were going to get worse before they got better. The United States had entered "a new kind of war," one fought on "every continent, every island, every sea, every air-lane in the world." He then described the Allied situation in different pockets of the globe and pointed out that in this new war, "the broad oceans which have been heralded in the past as our protection from attack have become endless battlefields."

This spread-out conflict inevitably brought the need to cross wide expanses of water—the Mediterranean Sea, the English Channel, the Atlantic Ocean, and the largest of them all, the sixty-four-million-square-mile Pacific Ocean, which meant increased air travel to reach distant destinations quickly. In the years since the Great War, air travel had become increasingly feasible. By World War II it had become a necessity. But crossing the ocean could be a risky endeavor in an era when airplanes were barely thirty years old, engines were small, and fuel capacity was limited. All too often planes crashed into the ocean either because of bad weather, pilots losing their way and running out of fuel, or because the enemy shot them down.

In October 1942, a high-profile episode involving Captain Eddie Rickenbacker, a famous World War I fighter ace, highlighted the danger of flying across the Pacific. Rickenbacker, a passenger aboard a Boeing B-17 flying from Hawaii to Canton Island, an atoll in the South Pacific Ocean, was on a special mission for Secretary of War Henry Stimson to evaluate United States Army Air Force combat units.

Ten hours into the flight, the pilot began looking for the tiny island. He circled, asked for course readings from air traffic control, and descended to five thousand feet, but he still couldn't spot the island. After agonizing minutes watching a fuel gauge ticking down to empty while desperately searching for land, the pilot advised the crew to don life jackets and prepare to ditch in six-foot swells.

After the plane hit the water the crew crawled out through a cockpit window and onto a wing where they divided up into three rubber life rafts. Although several of the men were injured in the crash, they managed to lash the rafts together for safety and settled into them for a journey of unknown duration, with few supplies, no water, and only four oranges to split among them. Over the ensuing days, they managed to live off of rainwater, a captured seagull, and several fish that flopped into the boat during rough seas.

The castaways were at the mercy of storms, a searing sun, and the constant threats of shark attacks. After two weeks, all were suffering from profound dehydration, blistering sunburns, and severe malnutrition. One of the most seriously injured men died. On day twenty, the pilot decided to take one of the rafts and set off on his own to look for help. Luckily, he was spotted by a navy patrol boat and picked up. On the twenty-first day at sea, navy floatplanes rescued the rest of the survivors.

Why had it taken so long for the survivors to be rescued?

The navy knew Rickenbacker's B-17 had crashed. They even had hints from air traffic control as to where the pilot had ditched the plane, but still it had taken four weeks to locate the men. Even then, the survivors were rescued, not because the navy had narrowed the search area and spotted the rafts, but because of the pilot's heroic action.

Men lost at sea in the Pacific were dying, not from the initial crash, but from extreme conditions at sea that resulted in dehydration, starvation, or illness. Mostly, they died because they hadn't been found in time. Rickenbacker's crash, widely publicized because he was a well-known public figure, raised the question of how to narrow the search area faster. As it turned out, oceanography would play a key part in finding an answer. At the root of the problem was the concept of drift, how winds and currents propelled an object through the water.

Predicting the drift of objects had proven to be a complicated matter that depended on numerous factors, including the shape of the wreckage and what portion of it was above the surface of the water versus submerged, a difficulty illustrated by the fate of the wreckage of a schooner near Nantucket on June 22, 1892. After a steamer crashed into the *Fred Taylor*, cutting it in half, the bow and stern portions drifted in opposite directions. One portion was found off the coast of Portland, Maine, and the other was located near New Jersey.

Not surprisingly, in the aftermath of the Rickenbacker crash, one of the first projects the Subcommittee on Oceanography assigned to Sears was to compile all available references on the surface drift of objects in the Atlantic and Pacific Oceans. Still working alone, she tackled the first high-profile assignment to come her way with her trademark focus and determination, gathering all the relevant published reports and also reaching out to her network of experts at Woods Hole and Scripps for unpublished data.

• • •

Sears had been putting together detailed information on short notice for decades. In an age that predated computers and Internet searches, she had other ways to find what she needed. She filled out an index card on every article, book, newsletter, or other reference she came across. She cross-referenced these by author and subject, and filed them alphabetically in a black box. Her Woods Hole colleagues marveled at the growing collection of black boxes taking over every inch of "the forest" of shelves behind her desk.

She had become the go-to person for answering queries from every direction: from fellow scientists around the world to vacationing beachcombers to schoolchildren working on science fair projects and book reports. Whether a query was typed on a sheet of letterhead embossed with the seal of a prestigious university, or scrawled by a youngster not yet in command of the cursive form, Sears took them all seriously.

In 1974, thirteen-year-old Mary Rimmele from Lombard, Illinois, wrote to Sears seeking help for an upcoming science fair exhibit on the life of a salmon. "I'd like to know if you have any information, especially on where the different kinds of salmon are located," she wrote. Young Rimmele likely had no idea that in writing to Sears she had unleashed the prodigious thought processes of a woman who went full throttle on any question lobbed her way and smashed the answer home like she was playing a match point at Wimbledon.

Sears frankly admitted that since she did not know what libraries were within reach, that the young student might want to start with the *Encyclopedia Britannica* for a general overview and then go to a public library to look for "The Homing Salmon," an article published in *Scientific American*. If all else failed she might be able to find a copy of *Salar, The Salmon*, published in 1935 by Henry Williamson, a tale about a salmon's last trip upstream that included scientific facts about the salmon life cycle.

Sears went on to suggest that Rimmele peruse the *Fishes of the Gulf of Maine* published by the U.S. Fish and Wildlife Service, noting that this volume, once out of print, had recently been reprinted by the Museum of Comparative Zoology at Harvard. The index of the *Journal of the Fisheries Research Board of Canada* would likely also be helpful, as the Canadians had probably done more research on salmon than anyone else, under the leadership of Canadian oceanographer A. G. Huntsman "who at ninety was seining in a salmon stream for salmon just three or four days before he died." Lastly, the multilingual Sears (fluent in Spanish, French, and German and passable in Danish, Norwegian, and Swedish), added, "If you read Russian, you would find quite a lot scattered in their scientific periodicals, especially those published by fisheries sections on the Pacific coast of the USSR."

Sears's collection of index cards grew into one of the more comprehensive oceanographic indexes, one that covered the entire world of oceanography, including just about every article written on any topic relating to every known body of water in the world, dating back to the turn of the twentieth century.

Her collection was so extensive that G. K. Hall and Company of Boston later filled fifteen oversize volumes with Sears's notations drawn from more than 250,000 index cards. As she explained in the preface to one of the volumes, "The convenience of a cumulative oceanographic card index was demonstrated to the author during World War II."

After the war, Sears had returned to Woods Hole and filled out index cards in earnest. The cards, as typed and handwritten by Sears and her assistants, were photographed "as is" from her collection with her personal notations left intact. As one reviewer mentioned, publishing the cards condensed them "from several hundred file drawers in Mary's Bigelow office to about two feet of bookshelf space." It also preserved one of Sears' many legacies for future generations of scientists.

Sears's review on drift for the subcommittee zeroed in on the most important issues—the easiest and most reliable way to calculate the drift of an object and how to train naval crew members in drift calculations so they could locate life rafts. The starting point for solving any drift problem, she found, was the surface current charts that covered major flight routes where pilots might ditch their planes. Naval personnel would also need to take into account the effect of local wind and how leeway, the sideways drift of an object such as a rubber life raft, affected its overall direction.

In May 1943, just one month after reporting for duty at Hydro, Sears submitted *The Drift of Objects under the Combined Action of Wind and Current* to the subcommittee. They endorsed Sears's conclusions and directed her to send the report to the Joint Meteorological Committee for approval. After completing such a critical report in record time, Sears had not only made inroads into assisting the rescue of hundreds of pilots and crew members, but had also started to make a name for herself at the Hydrographic Office and beyond. If there had been any doubt about the quality of her work as a female scientist, this report silenced it. Her colleagues realized that Sears could be depended on to provide the answers the military needed to wage war in the oceans.

Only weeks later, in June 1943, Sears got the exciting news that one of her former colleagues from Harvard, Fenner Chace, Jr., was transferring to the Hydrographic Office to work in the Oceanographic Unit. At the beginning of 1942, while Sears was still finishing her plankton research in Peru, Chace was working frantically in the catacombs of Harvard's Museum of Comparative Zoology, cataloging thousands of hard-shelled marine specimens collected on far-flung adventures from years before. In the wake of Pearl Harbor, the thirty-five year old marine biologist was hit with the reality that, any day, a wartime emergency might mandate a rapid evacuation of the museum's priceless collection of crustaceans, and he wanted to do everything possible to ensure it survived intact.

Chace sorted the specimens into bottles, replenished the alcohol preservative, and arranged the bottles into sections on trays. He created a system so that if the specimens had to be relocated to a safer location, they could be readily identified by the next archivist to unpack them. He numbered the horizontal rows, lettered the vertical columns and recorded each species type and its location in a logbook. Chace even left detailed instructions for a plan to pack the trays for emergency shipment.

At the same time that Chace was preserving his life's work, the clock was ticking on a difficult choice he needed to make. With the United States at war there was pressure on him to join the military. A handful of his colleagues had already enlisted, and with a mandatory draft in place, Chace would inevitably be conscripted. He could either enlist in the service branch of his choice and hope to have some say in where he was assigned or he could wait to be drafted, at which point he risked being deployed for combat overseas.

A native of Fall River, Massachusetts, and the son of a physician, Chace lacked the rough-and-tumble pedigree of a would-be soldier. Instead, at the age of six he had begun labeling insects and worms and putting them on display in refurbished display cases in one room of the twenty-three-room house where he grew up, an exhibition space he dubbed the "Wabsacook Museum."

The tall, handsome, dark-haired young man with large gentle eyes, attended Harvard University in the 1930s, and became acquainted with a much bigger museum than he had curated as a child—the Museum of Comparative Zoology (MCZ), one of the largest and oldest collections of natural specimens in the world. The MCZ had been founded by natural historian and preeminent paleontologist Louis Agassiz in 1859 to house specimens he had collected on numerous seafaring expeditions and to train future generations of zoologists. It was there that Chace, like oceanographers Mary Sears and Columbus Iselin before him, came into the orbit of Dr. Henry Bryant Bigelow and discovered his life's work.

Chace spent his first year as a graduate student working long hours in the darkest corners of the basement, dusting off crates that had been neglected for decades and reidentifying and relabeling the entire crustacean collection. He studied and sketched the anatomy of every species of shellfish. With his knack for detail and observation he identified several new types that had previously gone unnoticed and published his findings in the scientific literature. Poking under the shells of crustaceans

Chace found his calling. He was especially drawn to the decapods—the ten-legged crab, shrimp, and lobster species.

After obtaining his doctorate in zoology in 1934, the introverted scientist stayed on at the museum, where he met and married Janice Grinnell, who had assisted him in editing his doctoral dissertation while they were dating. Two years later, he was named the assistant curator of Marine Invertebrates and curator of Crustacea at the MCZ and started a new card catalog system for the entire collection.

The young crustacean expert liked nothing better than to work alone, dragging specimens out of the basement, lugging them back up to his office on the third floor, drawing and detailing each new species, and comparing them to other invertebrates depicted in the shelves of reference books in the MCZ. Intent on improving his craft, he took the Northwestern School of Taxidermy correspondence course to learn how to mount specimens to make them appear more lifelike, followed by painting lessons that helped improve his skills as an illustrator.

He later said, "It's the only way I can work, really. I have to draw things in order to see them."

While Sears was finishing her Ph.D. at Radcliffe, she met Chace through their mutual mentor Bigelow. They stayed in touch, both becoming members of the small circle of marine biologists on the East Coast. Sears had corresponded with Chace in 1939 requesting information on whether certain species of prawns could be sampled while working from the harbors of Woods Hole. Chace, clearly an expert on the subject, wrote back a detailed explanation of where the species could be found in nearby waters, including the depths, the diameter of net required to capture them, and the means of preservation.

In the world of oceanography that Chace grew up in there were "field men," who went out on expeditions and collected specimens and "research men," who studied and cataloged the catch, examining each one under the microscope and noting features that allowed them to be identified as a species. Although Chace ventured out on a couple of expeditions on *Atlantis* at Woods Hole early in his career, he was firmly in the research camp. He detested going to sea and preferred to work up collections brought back by his more adventuresome, seafaring colleagues.

Chace was not without his quirks. He wanted nothing to do with lecturing, tutoring, or the paper pushing that went along with administration. Afflicted with agoraphobic tendencies, he disliked travel of any kind, particularly flying, which he tried to avoid whenever possible. His fear of heights was so profound that he was known to plot routes that took him out of his way to avoid driving across bridges.

An additional weakness that would have posed major challenges had he been sent to the front lines was exposed one night while at a dinner party when a colleague got her finger caught in a mixer. After friends disentangled the woman's appendage from the appliance, they asked Chace to assess the bloody wound. He bit his lip and took a look despite his fear of the sight of blood. His wife, well acquainted with his florid hemophobia, later professed amazement that he hadn't passed out during the ordeal.

Chace found bliss in the role of museum curator, a position, in his words, best filled by "an individual who shuns controversy and even the company of others in order to preserve the tranquility conducive to complex cogitation." He stayed on at the MCZ for nine years, perfectly content with his perch on the lower rung of academia, completely absorbed with identifying crustaceans sent from around the world. And then the war broke out, threatening to interrupt his scholarly nirvana and catapult him to distant lands engaging in distasteful activities. As a draft-eligible male, he found himself faced with the inevitability that his career path was about to take a detour, one that he dreaded to even contemplate.

The young carcinologist found a temporary reprieve from enlistment when a former graduate student connected him to Lt. Richard Seiwell, the commanding officer of the Army Air Force's oceanographic group in Washington, D.C., the same Seiwell who would sit on the Joint Chiefs Subcommittee on Oceanography with Sears. After Chace had been working for two months as a civilian oceanographer at the AAF, Seiwell informed him it was time to "get into uniform," meaning he needed to go ahead and enlist. Chace knew that by joining the army, he would lose control over his career, but he couldn't side-step the issue any longer. He went to Officers Training School in Miami Beach, Florida, for six weeks where he lived for a dollar a day in a hotel with maid service.

While Chace was down in Florida, the Joint Chiefs carried out their plans to consolidate military oceanography, disbanding the AAF's oceanographic unit where he worked. When he returned to Washington, D.C., everyone in his unit had dispersed and he was assigned to Roger Revelle's office at the Bureau of Ships. Chace now found himself an army officer stationed in the navy, a somewhat unusual position, but Revelle had come across the perfect assignment for him.

Revelle gave Chace the task of creating ocean current maps for survival manuals and cloth survival charts, known as "silk handkerchiefs," for aviators. The hope was that these survival charts would become lifesavers for pilots lost at sea by helping them determine the direction in which they were drifting and guide them to a friendly island where they could be rescued. Chace's skill set as both an oceanographer and an illustrator accustomed to studying and copying details lent itself well to the assignment. Best of all for him, he could sit in a room by himself for hours, fitting all the pieces of the maps together.

The idea for the cloth maps had originated with Christopher Clayton Hutton, an agent working in the MI9 division of the famed British military intelligence apparatus. MI9 had been established in 1940 to design and create tools to enable lost soldiers to evade capture and help prisoners of war escape. This became a growing field of interest in World War II when airplane pilots and their crews were downed behind enemy lines in increasing numbers. Hutton came up with the concept of developing lightweight cloth survival maps that could not only withstand the elements but would also be easy to conceal.

He found small-scale maps in Edinburgh and reproduced them on either silk, man-made fiber, or a durable tissue paper concocted from mulberry leaves. Mulberry paper proved to be ideal for survival maps because it could withstand being balled up and soaked in water and would smooth out without wrinkling or fading. The British had allegedly hijacked a shipment of the exotic paper intended for the Japanese, who used it to make balloons for aerial bombs.

Hutton's maps were small enough to fit into a cavity in the heel of a flight boot. The compartment could later be opened with a wire saw that had been threaded into the boot's laces. MI9 devised numerous other clever techniques of disguising maps and escape tools, such as implanting compasses inside buttons or cuff links and inserting miniature telescopes inside cigarette holders.

MI9 found ways to get these items to captured prisoners who, under the Geneva Convention, were permitted to receive aid packages with recreational materials. In one instance, they collaborated with the British manufacturer of the ubiquitous Monopoly game to hide maps within the game board and to include tokens that could be taken apart and assembled into a small compass and a metal file. American companies also participated like the Playing Card Company of Cincinnati, Ohio, that downsized maps and then inserted them inside playing cards. Over the course of the war MI9 smuggled fifty different maps to British soldiers being held in German prisoner-of-war camps.

Before the war, in November 1941, a contingent of American intelligence officers traveled to England to visit MI9 to learn about escape and evasion techniques. MIS-X (Military Intelligence Service-X), formed during World War II, became the American military escape and evasion branch, modeled on MI9. MIS-X followed the MI9 playbook and worked with American companies to hide maps, radios, wire saws, compasses, and currency in items that could be shipped to POWs under the names of fictious aid organizations.

The Army Air Force (AAF) produced the first cloth maps used by MIS-X for pilots forced to land in enemy territory, mostly in the Asian and Pacific theaters. The navy produced another set of maps, designed to be used as drift maps for pilots who were forced to ditch their planes at sea. The navy charts were known as handkerchief maps because they measured approximately thirteen by sixteen inches, roughly the size of a standard handkerchief. The AAF and the Air Intelligence Group of the Office of Naval Intelligence coordinated their efforts to cover all geographic areas of interest.

Because standard paper was too bulky and fragile when exposed to the elements and mulberry paper was hard to come by, MIS-X began to search for a more durable material that could withstand temperature extremes and moisture without fading. Different samples of cloth were put to the test by exposing them to a hundred hours of light in a Fade-Ometer and immersing them for an hour in salt water. After extensive testing, rayon was selected as the most lightweight yet durable material.

American cloth maps were printed on a specially treated rayon-acetate fabric through a complex lithography process developed through hours of trial and error. Learning how to print maps on rayon was difficult enough, but printing double-sided maps on rayon, as specified by the military, was even more complicated. Map makers also had to develop a formula for ink that would not run or fade even in the extreme conditions of long-term exposure to sunlight and salt water. Developing an exotic map material and ink to go with it was the type of expensive and tedious endeavor that would never have been undertaken, but for the fact that there was a war on and the military had an urgent need.

Chace continued to work on the survival maps after being transferred to the Hydrographic Office to join Sears. He illustrated currents in the Pacific Ocean areas where amphibious invasions against the Japanese were planned. Sears, who had been researching drift, assisted him in the project.

Chace depicted the average surface currents with streamlines overlaid with arrows to show the direction of flow and used numbers to indicate average current speed in nautical miles per day. The steadiness of the current, that is, the consistency of flow in a given direction, was indicated by the thickness of the streamline. The thicker the line the more reliable the current. Additional shaded arrows were added to the chart to show the average wind direction, with numbers inserted to represent the expected Beaufort force of the wind. Chace worked on the maps published by the Hydrographic Office from the middle of 1943 to the end of the war. The navy sought periodic revisions, as in March 1944, when it requested that two seasons be depicted with a color-coded system on one map.

The maps provided a means of estimating both current and wind along with their intensity in any given location to help survivors calculate drift. Raft occupants could assess wind direction by lighting a smoke pot (included with rescue supplies), throwing it overboard, and watching which way the smoke blew. An additional chart helped translate sea surface characteristics such as ripples or whitecaps into an average wind speed. The maps included a full page of instructions for use in rubber raft navigation so that men on life rafts could use the maps to choose a direction in which to paddle. Officers directing air-sea rescue operations could use these same maps to plot out a search area and determine a method of search, for example by plane versus boat.

Many other scientists and engineers also contributed to the development and execution of the survival maps. Harald Sverdrup at Scripps Oceanographic Institution had designed earlier versions of current maps that the navy asked him to update after Rickenbacker's rescue in the Pacific Ocean. The United States Coast and Geodetic Survey supplied current and wind data for some of the maps as well.

Lt. Damon "Rocky" Gause, an Army Air Force pilot, became one of the seventy-eight thousand American and Filipino troops who retreated to Bataan after the Japanese attacked the Philippines on December 9, 1941, ultimately forcing the Americans to surrender. Even though he was taken prisoner, he escaped and fled to the nearby island of Corregidor, which was still held by the Americans. Eventually it too fell to the Japanese, forcing Gause to move stealthily from island to island for several months during which he stumbled upon Capt. William Lloyd Osborne, another stranded American. With the help of local natives the men were able to plot an escape to Australia on a twenty-foot fishing boat.

When the two first set out, their only navigational aid was an old National Geographic map supplied by one of the natives and a worn Australian pilot chart. When they stopped at a leper colony, an American doctor gave them a precious compass. With these limited tools and, after fifty-two days of dodging Japanese patrols, sharks, storms, and reefs, the two landed in Wyndham, Australia, on October 13, 1942.

The cloth maps didn't come soon enough for Gause's escape, but his saga demonstrates just how far a map and a compass could get a stranded pilot and how having one earlier in his plight might have aided his rescue.

At the request of the navy, in November 1944, the Hydrographic Office published *Methods for Locating Survivors Adrift at Sea on Rubber Rafts*, an instructional manual for intelligence officers to use in briefing pilots in navigation techniques and to train air-sea rescue units. This indispensable guide grew out of Sears's first research project for the Joint Chiefs and, with contributions from Chace and others, significantly expanded upon the original one-page of instructions included with the cloth survival charts. The final version incorporated concepts based on data from studies performed at the Woods Hole Oceanographic Institution, Scripps Institution of Oceanography, and materials contributed by the Bureau of Ships, the Bureau of Aeronautics, and the Hydrographic Office.

For the hundreds of airmen who crashed after Rickenbacker's plane went down, this new tool, which would help rescuers locate them somewhere within the vast Pacific Ocean, made the difference between life and death. Along with the over two million cloth escape maps printed by American companies, the drift manual dramatically improved the chances a pilot would survive being stranded at sea. According to the *Air Sea Rescue Bulletin*, hundreds of survivors praised the cloth maps and credited the "intelligent use" of them with their safe return.

After the war, when Sears came across cloth map scarves and skirts in a department store in Stockholm, she couldn't help but laugh. The maps she had helped develop during a time of crisis had found new life as fashionable attire.

Sears and Chace had teamed up to use their scientific know-how to improve methods for rescuing pilots and proven how valuable oceanographers could be to the war effort. Their first joint project had changed the way the navy approached air-sea rescues but their most significant contributions and greatest challenges still lay ahead.

CHAPTER 9

Oceanographers to the Rescue

— Suitland, Maryland, 1943 —

By July 30, 1943, a total of 342 WAVES, approximately a third of the workforce, had come aboard the "USS *Hydrographic*," and Admiral Bryan had experienced an epiphany.

"I recall that there were many misgivings at the time we first decided that a few WAVES might be employed in the Hydrographic Office. Now, I wonder how we could have functioned without them. . . . Some day when they look back on their service in the Hydrographic Office, I know that they will have a feeling of pride that their work was a vital contribution toward winning the war," Bryan wrote, in a letter congratulating the WAVES on their one-year anniversary at Hydro.

This had been quite the turnabout, as Hydro had been one of the agencies that responded to the Bureau of Navigation's survey of shore jobs in early 1942 by stating they had no need for WAVES. Just a few months later, under the crush of a labor shortage, Bryan had been forced to request them, and before the year was over, they had started arriving. The incoming WAVES were aware that only a few months before Hydro hadn't been able to identify a single job in the entire office that a woman was capable of doing. They hadn't forgotten it, and when they had the chance, they made sure no one ever said that about them again.

What had the WAVES done to change Bryan's opinion? The simple answer is *everything*.

Fifty-six WAVES had been assigned to Chart Construction, many of whom had previous design experience like Specialist Alma Mach, a freelance commercial artist and graduate of the Minneapolis School of Fine Arts who filled a position as a draftsman. Ensign Georgia Greer traded in creating fashion displays for Bullocks department store in Los Angeles for constructing nautical charts that took men to sea. Carolyn Chadwick of Newburyport, Massachusetts, a silverware designer turned camouflage painter for the U.S. Army's aircraft, was now using her artistic skills to make maps.

The women worked in teams at long, rectangular drafting tables, sketching landscapes, plotting surveys, computing Mercator projections for navigational charts, and recording bottom samples and rock formations from soundings. They mapped harbors, approaches, and coastlines, all features of critical importance to the amphibious missions of the Pacific Campaign.

After the WAVES transformed field surveys gathered by Hydro survey ships into finished plots, they routed them to the Lithography Division to be etched onto plates and turned into widely distributed charts. WAVES working in the Oceanic Sounding Unit added sonar data from Hydro's survey ships. They checked and rechecked every detail lest an inaccurate sounding cause a ship to run aground.

In a recruitment brochure, the photogrammetry section was described as the place where "the girls don coveralls, crawl over a large white projection board, sight through a transit and lay down 'paper dollies.'" They were compiling serial aerial photographs that would add important landmarks to nautical and aeronautical charts. WAVES learned to use complicated instruments like stereoscopes, sketch masters, and pantogravers for engraving on copper plates. They became skilled workers equal to or exceeding the capabilities of the men they replaced.

The greatest number of WAVES, a hundred or more, worked in Air Navigation, preparing aviation charts for navy pilots circling the seas, performing reconnaissance missions and dropping bombs on enemy targets. They drafted survival charts onto nylon fabric carried by pilots who might be forced to ditch into rubber life rafts, the same charts that Fenner Chace and Mary Sears had worked on earlier, making calculations and current drawings to use in drift prediction.

WAVES pulled charts from the collection of sixty thousand kept in the vault at Hydro from all around the globe where a military pilot might fly, including enemy territories. They gathered around large, flat tables designing plotting sheets for aviators to map out their courses. WAVES like Ensign Betty Shaper of Laguna Beach, who could fly her own plane, seemed like a natural fit for "Air Nav." Specialist Barbara Harvey brought advanced drawing skills as a graduate of the National Academy of Design. She later worked for Signal Corps Laboratories, where she made sketches and drawings of meteorological equipment, graphs, weather maps, and cyclone formations. Patrician Hollingsworth from Denver, Colorado, who had been a commercial artist sketching stylish outfits to include in the *Rocky Mountain News* fashion column now sketched coasts and cliffs for aeronautical charts.

The sixty-five WAVES assigned to the Lithography Division worked individually, using magnifying glasses and needle-tipped tools to painstakingly correct zinc plates and etch new ones for use in chart production. Each had the responsibility of spotting mistakes and making corrections before the chart was printed and distributed to combat forces. They knew that even a tiny inaccuracy on a chart could lead to a dangerous mishap for troops. Specialist Joan Hill, a trained photographer who spent her prewar days capturing shy smiles in a children's clothing shop, now turned that same sharp eye to geographic features that she photographed for the lithographers.

In the Division of Maritime Security, where Sears's Oceanographic Unit was housed, WAVES also worked in the Pilot Charts Section, transcribing urgent Teletypes. They alerted mariners to dangers at sea from around the globe and transmitted the information to the radio intelligence unit, who sent it out to the navy fleet and allied merchant ships. Lt. (j.g.) Sarah Walsh, a Phi Beta Kappa graduate of Boston University, had worked in the history department of the Boston Public Library before the war where she had taught many a navy man how to read indexes and atlases. She now hoped to help many more sailors by sending out urgent dispatches to keep them safe at sea.

In the Geographic Names Section, where the first group of enlisted WAVES went to work, the women abstracted topographical features from every available nautical chart and map of a given area, indexed place names in multiple languages with a particular map location, and compiled them into geographical dictionaries known as gazetteers. These proved to be invaluable references to the numerous departments of the army and navy that planned military operations because they helped pinpoint distant military targets that might be known by more than one name. During the war, the Hydrographic Office published sixteen hardcover gazetteers covering Japan, coastal China, Indonesia, and islands of the South China Sea and Pacific.

In the Oceanographic Unit, WAVES classified incoming data and organized it into an accessible filing system. When urgent requests arose for specific oceanographic information, they culled through the files so that Sears and her team could prepare a report on short notice.

Sears, already in her late thirties, willingly served as a mentor to the younger "enlisted girls," advising them on how to wrangle a weekend off and how to look good when a WAVE bigwig was making the rounds for an inspection. She had played the role of big sister to much younger siblings for so long that looking out for her less-worldly assistants, most of whom had left home for the first time to join the navy, came naturally to her. As the only officer-in-charge who was a woman, she was able to help smooth out the rough edges when the male officers, used to working solely with men, came across as overbearing or gruff.

After years spent working almost exclusively with men, Sears had walked into an agency where hundreds of bright, hardworking women were getting the chance to prove their capabilities in the technical areas previously reserved for men only and excelling at it. She wasn't the only naval officer who felt that way.

"We looked the first twelve over, decided that they were the cream of the crop, and put in for three hundred more. We knew that most of the

WAVES weren't engineers, but decided they would make everything but pressmen," Captain Walter Jacobs, the assistant hydrographer of the navy, said. Running the heavy printing presses was one job the women were happy to leave to their male counterparts.

Just over a year into their assignments, the WAVES had proven they could learn to master almost any technical position and had made themselves indispensable. Even though Hydro would continue to lose civilian employees throughout the war, the older male supervisors who had aged out of the draft remained and greeted their newest recruits with enthusiasm.

The presence of women had also livened up the formerly all-male agency. The Recreation Committee now held Wednesday night dances at the Suitland Recreation Hall with the live combo, the "Hydro Hot Shots," providing the entertainment. Because of the WAVES there were now holiday parties, guest lectures, teas, and rummage sales. After-hours class offerings included naval history, Spanish, typing and shorthand, sewing and personal grooming. Commander McMillan, an Arctic explorer, regaled the audience with stories of his adventures while showing footage from his trips. Captain Slayton, an amateur magician, put on magic shows.

The WAVES also took part in the existing Hydro–Census Bureau League, fielding their own softball and basketball teams. The barracks station wagon took WAVES once a week to the Anacostia Receiving Station near D.C. for pool outings. A WAVE lieutenant started an archery club sponsored by the National Archery Association. WAVES hiked, rode horseback, paired off for modern dancing, and planted seeds for Hydro's victory garden. The Hydro WAVES were even filmed for *Report to Judy*, a movie distributed nationwide by the War Activities Committee of the Motion Picture Industry.

Not surprisingly, when mixing a batch of mostly young, single female "sailorettes" with mostly young, single male sailors, on occasion a Hydro couple would fall in love and get engaged. For convenience, most would exchange vows in a military wedding held at the chapel at Anacostia. Some of the brides-to-be wore their dress "whites" or navy "blues" and others opted to wear traditional wedding gowns.

The WAVES hadn't taken over Hydro and they certainly weren't in charge, but they had moved in and made themselves at home as much as was feasible, given the fact that they worked and lived on the grounds of a naval installation, and the men seemed to be just fine with it.

"From the moment we arrived they truly 'welcomed' us and made us feel that we were wanted, needed and appreciated, and from that very first moment on we have been able to say truly and from our hearts that we are 'happy to be aboard, Sir!'" Lt. (j.g.) Bernice Boner wrote in the WAVES anniversary yearbook.

While the WAVES were making inroads into the agency as a whole, Sears had continued to settle into her role as the conduit for all military requests for oceanographic information. She had been busy tracking down data to fulfill requests from the navy, the army, the Joint Chiefs, and other intelligence agencies. The stack of requests in her in-box had been growing by the day as the military ramped up its plans to attack Pacific targets. Each site where an amphibious force might land required detailed intel on waves, currents, bottom sediments, and beaches. Any site where an underwater weapon such as a mine might be deployed required analysis. Bathythermograph data coming back from ocean surveys needed to be analyzed and published to the fleet. In short, Sears needed to review any military operation involving a body of water.

After working alone for the first few months, Sears had learned that the vice chief of naval operations had instructed Admiral Bryan to coordinate at the Hydrographic Office a "suitable oceanographic staff . . . for supplying oceanographic studies to the military and naval services." The word "staff" had a nice ring to it. It implied that Sears would be getting help. It was a good thing, because the vice chief had further directed that the army would submit requests to the navy for any oceanographic data they needed.

With the existing supply of oceanographers being so tight at the beginning of the war, Sears was desperate to add anyone with a scientific background who she could at least train in the basics of oceanography.

Fenner Chace had been the first to arrive in June. Then, in July 1943, she found out that the navy was about to send the rest of the promised staff she had been hoping for. Dora Henry, a civilian oceanographer, and Mary Grier, an oceanographic librarian, who both had worked at the University of Washington, were being transferred to the Oceanographic Unit from the Air Force Weather Directorate.

Even though Sears had not met them in person before the war, she knew and respected their work—Henry's extensive publications in marine biology journals and Grier's highly regarded oceanographic bibliography of the Pacific Ocean. Sears also knew the head of oceanography at the University of Washington, Dr. Thomas G. Thompson, one of the recognized leaders in American oceanography. These two women who spoke the language of the sea added exactly the type of expertise Sears's office had been lacking. She looked forward to welcoming her new colleagues from the Pacific Northwest and working side by side to prepare the most comprehensive oceanographic intelligence ever assembled.

Dora Priaulx Henry was born in 1904 in Maquoketa, Iowa, into the weight of the expectations her parents, both schoolteachers, held for her future—to get a good education and become an independent woman. Those plans took a slight detour when Henry, like Mary Sears, suffered the misfortune of losing a parent, her father, at a young age. Her mother, who had already defied stereotypes by working outside the home, further spurned tradition when she moved away from overbearing in-laws who thought she couldn't manage without a man in the house. She packed up her three children and relocated to Los Angeles to get a fresh start, setting an example for her five-year-old daughter in what a woman could accomplish on her own.

The move also allowed Henry to later enroll at Hollywood High School, a much larger school than any Maquoketa had to offer and one that presented a greater challenge to her academically. Her mother insisted that Dora put her studies first in lieu of wasting time learning to cook and sew, unnecessary domestic arts that she never bothered to acquire. In

Mrs. Priaulx's view, a woman must attend college, the same as any man, in the event she had to support herself just as she had been forced to do.

The strategy paid off when her studious daughter was awarded an undergraduate scholarship to the University of California, Los Angeles (UCLA), then known as the Southern Branch of the University of California in Berkeley. Once Henry had decided on a zoology major, she transferred to the more established University of California at Berkeley to finish her undergraduate degree, graduating in 1925, two years ahead of Sears at Radcliffe. Like Sears, Henry also completed a master's and then a doctorate in zoology.

In graduate school, Henry studied under Charles Atwood Kofoid, the chairman of Berkeley's Department of Zoology, a rare, forward-thinking academic who had already mentored several women scientists before Henry. Kofoid had broken into the field of parasitology after serving in the U.S. Army Sanitary Corps in World War I, where he was tasked with starting a laboratory to examine human parasites such as hookworms that frequently sickened soldiers. He steered Henry toward the study of the parasites of birds and mammals, a field in which she thrived.

While at Berkeley, the twenty-one-year-old, petite brunette with an impish smile fell in love with a fellow student, Bernard S. Henry, a tall, handsome, twenty-six-year-old veteran of World War I, who was working on his Ph.D. in microbiology. They married in 1926, the same year Henry completed her masters' degree in zoology. She completed her Ph.D. in 1931 just before the two moved to Seattle, Washington, when Bernard was offered a position as an instructor in the Bacteriology Department at the University of Washington.

Henry had published widely on the topic of parasites, showing academic potential every bit the equal of her husband, however, she was not offered a job at the university for at least a year and then, only at the level of research associate. Even though she had to wait, landing a position at the Oceanographic Laboratories of the University of Washington on Puget Sound proved to be an ideal fit for Henry. Dr. Thompson, the department chairman, had opened the labs in 1931, drawing staff members from the physics, chemistry, zoology, bacteriology, and botany departments at the university to bring together a stimulating mix of minds to explore the mysteries of the sea. Among the professors he recruited was Bernard Henry, an inaugural faculty member of the Oceanographic Laboratories.

One of the few chemists who had recognized the importance of the chemistry of seawater, Thompson was also ahead of his time with respect to women scientists. He frequently hired female researchers and, as early as 1932, not only allowed but encouraged women, including Henry, to take part in research expeditions on *Catalyst*, the institution's small research vessel.

Taking advantage of her new surroundings, Henry began to study the gregarines, intestinal parasites infecting Puget Sound barnacles. The necessity of identifying the barnacle hosts along with the parasite species led the young scientist to dissect and classify them also. It wasn't long before she was scraping barnacles from rocks, pilings, and buoys around Puget Sound to take back to the lab and dissect. Just as Charles Darwin had become fixated on barnacles, spending eight years of his life examining the tenacious crustaceans that attached themselves to ships' hulls, so had Henry.

Darwin would eventually move on from barnacles to publish *The Origin of Species*, but Henry would spend the rest of her career, another six decades, picking the encrusters apart. She became an expert in their taxonomy, identifying thousands of specimens, some collected while out on *Catalyst*, others from collections housed at the Smithsonian Institution. She also examined specimens sent by collectors from around the world. Whether they came in Coke bottles, jelly jars, specimen vials, or wet paper towels, Henry never turned down a barnacle, ever. She identified so many barnacles that she became known as "The Barnacle Lady."

One person who reached out to Henry for help with barnacle identification was author John Steinbeck, who had gone on an expedition in 1940 with biologist Ed Ricketts to collect marine specimens. They sailed to the Gulf of California, also called the "Sea of Cortez," a narrow strip of ocean that separates the Baja California peninsula from the Mexican mainland. When they returned, Steinbeck contacted Henry at the University of Washington to see if she would assist in cataloging his specimens.

She told Steinbeck to send them, and he did—nine lots worth. And when Henry was through examining them, she had identified five species, one of which was new. She later published a scientific paper noting that Steinbeck's collection "has added considerably to our knowledge of the barnacles of the Gulf of California."

Among the more unusual samples Henry examined were those from detectives in the Puget Sound area, retrieved when they pulled a corpse from the water. The Barnacle Lady was the logical person to render an approximate time of death as well as other possible clues from an analysis of barnacles clustered on shoes and clothing. Barnacle growth rates depended on the species, location, and the temperature of the water. Larvae or juveniles appeared after two weeks in the water and adults at seven months. She could also measure the circular barnacle footprint to construct a time line for how long human remains had been in the water.

"They're on everything," she would tell her friends about objects pulled from the ocean. You just had to know what to look for, and she did.

In 1941, Dr. Waldo Schmitt, curator of the National Museum collections at the Smithsonian Institution, encouraged Henry to study and catalog a collection of barnacles held at the Museum of Comparative Zoology at Harvard. Thus began a correspondence with Fenner Chace, then the assistant curator, responsible for shipping barnacles to her at the University of Washington. Chace also guided Henry through the process of getting her results published in the *Proceedings of the New England Zoological Club* in 1942, shortly before he entered the service.

As prolific as Henry was in her research, her academic advancement was hampered by the fact that, in addition to being a woman, she carried the label "faculty wife" because her husband also taught at the university. The University of Washington, like many major universities, had strict anti-nepotism rules, meant to keep undeserving family members from being appointed to coveted positions. The predictable consequences of such sweeping rules were that wives who happened to be scientists were penalized even if equally qualified.

Women carcinologists often worked with little or no financial compensation. It was not unusual for women to be offered lower salaries or for them to take decreases in salaries to allow their male colleagues access to more funds. Pioneering women scientists who studied crustaceans still managed to succeed despite "personal difficulties, scorn by male counterparts, and poor working conditions." Even though many of these women made discoveries that exceeded the accomplishments of the men with whom they worked they were treated like the farm league of researchers. In Henry's case, she received a part-time salary for decades, even though she worked the same hours as the men.

Women seeking to enter male-dominated fields like science, medicine, and law in the 1930s were well aware of the discrimination toward married women, whether they were subject to the constraints of nepotism laws or not. Married women were perceived as subpar employees who would not work as hard as a man, especially when they began to have children. Perhaps this is why Sears often said that a woman had to choose between marriage or a career, as she and many other female scientists of her generation did by remaining single.

The sentiment surrounding women scientists, and specifically Dora Henry, was echoed by the groundbreaking microbiologist and former head of the National Science Foundation Dr. Rita Colwell in *A Lab of One's Own*, a memoir of her career as a scientist, beginning with her training in the 1950s at the University of Washington:

"Two other women scientists who might have mentored me occupied such lowly positions on campus that I felt that I could hardly consider them authorities on academic career building. Dora Priaulx Henry was a world expert on barnacles, and Helen Riaboff Whiteley was the university's star microbiologist. Yet both were 'associates' because their husbands were professors at the university and the state's anti-nepotism laws and university regulations forbade hiring relatives."

Colwell goes on to explain that while modern nepotism rules still prevent professors from supervising relatives, the ones she and Dora Henry were subject to were enforced "almost exclusively against wives of faculty members," at most universities and colleges in the United States. The anti-nepotism rules at the University of Washington went so far as to prohibit wives from paid work anywhere in the university except as clerks, secretaries, or laboratory assistants.

Dora Henry, a woman whose scientific discoveries in barnacles would be considered on a par with Darwin's by her peers, a woman who had been awarded yearly National Science Foundation grants for decades and was the leading American expert on barnacles for over half a century, would remain a part-time research associate at the University of Washington for almost thirty years, finally being promoted to a research associate professor in 1960.

While working at the University of Washington, Henry learned that the Naval Station at Bremerton, Washington, built as a shipyard for the overhaul and repair of the fleet, was conducting research on the bottom fouling of ships, a condition where an accumulation of organisms and vegetative matter adheres to a ship's hull. This buildup caused hydrodynamic drag at sea that slowed ships and increased fuel consumption. This was the same issue that researchers at Woods Hole had been working on for the navy and that Sears had been assigned to when she returned from Peru.

Henry had studied thousands of barnacles. She knew more about the cement-secreting glands that enabled them to adhere to ships than anyone in the country. The Barnacle Lady drove over to Bremerton Naval Station and offered to help find a solution to the fouling problem. But when she explained to naval officers in charge of the project that she was there to help them with their experiments to address the fouling problem, they weren't interested.

"There were two strikes against her," biologist Ed Ricketts later explained to John Steinbeck, as recounted in *The Log from the Sea of Cortez*. "One, she was a woman, and two, she was a professor. . . . She was thanked and informed that the navy wasn't interested in theory."

Several months after her visit to Bremerton, Henry heard there were problems with the antifouling project. The navy hadn't been able to grow a single barnacle on their test materials. Still anxious to assist in the war effort, she drove back out to the naval base to see what she could do to help. The navy's research technicians thought they had replicated the exact conditions required for barnacles to breed, adding seawater to their large concrete tanks and monitoring the temperature. *What could they be doing wrong?* Henry had them retrace every step and minutes later identified the problem. She told them it had to be the filter.

The seawater around Bremerton brimmed with harbor debris, oil, decaying fish and algae. In the navy's zeal to eliminate "the filth" from their experiments, they had filtered the seawater before filling the test tanks, and in doing so they had completely purged the population of barnacle larvae. Without them, adult barnacles would never form.

Using a filter was an amateur mistake and one that the navy might have avoided if they had simply allowed Henry to review their experimental protocol. But that was never going to happen, because when Henry first walked into the Bremerton Naval Base she wasn't taken seriously. The navy researchers did not see a scientist wearing a white lab coat. They saw a woman. Nothing that she said after that mattered. The navy was not going to take advice from someone in a skirt, not until there was absolutely no other alternative.

World War II brought big changes to the Henry household. Dora Henry's husband, Bernard, who had served in France during the Great War at age eighteen was now faced with serving again. The difference was that at age forty-three he was a professor of bacteriology at the University of Washington and had a technical skill that the army could use. He was able to parlay his training into a position with the army's Sanitary Corps, tasked with overseeing sanitation and preventative health services for the army's medical department. Bernard was commissioned in 1942 as a major and placed in charge of the Ninth Service Command Laboratory at Fort Lewis, Washington, where he identified gastrointestinal parasites and other infections. Bernard Henry would spend the duration of the war in the Pacific Northwest.

Dora Henry, on the other hand, had no obligation to enlist in any branch of the service or to work for the government. But, the oceanographic labs at the University of Washington had been shuttered because of the war and she was determined to find a position helping to defend her country. After the Bremerton experience, she knew she had something of value to offer, something that pertained directly to a war being fought in two oceans.

Through the close-knit network of American oceanographers, she learned of the Army Air Force's oceanography group stationed in Washington, D.C. Unlike the navy, when she offered her services to the army, they recognized her expertise and offered her a position as an assistant oceanographer. It would take her across the country and away from her husband, but she too wanted to serve a vital role in the war.

Once in D.C., she met Fenner Chace, the young carcinologist from the Smithsonian Institution who had once shipped her a collection of barnacles to examine. The two would meet again in April 1943 when Army Air Force personnel reassembled under the direction of Lt. Mary Sears at the Hydrographic Office in Washington, D.C.

While having marine scientists on board to analyze and interpret oceanographic data was critical to the Oceanographic Unit's mission, it was equally crucial to gather the best available references. In 1942, Mary Grier was the most knowledgeable oceanographic librarian in the country, having worked in that role for twelve years at the University of Washington. Evidence of her expertise was her towering accomplishment *Oceanography of the North Pacific Ocean, Bering Sea and Bering Strait: A Contribution Toward a Bibliography*, published in 1941. It had taken Grier two years to compile the list of over twenty-nine hundred published references by topic. In the introductory note to the bibliography Grier had thanked Dora Henry for her "helpful criticisms."

The methodical Grier had scoured books, magazine articles and scientific journals from around the world as she hunted down every single oceanographic reference in existence. In doing so, she had developed relationships with a network of librarians across the country, including those at the American Museum of Natural History in New York, the New

York Public Library, and the Library of Congress. If an article had been published in the oceanographic literature pertaining to the North Pacific Ocean, even if it was in a foreign language, Mary Grier knew about it. Little did she know, as she hunted down obscure references, that her bibliography, along with the contacts she made working on it, would prove to be a valuable source of intelligence to the United States Navy in fighting World War II.

Soon after the publication of her landmark volume, Grier, like Dora Henry was out of a job when the Oceanographic Laboratories at the University of Washington closed due to the war. The closure forced her to find work as an inspector at the Boeing Aircraft Company in Seattle, a position left vacant by a male employee entering the service. While she was grateful to be employed, a position reviewing shop records and checklists for aircraft engine maintenance was not exactly her dream job. She missed the intellectual stimulation of working with scientists who shared her interests.

In early 1943, Grier received an offer she could not have imagined would come her way. Major Dick Seiwell called asking if she would be interested in coming to Washington, D.C., to join Dora Henry at the Army Air Force Weather Directorate. Grier could barely contain her excitement over the phone as she told Seiwell that yes, she was very interested in joining his group of oceanographic researchers and would get there as quick as she could. Grier, a single thirty-six-year-old, still living at home, turned in her resignation at Boeing and raced home to tell her parents the news. She packed up her clothes and toiletries and took the bus to D.C. She wanted to get there before anyone changed their mind about giving her the job she so desperately wanted.

In Washington, on her first day at the Weather Directorate, Grier was greeted by the familiar warm smile of Dora Henry. Having worked with her in Seattle, she knew Henry's outward appearance belied her true determined nature. Henry had pushed her way into a man's field and leveraged her iron will to extract the best from everyone she worked with. But Grier didn't mind working with tough women because she always felt like she knew where she stood with them and that if she did her job well, they would get along just fine.

She also met the young carcinologist Fenner Chace, someone she'd only "known" through his papers on crustaceans, which she'd included in her bibliography. Chace was meticulous, like most of the scientists she knew, but he had a reserved, almost shy manner about him and a wry sense of humor. She liked that about him. All in all she felt like she'd landed in a good spot, among one former colleague she admired and new ones she equally respected.

Grier found out right away that there was no true library at the Weather Directorate, only some reference books on a shelf in the large room crowded with desks where the researchers puzzled over questions about the oceans. Her specific task would be to go out to libraries in D.C. and New York City to locate published oceanographic data. She would need to transcribe the relevant information by hand and bring it back for use in intelligence reports prepared for military units and she would need to do so quickly, as many of the requests were time sensitive. Some of the scientific information the oceanographers needed had already been published in various formats, including in scientific journals. This was Grier's wheelhouse. No one knew the scientific literature on oceanography better than she did.

When Grier found out she would be transferred to the navy's Hydrographic Office to continue her work under the direction of Sears she was relieved. First, because she wouldn't be packing up to go back to the Boeing plant when the AAF unit was dissolved. But also because she had known of Sears's work as a planktonologist at Woods Hole and of her numerous collaborations with the legendary Henry Bryant Bigelow. If Sears had kept Bigelow happy and managed to make a name for herself in the male-dominated world of marine science, she was bound to be top-notch.

The core of Sears's team at the Oceanographic Unit of the Hydrographic Office had begun to take shape. Fenner Chace, the curator of shrimp and crabs, would help review oceanographic data and act as the chief illus-trator for reports. The Barnacle Lady, Dora Henry, would assist in draft-ing reports and hone her editing skills working under the exacting Sears as she translated voluminous reports into copy that nonscientists could comprehend. Mary Grier, one of the nation's best oceanographic biblio-philes, would hunt down obscure sources, including in foreign languages, that could be distilled into confidential oceanographic intelligence to give the troops an edge. Sears, would be the go-between, attending meetings in D.C. and bringing back the top secret locations for military operations. She would also function as the chief analyzer of oceanographic data, checking for accuracy and performing last-minute calculations.

This gifted group of marine scientists, educated to study the creatures of the sea and now analyzing combat zones, toiled far away from the front lines of war, under the radar and out of the spotlight. As they assembled complex oceanographic intelligence reports, Sears and her team reached out to their contacts in the small world of oceanography. Dr. Harald Sverdrup, who had become director of Scripps just prior to the war, was a major resource for the team, particularly in the area of wave prediction. Likewise, Columbus Iselin, the director at Woods Hole, stayed in frequent contact with Sears throughout the war, exchanging information related to the naval research he was overseeing. Dora Henry consulted with her former mentor, Dr. Thompson, who served in the Chemical Warfare Ser-vice of the Army throughout World War II. Sears also met regularly with fellow oceanographer Roger Revelle, now assigned to the Bureau of Ships. All the major schools of thought in cutting-edge oceanography would be represented under one roof.

Personnel would come and go at the Oceanographic Unit, which av-eraged twelve to fifteen members—enlisted men, who Sears would refer to as "the little boys," the WAVES Sears dubbed "the enlisted girls"—who helped pull references for reports, and even an occasional scientist who would rotate through and then head out to Woods Hole or Scripps to work on another naval research project. The four-person core, however, would stay intact for the duration of the war, putting their careers and their lives on hold for as long as it took to defeat the Empire of Japan.

Part Two

THE MISSION BEGINS

CHAPTER 10

Closing the Intelligence Gap

— Washington, D.C., 1943 —

Four months into her job at the Oceanographic Unit, Sears had learned a lot about what the military needed from oceanographers. She had learned it from meeting with Roger Revelle and his cohorts on the Joint Chiefs Subcommittee on Oceanography where she listened to concerns about what the navy was lacking and took detailed notes. She had learned it from answering requests from every branch of the military for tidal data, wave forecasts, and currents to support tactical operations overseas. She had learned it from gathering all the known references on drift and drafting an urgently needed manual to help locate men lost at sea. The more she took in, the more she understood exactly how dire the lack of oceanographic intelligence was and how it could undermine military operations. And now she was going to have to do something about it.

Sears was no longer at Woods Hole, where she had been sidelined by her male colleagues who sailed on *Atlantis* and collected *her* specimens while she stayed onshore. For the first time in her life, she was in charge. It was now her responsibility to set up and direct the operations of an oceanographic intelligence unit researching vital questions that impacted the war. She had never been asked to set agendas, call meetings, or give people orders, much less make sure they carried them out, but she was going to have to do those things to get the military the information they needed to win the war. She was going to have to take the lead.

To assume the role of leader, Sears would need to push through her innate reserved tendencies and any thoughts racing around in her head that screamed *you don't belong here*. Taking charge of a team of ocean-ographers did not come naturally to a bench scientist who worked alone all day staring into a microscope, especially if that scientist was a woman, but Sears had learned from watching Revelle. He had started as an aca-demic in a tweed jacket with elbow patches, but when the navy made him a lieutenant he took on the persona of "the man in charge."

When Revelle walked into the conference room of the Munitions Building—tall, broad shouldered, and uniformed—he was in complete control. He spoke in a booming, decisive voice. He had an answer for every question. He solved problems. Now, thanks to the overly confident Revelle, Sears was wearing the uniform too. She had stepped into his shoes at the Hydrographic Office. She was not going to let anyone think she couldn't fill them.

During the first year of the war there had been a mad scramble in Wash-ington to gather information about the countries where troops might be fighting, especially distant locales like New Guinea, Indochina, Formosa, and all the tiny islands dotting the sixty-four million square miles of the Pacific Ocean. World War II spilled across the globe into places most Americans had never heard of and where the military had never been. It was unlike any other war Americans had fought.

Getting to these places would be the easy part. The navy could navi-gate its way to just about any far-off target anywhere in the world, thanks to the nautical charts maintained by the Hydrographic Office, but what would it find when it got there? *Were the beaches flat and wide or would they be narrow, steep, and difficult to land on? Was the terrain mountain-ous, volcanic, or swampy? Would high winds and waves impede a smooth landing? Would they land during the rainy season? Who were the native people and what language did they speak? Were there drivable roads once troops got across the beaches?*

All these details mattered because going to war was more than hauling men, tanks, rifles, and ammunition to a designated site and attacking the enemy. The troops needed to come prepared for whatever they might find, which meant knowing everything they could about an area in advance.

The military searched their files for background materials. They found spotty reports scattered among files of government agencies but no comprehensive references that spanned the globe and nothing that left them with a sense of what to expect when they went to war. The years between World War I and World War II stretched across the lean budgets of the Depression years. The military had languished along with the rest of the country—training soldiers with Springfield rifles manufactured in 1903 and using borrowed cruise liners to transport troops. With Congress keeping the purse strings tight, there had been no money to spend gathering intel for wars that might pop up one day in some remote corner of the world. The file cabinets were all but empty. As one intelligence official summed it up, "We were caught so utterly unprepared."

What would the armed forces do now to catch up in the midst of an ongoing war?

It was a problem that had vexed Roosevelt even before the war. To help remedy the intelligence gap, he had appointed General William Donovan in mid-1941 as coordinator of information, a role that morphed into the director of the Office of Strategic Services (OSS) during World War II. But Donovan too was getting a late start, and his mission was focused on espionage and sabotage, not foreign terrain.

The logical source of information for the military was its own intelligence agencies. The Office of Naval Intelligence (ONI), the OSS, the Army Corps of Engineers, and G-2, the army's intelligence unit, had all started spinning out their own internal intelligence reports, duplicating effort and expense. But like jealous siblings guarding their toys, the agencies kept their reports to themselves, which only hampered preparations in the long run. Furthermore, these groups had not antic-ipated the massive landscape this war would cover and there were still many gaps to fill.

"Who would have thought, when Germany marched on Poland, that we would suddenly have to range our inquiries from the cryolite mines of Ivigtut, Greenland, to the guayule plants of Yucatan, Mexico; or from the twilight settlements of Kiska to the coral beaches of Guadalcanal. Who even thought we should be required to know (or indeed suspected that we did *not* know) everything about the beaches of France and the tides and currents of the English Channel," a CIA official later mused.

That was exactly the problem: there was no predicting just what in-formation might be needed in a war of global proportions. Whether it was knowing where to collect an essential mineral or finding the latest tidal data, the need for information, beyond just estimating enemy troop strength or weaponry, was enormous. The military leaders trying to plan the war—where to send troops first and what operations to execute when they got there—were particularly hindered. Their information needs were unfolding in real time, and without a centralized forum for gathering, collating, analyzing, and disseminating information, the United States found itself at a disadvantage in war planning.

Roosevelt began to realize the extent of the problem when he started meeting with Churchill and the British Chiefs of Staff in a series of war planning conferences. At the Arcadia Conference held two weeks after World War II began the British had the edge in strategic planning. They had operated under a system for almost two decades where the British Chiefs of Staff served as a supreme, unified command, reaping the ben-efits of cooperation between the Admiralty and the British Army. The United States had no such corresponding body.

Weeks after the first conference Roosevelt formed his own Joint Chiefs of Staff, a unified, high command in the United States composed of Ad-miral William D. Leahy, the president's special military adviser; General George C. Marshall, chief of staff of the army; Admiral Ernest J. King, chief of Naval Operations and commander in chief of the U.S. Fleet; and General Henry H. Arnold, deputy army chief of staff for air and chief of the Army Air Corps. This impressive array of leaders could draw up battle plans, but it would take time to turn themselves into a truly cooperative body.

At the next war planning conference, at Casablanca in January 1943, Roosevelt noticed yet another fault in the American war planning apparatus—the information gap between the British and the Americans. No matter what subject came up in any corner of the world, the British had prepared a detailed analysis on the area at issue and pulled those reports out of their briefcases. The Americans weren't able to produce a single study that could match the quality of the British reports, a failing that frustrated and embarrassed the president.

"We came, we listened and we were conquered," Brigadier General Albert C. Wedemeyer, the army's chief planner, shared with a colleague following the Casablanca Conference. "They had us on the defensive practically all the time."

The British had a two-year head start on the Americans in this war and they had learned the hard way about the need to collect reliable topographic intelligence. During the German invasion of Norway in 1940 the Royal Air Force Bomber Command had been forced to rely on a 1912 edition of a *Baedeker's* travel guide for tourists as the sole reference in planning a counterattack. In the same offensive, the Royal Navy had only scanty Admiralty charts to guide an attack on a major port, an intelligence deficiency that could have easily doomed the mission. The British had gotten away with one in their Norway mission, but they knew they had to do better.

So they had formed the Interservices Topographical Department to implement the pooling of topographical intelligence generated by the army, navy, and the Allies, and tasked it with preparing reports in advance of overseas military operations. This was where Churchill's reports came from and why his aides could pull them out of their briefcases when the most sensitive joint operations were being planned. To be on an equal footing with the British, the Americans needed to be able to do the same, which meant they were going to have to find a way to rectify the lack of information and fast.

. . .

In April 1943, the same month Sears started at the Hydrographic Office, the Joint Chiefs put into action a plan to close the intelligence gap with the British. They appointed a Joint Intelligence Study Publishing Board (Joint Publishing Board) to oversee the preparation of comprehensive reports that would be titled "Joint Army Navy Intelligence Studies" (JANIS). The JANIS mandate—"To make available one publication containing all the necessary detailed information upon which may be based a war plan for military or naval operations in a given area"—was lofty, expansive, and difficult to achieve. A year and a half into the war, it was also long overdue.

The idea was to prepare an all-inclusive intelligence report "under one cover" that would describe the geographic, physical, demographic, and socioeconomic characteristics of a particular strategic location—every detail that could affect a combat operation by land, sea, or air. To get the most accurate information, interpreted by experts in their fields, would require the input of at least twenty separate government agencies. By bringing these intel reports under one umbrella, the Joint Chiefs hoped to improve the quality of the reports and overcome the reluctance to share data that had swirled around the intelligence community.

The Joint Chiefs appointed representatives from the three major intelligence agencies—ONI (Office of Naval Intelligence), G-2 (United States Army intelligence), and the Office of Strategic Services (OSS)—to the Joint Publishing Board. The first step was to develop a format for these unprecedented, all-encompassing studies.

The board came up with an initial thirteen-chapter outline to include an introductory brief and sections on military geography, oceanography, coasts and landing beaches, climate and weather, port facilities, telecommunications, cities and towns, resources and trade, people and government, health and sanitation, and aviation. The topics would be divvied up among the twenty agencies, known as "the contributors," who were to prepare their sections by a set deadline. These draft reports would be submitted to the Joint Publishing Board, which would collate, edit and print the information, and get it out to the Joint Chiefs, military commanders, and government agency heads, hopefully, in time to make an impact on the war.

Sears may not have been aware of it, but in the process of completing the many tasks that had been dumped in her lap in record time, she had started to make a name for herself among the men who outranked her. Here was someone who really seemed to understand how tides worked. She could even compute them for distant locales where no tide tables existed. She knew a lot about currents too, as she proved with her extensive report on the drift of objects at sea. She had learned everything there was to know about sea and swell by reviewing Sverdrup's work on them. She took every request for data seriously and never punted an assignment. Sears's attitude and skills made an impression on the higher-ups in the navy who knew just how pivotal data about the ocean could be to the fate of amphibious missions and the success of the Pacific Campaign.

Each amphibious mission involved moving men and massive amounts of cargo through a series of ships, starting with transport vessels that could carry Higgins boats, amphibious tractors (LVTs), troops, supplies, and equipment for amphibious landings. Next came the ship-to-shore movement, the most critical stage of an amphibious operation. It was in this transition, vulnerable to high waves, rough seas, and variable tides that most trouble occurred. Lowering boats and tractors into a turbulent ocean was dangerous enough, but the added step of transferring men and equipment to them increased the risk. A low tide, too low to float even the shallowest keel, could strand landing boats on an intervening coral reef and expose vulnerable troops to a blizzard of fire. A steep landing gradient onshore might incite a torrent of towering waves that caused vessels to capsize and break apart. Oceanographic intelligence could be key to fighting these ocean-based battles, and now the navy had someone who could deliver it.

Despite Sears's strong start she still had to be taken aback when Admiral Bryan called her into his office in July 1943 and explained that he had a new project for the Oceanographic Unit. The Joint Chiefs had ordered the preparation of JANIS reports, long-range strategic intelligence reports that would help them plan the war. Bryan informed Sears that she would be heading up the preparation for "Chapter III, Oceanography," of the JANIS reports. The report would be based on the thirty-three-topic outline Revelle had presented at an earlier meeting of the Subcommittee on Oceanography.

The Joint Publishing Board had initially assigned this responsibility to a much more seasoned officer, Colonel Sturdevant of the Office of Naval Intelligence (ONI). But shortly after getting the assignment he had become aware of the newly formed Oceanographic Unit and realized they could do a much better job. "A large portion of the necessary basic hydrographic and oceanographic information, both for landing places and for offshore areas, can best be compiled by the Oceanographic Unit of the Hydrographic Office," read a memo to Bryan requesting the change. The head of naval intelligence had just handed off a report that would go straight to the Joint Chiefs. He must have had tremendous confidence in the newcomers to do so.

Sears and her fledgling crew were untested in the intelligence arena, but no one could doubt their expertise in oceanography. The Joint Chiefs would be using these reports to make pivotal decisions about every phase of the war, Bryan informed Sears. This project would take priority over everything else they were doing. The oceanographers would still be preparing urgent reports for tactical operations. They would still be putting together monographs on oceanographic topics like they had for drift and waves. They would still be analyzing bathythermograph data and preparing dispatches to the fleet. And now on top of it all, they would be sifting through mounds of articles, data, charts, and observations from merchant ships and deciding what the Joint Chiefs needed to know that would impact their plans to assault island targets.

It was a heady responsibility for Sears to be entrusted with this high-priority assignment for the highest level of command. Each JANIS report would have to anticipate all issues that might impact a military operation that originated or took place in the ocean. It would take a massive effort to amass the data needed to cover all thirty-three oceanographic subjects for just a single report. Sears would have to meet the deadlines and accommodate last-minute schedule changes. Any mistakes would be magnified across the entire spectrum of the United States armed forces.

Sears knew this latest assignment would add to the workload and pressure on the team. But, if "Chapter III, Oceanography," did what it was intended to do, numerous hazards of the sea might be avoided, which meant saving lives. Who better to point those out than her Oceanographic Unit?

With the Joint Publishing Board still organizing for the production of the JANIS reports, the nation's first offensive amphibious landings in the Pacific theater had already begun, starting with the amphibious assaults on the Solomon Islands in August 1942.

The Solomons, British territory before the Japanese wrested them away in a flurry of invasions, were virtual unknowns to the United States Navy in the distant South Pacific, twelve hundred miles east of the northern tip of Australia. The Japanese, wholly unprepared for and surprised by the early morning beach landings on Guadalcanal and Tulagi, could not muster an opposition force. The marines splashed ashore virtually untouched. Such was not the case for the landings at Gavutu and Tanambogo that took place later that afternoon because there were not enough landing boats to launch all the assaults at once.

A coral reef encircling Gavutu mandated that landing boats approach from the northeast. They had to funnel into a single channel to cross the barrier, fourteen thousand yards out from the beaches, against a stiff wind. As the United States Marines approached the beach, the Japanese, warned by the earlier landings, sighted on the invaders and opened fire. Although the Marines ultimately prevailed after vicious fighting, the 1,300-man assault force suffered 157 casualties over the two-day mission, which was fraught with chaos and confusion.

The overarching lesson was that opposed landings, where the Japanese defended the beaches with a hailstorm of machine-gun fire while marines slogged their way to shore in rough surf, allowed little margin for error. The execution of the Gavutu-Tanambogo operation not only exposed the need for more in-depth amphibious training and better equipment but also demonstrated that oceanographic intelligence on tides, reefs, surf zones, and beach gradient was just as essential to the mission as advance knowledge of enemy strength, weaponry, and defensive tactics.

As the Pacific Campaign continued, the Joint Chiefs set dates for the next rounds of assaults, making decisions that were complicated by the fact that many of the strategic targets were complete unknowns to the American military. The newly conceived JANIS reports could help with planning operations on islands that had been shrouded in secrecy by the Japanese for decades. The reports couldn't appear soon enough for their purposes.

Meanwhile, the Joint Publishing Board slogged along, inching its way through the layers of government bureaucracy. They had to hire editors and secretaries, find space in the crowded office buildings around Washington, D.C., and requisition the hundreds of other items needed to start up a new government publishing enterprise dedicated to churning out confidential intelligence reports for the military.

Throughout the first summer of their existence, the Joint Publishing Board held meeting after meeting to discuss technical issues like formats and font size for the printed text, page size, photographs, map layouts, and cover design. They worked out reporting responsibilities and deadlines. Forced to find an outside printer because the government printing office was backed up, a team made numerous site visits. In the meantime, the war in the Pacific intensified against a determined enemy and no reports were forthcoming to aid the cause.

In spite of the delays, Sears needed to start thinking about the future, which meant rearranging the Oceanographic Unit's workspace. With the hope that she could nab a few more WAVES to help out, she had squeezed more desks into the one large room where the Oceanographic Unit worked.

Sears approached her new assignment with confidence, knowing that she had the right people in place to take on this monumental responsibility. Her team had started to fall into their natural roles based on their talents and expertise. Mary Grier would be dispatched to the libraries around Washington, D.C., and anywhere else she needed to visit to retrieve the best oceanographic data. Fenner Chace, who had already been mapping currents and wind speeds, would take the lead on charts and graphics for the reports. Dora Henry, who had marked up many a graduate student's thesis at the University of Washington, would serve as editor, compiling the report sections while reviewing them for errors. Sears would help analyze the stacks of data Grier brought back and translate complicated scientific concepts into language that a lay person could understand. She would have the final say in what to include in the report.

As a member of the Joint Chiefs' Subcommittee on Oceanography, which met in the Public Health Building, Sears was used to trekking across dusty, crowded, and, during the summer of 1943, blistering hot, Constitution Avenue, the major conduit between military and governmental agencies and the White House. When the organizational meetings for the JANIS reports began, she attended them in one of the eight wings of the Munitions Building, which had been erected on the National Mall. Each wing was longer than a football field, its own microcosm of wartime administration. Between the time spent walking down Constitution Avenue and through the hallways of the Munitions Building, Sears was getting plenty of exercise, which suited the fitness buff just fine.

The proposal for these temporary buildings had first been pitched by Franklin D. Roosevelt, then the assistant secretary of the navy, to President Woodrow Wilson to alleviate an office space crunch during World War I. FDR had then proposed constructing the "tempos" on the Ellipse, a fifty-two-acre parklike expanse in front of the White House. Wilson vetoed the idea because he wanted to avoid the cacophony of construction. Roosevelt moved the project farther away to the Potomac Park section of the National Mall, knowing that reallocating the people's parkland would not be a popular move.

Three stories tall and built mainly of reinforced concrete with gray "cemento-asbestos" exterior walls, the structures lined the National Mall along Constitution Avenue for a third of a mile. The five-hundred-foot-long east–west main hallways branched at right angles into north–south wings, eight for the Munitions Building and nine for Main Navy, each building housing fourteen thousand workers. From overhead, the structures looked like gap-toothed combs. As the government ran out of space, it added even more rows of the cheap, drab structures, extending along both sides of the Reflecting Pool east of the Lincoln Memorial and nearly surrounding the Washington Monument.

"When I first came down here in 1933, I said I didn't think I would ever be let into the Gates of Heaven, because I had been responsible for desecrating the parks of Washington," Roosevelt later commented.

Even after the War Department moved out of the Munitions Building and into the newly built Pentagon in November 1942, then the world's largest office building, the vacated space quickly filled up with more government agencies. By 1943 the National Mall was almost completely covered with boxy, cookie-cutter buildings lacking in even the most basic architectural flourishes. Although some of the buildings were disassembled after the war, the Munitions Building and Main Navy lasted more than five decades, a span during which they were a constant source of controversy, not just because they were eyesores, but also because they stood on parkland, part of which would eventually be occupied by the Vietnam Veterans Memorial.

When it came to finding offices for the massive influx of workers and enlistees, the government had no choice but to shoehorn them into unconventional spaces like the "tempos." Military housing spread into borrowed building sites at George Washington University. Necessity transformed mansions from social hubs to stenographer pools. Mobile homes were squeezed into any patch of land big enough to fit one while prefabricated defense housing sprung up on the outskirts of the city. The government even called on local citizens to rent out rooms to help house the flood of workers.

• • •

Over that first long, hot summer in the three-story federal building wrapped with security fencing in Suitland, Maryland, Sears had her team ready to start gathering critical information for the first JANIS assignment that reached her desk. She expected it to be an important landing site in the Pacific, but she was wrong. When the team of oceanographers excitedly pulled up their chairs to the large, flat wooden table, instead of unfurling maps of critical targets in the Pacific, they found that the subject of the first JANIS was Bulgaria, followed by Albania and Yugoslavia. The United States had already notched at least four major victories in the Pacific and had many more to go, but the first JANIS priority list didn't have even a single Pacific target on it.

How could this be? Wasn't the Pacific Campaign their focus? Wasn't that where their skills as oceanographers would have the greatest impact? Their excitement gave way to frustration and groans of disappointment.

Admittedly, the perplexed scientists were far from the level of strategic war planners, but still, they knew the Pacific Campaign, where amphibious forces were approaching harbors and beaches, was in progress. If they were going to double their workloads, spend nights and weekends hunched over tide tables and reams of data, review wave observation reports and study reconnaissance photos until they were bleary-eyed, they wanted the end result to make a difference.

The British had already agreed to supply oceanographic intelligence for regions adjacent to the Atlantic Ocean, including all of Europe, since they had a two-year head start in the region and access to excellent oceanographers in London. Bulgaria, Albania, and Yugoslavia certainly seemed to be in their sphere. The oceanographers must have felt like they were wasting their time on these first assignments, but they also knew they were working for the navy now. They didn't get to pick their areas of research like they did in civilian life at universities and research institutions. Here, they did what they were told, and if their first JANIS assignment was Bulgaria, they would get to work on it.

It turned out the oceanographers' intuition was correct. Eventually it came to light that the source of the first JANIS priority list had been an outdated Military Intelligence Service's (MIS) to-do list that had little relevance to current military operations. It was a glaring and costly oversight that failed to incorporate the pressing needs of the Pacific Campaign.

In September 1943, the Joint Publishing Board finally issued an amended priority list. Bulgaria, Albania, Yugoslavia, and France were still on the list, but relevant Pacific targets had all of a sudden appeared—the Marshall, Caroline, Palau, and Mariana Islands. Commander Bailey, the board chairman, was most likely acting on directives resulting from the proceedings that took place at the Quadrant Conference held in August in Quebec City, Canada. The agenda had included a discussion of specific targets for the Pacific Campaign by the Combined Chiefs made up of the British and American Joint Chiefs.

This change in priorities signaled that war planners had recognized the need for up-to-date topographic information on future targets in the Central and Southwest Pacific. The road to Tokyo the Joint Chiefs were mapping out in real time would align the JANIS reports with potential invasion targets, increasing their relevance. This was exciting news for the contributors gathered around the table, who wanted to do something to help win the war. The JANIS reports would become more valuable war planning tools, not only for strategists in Washington, but also for operational planners in the field, who soon began to extract text, diagrams, and maps from JANIS reports and insert them into their own battle plans. This newfound combat relevance boosted morale for the JANIS contributors, especially for Sears and the oceanographers.

It didn't take Sears long to catch on to the fact that after each Combined Chiefs Conference, when Churchill and Roosevelt got together to flesh out their war strategy, more requests came rolling into the Oceanographic Unit. Some were for "quickies," top secret urgent reports Sears fast-tracked within her group and hand-delivered without delay to the requesting party. She also learned to expect a change in JANIS priorities as war strategy evolved, as had happened at the Quadrant Conference.

Six weeks later, Commander Bailey announced a reshuffling in the administration of the JANIS reports. Because there had been so many requests for JANIS studies and other briefer queries, the Joint War Planners had established the Joint Topographical Committee to help establish priorities. The committee would also determine if an area required a complete JANIS report or whether a preliminary "Phase Two" or "Phase One" study, would suffice to supply the needed information.

Bailey also noted that the next JANIS report would be on Netherlands New Guinea, a Dutch colony seized by the Japanese in early 1942. The Japanese had constructed a network of airfields across the island that the Americans were intent on seizing so they could launch their own aerial attacks as they proceeded across the Pacific Ocean. New Guinea now moved up the list to become the second JANIS report, bumping the other European targets.

Before the planning meeting on New Guinea in late November 1943, Bailey sent a terrain study prepared by the Allied Geographical Section (AGS) to the contributors for review. AGS, headquartered in Melbourne, Australia, was formed in 1942 at the direction of General Douglas MacArthur to address the critical lack of geographic information in the Southwest Pacific. AGS had since drafted detailed reports by trained geographers for combat missions. Bailey asked the contributors to review the AGS study and weigh in on whether it would suffice in lieu of a JANIS report. At the meeting, Bailey went around the table, asking for the contributors' assessments.

Sears delivered her response without hesitation. "More could be added on tides, seas and swells, sound ranging, bottom sediments, currents and salinity," she said, indicating that the report was lacking in key oceanographic data that could affect military operations. Sears might be new to the JANIS group and to the navy, but she was not new to the science of the sea, and knew an inadequate report when she saw one.

Captain Caskey of the AAF Weather Directorate felt similarly about the climatology section and stated that "a much better report" could be compiled on the weather. Lieutenant Colonel McCaffery from the Corps of Engineers agreed, stating that considerable new data could be added on points where port facilities could be established. The areas of the AGS report that covered the hard sciences of oceanography, meteorology, and engineering were the areas of greatest concern.

Yet not everyone around the table found fault with the report. Contributors from the military intelligence services preparing sections on defenses and military installations, which were nonscience-based topics, judged the report to be adequate. Swayed by those arguments, Bailey concluded that the New Guinea JANIS should be scrapped. Later, though, someone up the chain of command overruled him. New Guinea remained the focus of the second JANIS report and was published as scheduled.

The oceanographic chapter for the JANIS on New Guinea was the first JANIS drafted by the Oceanographic Unit for an amphibious invasion target. The scientists worked late into the night to complete it on time, with only snacks out of the vending machines to tamp down their hunger. When they finally completed "Chapter III, Oceanography" and Dora Henry had edited all the sections, they were wiped out, but it was a good feeling, like they knew they had accomplished something important to the war.

Sears and her team managed to find and digest numerous sources on short notice drawing from sixteen different sources. Their eleven-page report included publications and tide tables from the British Hydrographic Department, Dutch periodicals, a report on oceanographical observations from the Japanese Imperial Fisheries Institute, tide tables and publications from the U.S. Hydrographic Office, as well as data from two expeditions, the HMS *Challenger* in 1875 and the *Snellius* Expedition in 1929.

This broad constellation of references demonstrated not only just how difficult it was to find information about some of the more esoteric targets, but also how antiquated the data could be. These were not well-traveled areas, especially not by Americans. In this case, to get the necessary data, the group had reached back to references that were sixty-eight years old.

Despite the difficulty in tracking down sources, the oceanography chapter on New Guinea allowed the oceanographers to flex their scientific muscles and show the group's capabilities. One criticism that was outside of the oceanographers' control was that the report, which did not officially roll off the presses until March 1944, was delivered only six weeks before the New Guinea offensive took place. Even though it had been available to the Joint Chiefs War Planners in time for critical decisions, word filtered back from the field that getting the JANIS reports out sooner would allow more extensive distribution throughout the theaters.

The stated purpose of the JANIS reports was for strategic war planning at the Joint Chiefs level, not to prepare battle plans, but operations planners wanted as much intelligence as they could get before sending men into the ocean. The Joint Publishing Board took this feedback to heart as they spent the rest of the war streamlining their processes to expedite delivery of reports to the field. Subscribers grew from 750 for the first JANIS to over 2,500 recipients, including all echelons of military command, government agencies, the State Department, the Joint Chiefs, and FDR's map room at the White House.

Regardless of how the initial JANIS reports were coming across, at least one naval officer had already reviewed other tactical studies compiled by the Oceanographic Unit and found them to be more than satisfactory for his purposes. "Please thank Miss Sears for me in regard to the studies put out by her unit," wrote Lt. Charles L. Burwell, USNR, Amphibious Force, Atlantic Fleet, to Lt. Commander B. E. Dodson, Mary Sears's immediate supervisor at the Hydrographic Office.

This rare personal recognition of a fellow officer's contribution to the war effort, came from a highly respected naval intelligence officer. When Dodson passed the praise along, the oceanographers rejoiced that a report they had turned out had made a difference. Less than a year later, Burwell would be among those briefing commanders and troops on weather and surf conditions at Utah Beach on D-Day at Normandy. He would provide these same services at the Pacific invasions at Lingayen Gulf and Luzon in the Philippines and at Okinawa where he would come to incorporate even more of the Oceanographic Unit's research into operational plans.

Burwell's accolades seemed to echo the conclusions that Sears's superiors had already reached about the hardworking marine biologist. In December 1943 she was promoted from lieutenant (junior grade) to lieutenant (senior grade), a testament to Sears's mastery of her duties and the leadership she had shown in carrying them out. It was also a move that made her among the highest-ranking women in the navy and put her on a more equal footing with the male colleagues she worked with on the Joint Publishing Board and on the oceanographic subcommittee.

In November 1943, while the oceanographers were still drafting the Bulgaria study, the assault on Tarawa in the Gilbert Islands, one of the first major amphibious landings of the war, was just getting underway, without the benefit of a JANIS report or the best oceanographic intelligence available. Tarawa had never made it onto the JANIS priority list, probably because there wasn't time to prepare a full study. "The navy went to war without knowing enough about the oceans," Sears later said. The Battle of Tarawa became the poster child for this sentiment and would haunt the navy and the marines for the rest of the war.

Mary Sears (end of third row, far right, hair in bun), shown in her eighth-grade graduation photo, class of 1923, attended the all-female Winsor School in Boston, where she broadened her horizons both educationally and culturally.

Sears (shown at left in the Bigelow Library with two colleagues) attended graduate school at Radcliffe College and worked at Woods Hole Oceanographic Institution (below) in the summers.

During World War II, Mary Sears transformed from a marine biologist researching undersea organisms into a naval oceanographer churning out intelligence reports.

Fenner Chace left the study of crustaceans temporarily to join Sears at the Hydrographic Office. After the war he returned to the Smithsonian Institution, where he spent the rest of his career as its director of carcinology.

Dora Henry, known as the Barnacle Lady, also enjoyed deep-sea fishing.

Mary Grier, one of the best oceanographic librarians in the country, joined Sears's Oceanographic Unit in 1943, where she scoured the nation's libraries for oceanographic data to include in intelligence reports.

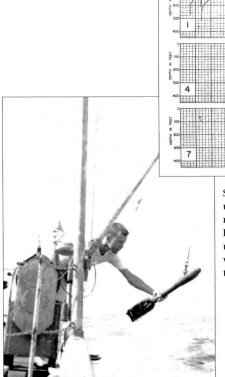

Sears interpreted bathythermograph (BT) data used in submarine warfare. To record a BT measurement the cumbersome instrument had to be lowered into the ocean (left) and reeled back up again. The BT etched tracings of temperature versus depth (above) that were used to predict thermoclines in the Pacific.

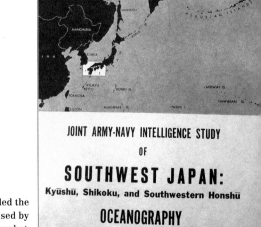

JANIS 84
CHAPTER III

Non-registered

JOINT ARMY-NAVY INTELLIGENCE STUDY
OF
SOUTHWEST JAPAN:
Kyūshū, Shikoku, and Southwestern Honshū
OCEANOGRAPHY

Sears and her team of marine scientists compiled the Joint Army Navy Intelligence Studies (JANIS) used by tactical planners and the Joint Chiefs to plan combat operations and the war.

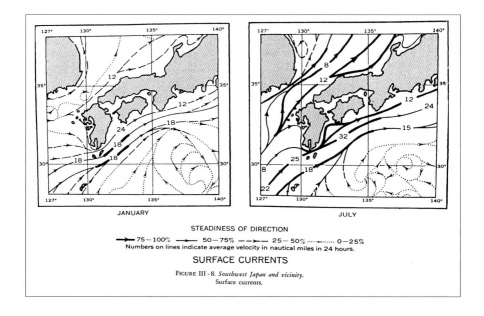

JANUARY   JULY

STEADINESS OF DIRECTION

→ 75—100% ⟶ 50—75% – –▸– 25—50% ⋯⋯▸ 0—25%
Numbers on lines indicate average velocity in nautical miles in 24 hours.

SURFACE CURRENTS

FIGURE III - 8. *Southwest Japan and vicinity.*
Surface currents.

JANIS reports included data on thirty-three oceanographic parameters, including surface currents (above) and the size and distribution of ocean waves (below) for island targets.

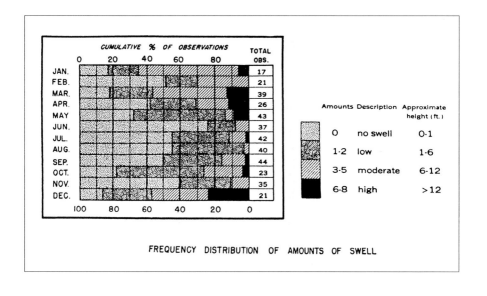

FREQUENCY DISTRIBUTION OF AMOUNTS OF SWELL

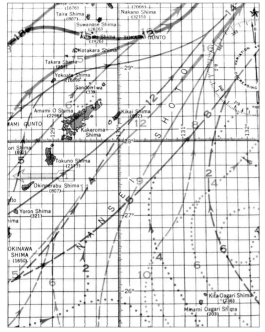

Fenner Chace used his illustration skills to depict ocean-current strength and direction on cloth rescue maps for downed pilots in the Pacific Ocean. Sears used her expertise in currents and drift to assist in the project.

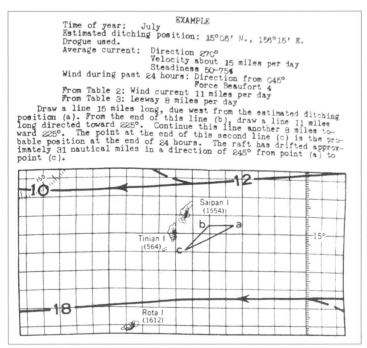

EXAMPLE

Time of year: July
Estimated ditching position: 15°05' N., 156°15' E.
Drogue used.
Average current: Direction 270°
Velocity about 15 miles per day
Steadiness 50-75%
Wind during past 24 hours: Direction from 045°
Force Beaufort 4
From Table 2: Wind current 11 miles per day
From Table 3: Leeway 8 miles per day

Draw a line 15 miles long, due west from the estimated ditching position (a). From the end of this line (b), draw a line 11 miles long directed toward 225°. Continue this line another 8 miles toward 225°. The point at the end of this second line (c) is the probable position at the end of 24 hours. The raft has drifted approximately 31 nautical miles in a direction of 245° from point (a) to point (c).

The cloth maps included a set of instructions to aid in navigation.

VOL III 1 45

The Hydrographic Office's weekly newsletter, the *Scuttlebutt*, included a mix of gossip, social activities, jokes, and intramural sports scores; it also provided updates on the whereabouts of deployed former coworkers.

Picture yourself in

It's a proud moment when you first step out in brand new Navy blues. The trim, smart uniform was especially designed to flatter every figure and make you look—and feel—your best.

When you arrive at recruit school as an enlisted WAVE, you will be provided with an allowance of $200 for uniforms and other clothing. The official uniform consists of "everything that shows," except shoes and gloves. The cost—about $180—is paid from the $200 allowance. The balance of about $20 is given you for shoes, underclothing and anything else you may need.

After one year's service you will get $50 a year for clothing replacements.

The regular uniform for enlisted WAVES consists of the following articles:

Soft hat, rolled brim, black band.

Navy blue wool suit. Jacket has slightly built-up shoulders, rounded collar and pointed lapel. Flattering six-gored skirt.

*Summer white dress uniform, same design.

White and dark blue shirts.

Black and reserve blue seaman's ties.

Over-shoulder leather pouch bag.

Cool, gray-and-white, pin-striped seersucker work uniform for summer.

White gloves and black gloves.

Beige hose.

Black oxfords (heels not over 1½") or "pumps (heels not over 2").

Rain-proof havelock and raincoat.

*Overcoat.

Blue denim work coverall, slacks or reserve blue smock—for special jobs.

*Optional.

—18—

these smart Navy Uniforms

Light-weight whites for summer dress

Summer gray-and-white seersucker shirtwaist dress and jacket

Navy blue wool winter work uniform

Attractive raincoat and rainproof havelock

Blue work smock

—19—

The tailored WAVES (Women Accepted for Volunteer Emergency Service) uniform, created by fashion designer Mainbocher, served as a recruitment tool drawing in young women who wanted to wear the stylish attire.

WAVES assigned to the Maritime Security Division assisted Sears and her team of oceanographers in researching JANIS reports and urgent requests for oceanographic data from branches of the military.

Hydrographic Office WAVES take a break from drafting. Specialist Lucy Berkey (center, head turned to the right), a former art teacher, used her skills to etch fine details on charts used in combat zones.

When World War II began, the demand for nautical and aeronautical charts to guide the military to foreign targets surged, quadrupling the workforce needs at the Hydrographic Office. Over three hundred WAVES arrived to fill in the gaps, including Sylvia Adams, who plotted hydrographic features on charts.

When WAVES joined the workforce at the navy's Hydrographic Office in 1943, they showed they could perform any task required of them, including using aerial photographs to construct nautical charts as Specialist Lillian Boschen does here.

Specialist Mary Palmquist, a WAVE working at the Hydrographic Office during World War II, uses a magnifying glass to inscribe features onto a nautical chart, a task that required accuracy and attention to detail.

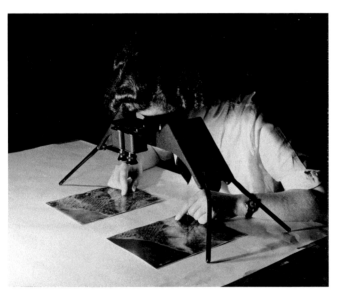

WAVES learned to use specialized equipment like the stereoscope Francis Bochner is using here to pinpoint geographic features that would later be added to charts.

Lt. (j.g.) Muriel Braeutigam transfers details from a Japanese chart to a naval chart. During the war, oceanographers used data from captured Japanese charts and publications to compile intelligence reports on targets in the Pacific.

Adm. Chester W. Nimitz, who commanded naval Pacific forces during World War II, issued a commendation to Mary Sears recognizing her role in compiling oceanographic intelligence for combat missions for the Joint Chiefs.

OFFICE OF THE CHIEF OF NAVAL OPERATIONS
WASHINGTON 25, D. C.

Op43-B4-hmw
Ser 10455P43

20 MAY 1946

From: The Chief of Naval Operations
To: Lieut.Commander Mary SEARS, (W),USNR, 218870

Subj: Commendation

1. The Chief of Naval Operations takes pleasure in commending you for your outstanding contribution to the war effort as Chief of the Oceanographic Unit of the Division of Maritime Security of the Hydrographic Office, and later as Officer-in-Charge of the newly formed Division of Oceanography at that Office. Your technical knowledge and administrative skill were instrumental in the selection, compilation, and publication of oceanographic data of great value to the armed forces of the United States. In your capacity of oceanographer you were frequently called upon by the Joint Chiefs of Staff to furnish critically valuable information for use in combat operations. Your performance of all these duties was at all times exceptional, and beyond the high standard normally expected.

After World War II Sears returned to Woods Hole Oceanographic Institution, where she became known for her extensive index-card collection summarizing oceanographic publications. Sears's cumulative *Oceanographic Index* was later published in fifteen oversized volumes.

Mary Sears (center, middle row) served as clerk of the otherwise all-male Woods Hole Corporation. Her mentor, Henry Bryant Bigelow (center, first row, hat on lap), was the first director of the Woods Hole Oceanographic Institution. Columbus Iselin (first row, third from left) served as the institution's director during World War II.

The USNS *Mary Sears*, the first oceanographic survey ship named after a woman, was launched on October 19, 2000. Leila Sears christened the ship named after her sister.

CHAPTER 11

Tarawa

— Tarawa, 1943 —

On the eve of the Battle of Tarawa in November 1943, Admiral Chester Nimitz, commander in chief of the Pacific Fleet, had a foolproof plan
to ensure victory with only minimal casualties. The navy would soften
enemy positions before the landing by shelling the Japanese-held island
in the Central Pacific Ocean from battleships and cruisers offshore. It
would then attack mercilessly from the air with hundreds of planes—
torpedo bombers, dive bombers, and Hellcat fighters. Nimitz believed that
this kind of large-scale overpowering attack, when launched in the early
morning hours before the landing boats headed to shore, would hobble
Japanese forces so severely that they would be easily overrun by marines
storming the beaches.

The need to wrench captured islands out of Japanese hands made
amphibious assaults, an untested form of warfare, necessary, but the
operations were inherently complex and risky.

"There are no amphibious cakewalks," wrote historian Joseph Alexander, an amphibian assault commander in later years. "The work is extremely hazardous. Even under the most benign tactical conditions men
drown, or get crushed by shifting cargo, or get run over by heavy equipment."

An amphibious landing was an orchestra of moving parts, each one essential to the execution of the whole and each presenting an opportunity for catastrophe. Even with the best planning the operations carried inevitable hazards—hostile fire, barrier reefs, swirling currents, a rough surf zone, and underwater obstacles. There were also unexpected failures to contend with, the kind that could throw off an entire operation, like the sinking of landing craft and tanks, communication breakdowns between the ships at sea and the men onshore, and the paralyzing hypothermia induced when men were forced to wade ashore in frigid waters.

The engagements of the Pacific Campaign had to be staged thousands of miles away from the navy's home bases of San Francisco and Pearl Harbor, from where all the equipment, supplies, and troops had been shipped over weeks in preparation. If the marines lost something they needed either in transit or during the approach, there was no ability to ship it on short notice. Like a theater troupe on opening night, they had to make do with who and what they had and improvise if necessary, because the curtain was going up on the next battle and nothing short of a Japanese surrender was going to stop it.

The marines would be going ashore in LCVPs (landing craft, vehicle, personnel), known as "Higgins boats," barge-like vessels, measuring thirty-six feet in length with a minimal four-foot draft, needed to cross shallow waters. New Orleans shipbuilder Andrew Jackson Higgins had visited the marines several times over seven years to pitch the boat he designed for fur trappers and oil drillers working in the low-lying swamps of Louisiana. His first iteration, the Higgins "Eureka" boat, was outfitted with a hollow tunnel to protect the propeller from sandbars and underwater obstructions, a flat bottom with a shallow draft, and a blunt bow that would push obstacles out of the way. This unique design allowed the boat to navigate through shallow, root-infested waters without fouling the propeller.

When Higgins finally got his boat in front of the right audience and tested it in a series of beach landing exercises, the naval officers could not believe what they were seeing. After years of trying and failing to develop an effective landing craft they had found one, along with a knowledgeable and willing collaborator for the duration of the war. After Higgins

tweaked the bow design to add a ramp that could be lowered as it hit the
beach, thus making it easier for troops to disembark, the navy adopted
the Higgins boat as their standard landing craft.

In planning for the assault on Tarawa, operational planners had concerns
about the tide levels the troops would encounter in trying to traverse the
reef in Higgins boats. The daily tidal cycle when the sea rises and falls varies with the gravitational pull of the moon and the sun. Neap tides occur
during the first and third quarter moon when the sun and moon are at
right angles creating a narrower tidal range.

D-Day at Tarawa Atoll coincided with the occurrence of a neap tide,
when the difference between high and low tide is minimal. If the tidal
level became too low, landing boats could have a difficult time crossing
the extensive barrier reef outside of Tarawa. Yet, ship captains and former
residents of the island, predicted the tides would rise to at least five feet.
Planners believed five feet would be plenty if landing boats headed toward
the island at peak tide level on D-Day.

The potential impact of tidal variations on military operations had
been discussed among the members of the Joint Chiefs Subcommittee
on Oceanography at least seven months prior to the Battle of Tarawa at
their April 23, 1943, meeting. When Roger Revelle had first introduced an
outline of oceanographic data, among the numerous topics suggested for
study was a detailed analysis of tides that covered the character and time
of the tide, tidal range, and "special tidal phenomena." Specifically mentioned in this section were concerns for "low water, lower at neaps than at
springs" and "excessive duration of high or low water." Reports based on
this outline had, unfortunately, yet to be generated before Tarawa.

With the history of unpredictable tides around Tarawa and knowing it
was encircled by a coral reef, military planners decided that the initial
assault waves would deploy the LVT (Landing Vehicle Tracked), an amphibious tractor capable of traversing water or land.

"Swamp areas and coral reefs encountered near the beachline are passable by no other means," Major General Holland Smith had said advocating for the role of this early generation of LVTs. "The use of the amphibian tractor permits a wider selection of landing places and more freedom of maneuver for the attacker."

Smith would end up being correct, not only for Tarawa but for every other amphibious assault where it was necessary to traverse a coral reef. The small tractor boats could grind over a coral shelf no matter how shallow the water, track up to the beach, and drop the men onshore. In the worst case, the amphibious tractors could shuttle troops between landing boats on the ocean side of the reef and the shore, a distance of about five hundred to eight hundred yards. The downside of that scenario was that even one additional handoff of troops to another craft while under fire added risk and delay.

Tarawa would be the first time the newly acquired LVTs, designed for hauling cargo to the beach, had been used during combat to transport marines. This early generation of amphibious tractors, known as "amphtracks," "amtraks," or "tin cans," were not armored or designed to withstand heavy fire. Even though the military directed some last-minute modifications before the Tarawa assault—mounting machine-guns on the bow and riveting boiler plates to the sides—the LVTs were still susceptible to large gun and machine-gun fire and could easily explode if the gas tanks were hit. But in a pinch, they would have to do.

Further complicating the plan to use amphibious tractors was that the navy could only scavenge 125 of them in time for the Tarawa invasion, not nearly enough to transport even half the troops to shore. The later waves of troops would have to ride to shore in Higgins boats, hoping that by the time they got to the coral shelf the tide would have risen enough for them to clear the shallow bottom.

The morning of the invasion, November 20, 1943, war correspondent Robert Sherrod was packed into a Higgins boat along with thirty marines heading toward Tarawa atoll. Tarawa was just two and a half miles long and seven hundred yards across, only one square mile of land, useless but for its strategic airstrip, which was essential to provide air cover for the Americans' continued march across the Pacific.

The relentless thunder of missiles launching from navy destroyers echoed in Sherrod's ears on the way to the battle. Red-orange flashes lit up the horizon and booming shells thickened the air with smoke and ash. Sherrod counted over a hundred explosions a minute and ninety-two planes overhead. The town of Betio, near the airstrip, was on fire, a reassuring sign that the navy's prelanding bombardment was hitting its intended targets. Surely the Japanese large guns had been knocked out by now.

A half a barrel of water per minute splashed over the boat's bow as it motored to shore, soaking the troops on board and prompting Sherrod to unclasp his watch, dry it off, and slip it inside a waterproof envelope he zipped into the pocket of his olive-green field jacket. He tucked away the rest of his valuables—photos, a lighter, a pack of cigarettes—and then huddled with the men on board, shaking with a mixture of cold, fear, and excitement.

When Sherrod's boat reached the rendezvous point about a mile from shore it circled in the rocking waves, awaiting a signal to assault the beach. They were close now, close to risk, close to reward, nearing the moment of attack and almost certain engagement with elite Japanese marines. Sherrod was in the fifth wave, which meant that four waves of Higgins boats filled with Marines had gone before him and should have scooted onto the scorched sand of the beach already. As Sherrod searched the shoreline for some sign of the preceding waves of boats, he swallowed hard. He couldn't pick out a single Higgins boat. All he could see on the beach were a few scattered amphibious tractors.

Where were they?

The mystery was solved when a naval officer in a command boat pulled up alongside and yelled, "You'll have to go in right away, as soon as I can get an amphtrack for you. The shelf around the island is too shallow to take the Higgins boats."

And just like that the excitement of the mission drained out of the veteran reporter and fear rushed in. If the first four waves hadn't made it to shore, what had happened to the men? Who was on the beach? And what would be Sherrod's fate, pitching about in a plywood bathtub in the middle of the Pacific Ocean, approaching hostile territory and the relentless fire of seasoned Japanese snipers?

Sherrod knew that the amphibious tractors had been intended as emergency backups and that there were not enough of them to land all the marines in the initial waves. Waiting for a shuttle to the beach would slow down the landing and give the Japanese even more of an upper hand. If too many of the thin-walled tractors were knocked out by enemy fire, there would not be enough to get his crew safely to shore.

Charles Pase, a seventeen-year-old marine machine gunner from West Virginia, was aboard a nearby troop ship watching the tragic scene unfold with field glasses. He later recalled a sight that would forever be seared into his memory: "We'd watch these lines of marines climb out of the Higgins boats as they worked up on to the reef, and then try to walk ashore and occasionally we'd see a man disappear. Then, maybe two or three men away another man would disappear, and they would just drop into the water. We couldn't see the blood but we knew what was happening. These men were being picked off by the machine guns because we could see the machine gun bullets hitting the water like raindrops."

After waiting interminable minutes in a drifting Higgins boat with 40 mm shells getting way too close, Sherrod jumped onto an amphibious tractor that was shuttling marines close to a pier, seven hundred yards from shore.

"It's hell in there," the crew chief said. "They've already knocked out a lot of amphtracks and there are a lot of wounded men lying on the beach." He pointed toward a rusty hulk of a Japanese freighter in the distance. "You can wade in from there," he said.

Like most of the men aboard, Sherrod was shaking when he flopped over the side of the eight-foot-tall vessel into neck-deep water and started wading into machine-gun fire pelting the surf. As the marines sloshed through a sea of bodies and debris, they rose up out of the water, becoming larger targets. That was when the Japanese really opened up, timing their fusillades for when the marines were most exposed.

"I could have sworn that I could have reached out and touched a hundred bullets," Sherrod later wrote.

Almost any other week, almost any other day, the marines would have gotten the minimum four feet they needed to clear the reef, but what they got on November 20, 1943, was closer to three feet. Instead of sailing to shore, the bottoms of the Higgins boats scraped across the coral reef and stopped. No boats crossed that barrier the morning of the assault, and none for the next forty-eight hours. The men were stranded, and they had to evacuate in heavy surf. Even the ingeniously designed and rigorously tested Higgins boat, the same boat that Dwight Eisenhower would later credit as the reason the Allies won World War II, could not get them to shore. Tarawa vividly and tragically demonstrated that minimum tide levels could not be taken for granted where coral atolls ringed the shore. Tides mattered, and on some days, tides were everything.

As the thinly armored tractors rolled toward shore with the first waves of men and into blizzards of machine-gun fire their weaknesses too were exposed. At two hundred yards, the Japanese began to hit their targets with deadly precision, strafing the LVTs, causing some to explode and others to catch fire. Twenty-five of the tractors were disabled in the first wave.

Any tractors that could still run had to maintain a safe distance from enemy fire, which meant dropping the men off the length of two football fields from shore. From there, troops were forced to jump into the ocean with eighty-pound packs strapped to their shoulders, hoisting their rifles overhead to keep them dry, while wading ashore over razor-sharp coral that slashed uniforms and skin alike. The landing devolved into chaos with bullet-riddled Higgins boats stalled on the coral reef, LVTs set ablaze, and the relentless slap of machine-gun fire on surf as wounded men stumbled into deep red pools of ocean and drowned.

All the troops could do was keep wading forward, doing their best to dodge fire and find cover. Those who made it ashore that first day weren't safe even then. Trapped between the sea on one side and Japanese machine-gun fire on the other, they clung to piers, hid behind the burned-out shells of scorched LVTs, or dug into the sand and prayed.

For Vice Admiral Raymond Spruance, commander of the Central Pacific Force, and Major General Julian Smith, of the Second Marine Division, who were watching from offshore, the floundering of the troops and the mounting casualties were excruciating. This was not the landing they had expected.

"Get the hell in and get the hell out," Nimitz had instructed them, and now the fate of the entire mission was in jeopardy.

On the second day of the ill-fated offensive Private Pase loaded machine guns into a rubber raft and motored through a sea of corpses, "hundreds of marine bodies," men who had not made it to the beach.

"We steered our way through them as carefully as we could," he said.

Because the tide remained low, Pase's rubber raft was the only boat that could make it across. He watched as a marine battalion in Higgins boats, unaware of the continued low tide level, smashed up against the reef. The Japanese took advantage of the mishap, using shore-based anti-aircraft guns to blow up several of the boats while troops were attempting to disembark, resulting in yet another round of casualties.

Fierce fighting continued on that second day. There were moments when the outcome was in doubt, but the marines kept fighting their way inland. They used a combination of the only two Sherman tanks to make it to the beachhead, close-in naval gunfire, and expert riflemen to make their way. Finally, by the morning of the third day, the tides reached normal range, allowing the rest of the Higgins boats and reinforcements to shoot across the reef and onto the beach.

The marines prevailed in seizing Tarawa, but the magnitude of the casualties cast a pall over the victory. Of the 5,000 marines in the landing force, 1,027 were killed and 2,100 were wounded. An estimated 300 had been killed just trying to cross the barrier reef after their boats had gotten stuck.

After it was all over—after the flag of the U.S.A. had been firmly planted into the sandy soil of Betio, after the bodies had been counted, after some of the dead had been tagged and taken back to the ships for burial at sea and more were covered with ponchos and placed into hastily dug mass graves—military strategists cataloged and studied the tactical errors and miscalculations of the Battle of Tarawa.

First, the naval and aerial bombardment had fallen short and left the enemy relatively unscathed. Second, the three-to-one ratio of attack force to enemy combatants had not been assembled, and that added to the calamity. Third, the shortage of amphibious tractors slowed the momentum of the attack and left the first waves of marines desperate for reinforcements.

But, in the end, the greatest error, the final common pathway that hampered the offensive and turned the shoreline into a killing field, had been misjudging the tides. When the boats couldn't cross the reef, the timing and momentum of the entire operation was thrown off. The troops who had managed to get ashore under heavy fire from the enemy, desperately awaited reinforcements, many of whom were floating face down in the surf.

Operational planners had worried that oceanographic intelligence was spotty. The best existing charts of Tarawa had been compiled a hundred years before. The offshore measurements necessary for accurate tidal calculations had been impossible with the island in enemy hands. Without that data, planners were simply guessing at tide variations and relying on the fallible memories of locals.

Another four decades would pass before the tides at Tarawa were fully explained when a history professor in Texas asked a physics colleague if he could figure out what happened that fateful day. In 1987, Dr. Donald

Olson determined that on November 20, 1943, in addition to a neap tide, the moon was in apogee, at its farthest point from Earth, during which the tidal range is even narrower.

It was the navy's bad luck that the Tarawa operation fell on one of only two days in 1943 when an apogean neap tide occurred. As a result, from 0900 to 2200 on November 20, 1943, the water level stayed within six inches of its mean level of 3.3 feet.

The Battle of Tarawa had taken place in a far-flung location in the middle of the Pacific Ocean, foreign territory to the United States Navy. In the future, military planners would find ways to gather critical intelligence for these remote operations. They would rely on oceanographic intelligence reports compiled by the newly formed Oceanographic Unit well in advance of operations. They would augment that information with aerial reconnaissance and the observations of frogmen working in underwater demolitions teams. But Tarawa, one of the first major landings, and the one that came closest to failing, had laid bare the necessity for gathering as much data as possible and putting it in the hands of expert analysts.

The casualties of Tarawa spawned nationwide shock. An outraged public demanded answers and Congress convened hearings. *Why were so many mistakes made and what could be learned from them?* The flood of questions swirled around the hearing room and washed over the military leaders called to testify.

"There had to be a Tarawa," Major General Julian Smith told Congress. There had to be a first large-scale attack with all its inherent flaws in decision-making, logistical fiascos, and spotty oceanographic intelligence. Even though the marines had ultimately prevailed, there were lessons to be learned about making amphibious tractors more combat worthy, about the timing of assault waves, how to better "soften" a hostile shore, and about gathering reconnaissance in advance of high-risk missions.

"There were no foxholes offshore," General Alexander Vandegrift, commandant of the Marine Corps, told the Senate Naval Affairs Committee after Tarawa. "The American public would have to steel itself," he said. Heavy losses would continue throughout the gritty Pacific campaign to wrest islands from a tenacious enemy.

Unloading thousands of men, heavy equipment, and supplies into a turbulent sea under intense fire presented numerous opportunities for calamity no matter how many calculations were made and rehearsals performed. Japanese soldiers were professional and tenacious. Their battle tactics would surely evolve to blunt American offensives.

No one expected amphibious landings to be easy or simple, but the outcome at Tarawa horrified the public. With no means of evacuation, the Japanese fought to the last man, deploying every bullet, bomb, and bayonet at their disposal. Such desperation lent a fierceness to the combat unseen in other theaters. The likelihood that the pattern of reckless slaughter of marines would continue unabated was unwelcome news both to the military and the American public.

In the rush to procure the optimal landing craft, scavenge amphibious tractors, and build ships to transport troops and heavy artillery, the military had failed to take into account the complexity of the ocean. At Tarawa, the navy had gone to war largely ignorant of this new aquatic battlefield, with its waves, surf zones, and underwater hazards. The resulting lack of preparation manifested on the blood-stained beaches of Tarawa.

It wasn't just the enemy that had ravaged American forces.

They had just about beaten themselves.

CHAPTER 12

Reversing the Mandate

— The Mariana Islands, 1944 —

As the Oceanographic Unit geared up to compile the next wave of JANIS reports in January 1944, it was clear that neither the country nor its leaders were in the mood for another Tarawa. Although Admiral Nimitz publicly praised the marines' efforts and restated the significance of the mission, privately he agonized over why the invasion had unfolded the way it had. His entire Pacific strategy rested on one amphibious assault after another. Nimitz knew it was unsustainable to repeat the mistakes of Tarawa.

"You killed my son on Tarawa," one mother wrote to Nimitz after the casualty report was released to the newspapers, one of many letters he received from distraught relatives.

Before Tarawa, the plan of attack had been a dual advance across the Pacific, with General MacArthur proceeding along the northern coast of New Guinea to the Philippines and Admiral Nimitz driving across the Central Pacific, launching a series of island assaults. After Tarawa, and the shocking number of casualties it cost the marines, the high-risk strategy began to look shaky.

The outspoken MacArthur began to advocate for abandoning Nimitz's central prong of attack altogether. Tarawa had reinforced the inherent dangers of amphibious assaults. Even Nimitz, fresh from the sting of intense congressional questioning and an avalanche of letters from grieving mothers, reexamined his strategy.

Tarawa reflected the ultimate truth about amphibious landings. Each one was its own story, a fusion of hazards, some known and others that would sneak up unannounced. If the navy were going to avoid another Tarawa, they would have to study the ocean like never before. And they would have to do so in the midst of a war that would not wait for them to catch up.

As was the military's way, no express mention was ever made at the JANIS meetings of how the early misdirection in priorities might have affected events at Tarawa, but everyone, especially the oceanographers, was aware that Tarawa had been a disaster and, worse, one that could have been avoided.

Secretary of the Navy Frank Knox informed the press that a "sudden shifting of the wind" had lowered the waters around Tarawa and caused landing craft to be stranded on the coral reef. One can only imagine Sears's dismay at Knox's explanation, knowing it lacked any scientific basis.

Sears was no doubt quite aware that her team might have predicted the prolonged neap tide through extrapolation. They could have provided a detailed description of the coral reefs outside of Tarawa and predicted how the combination of the two conditions was a setup for disaster. But with the crowded schedule of future landings in the Pacific, there was precious little time to waste lamenting what might have been. Still, to Sears, the importance of her mission had never been clearer.

The tragic mishaps at Tarawa soon changed things for the Oceanographic Unit, starting with a shakeup in the priority list for JANIS studies. On December 7, 1943, just two weeks after Tarawa, the Joint Publishing Board had its first planning meeting for targets in the Philippines. By the first of the year, the Joint War Planners were in urgent need of information on the Marianas, the Carolines, and the Palaus. Reports on potential targets for these Pacific Islands would be fast-tracked in the following months.

"Present war conditions are such that speed is a primary consideration in the publication of JANIS," Colonel Bicknell stated in a new memo issued in early 1944. "There is neither time nor necessity to carry out a textbook type of editorial work in a publication such as JANIS."

Bicknell had taken over as chairman of the Joint Publishing Board from Commander Bailey. While Bailey had been a stickler for accuracy, insisting that reports be checked and rechecked before publication, which caused needless delays, Bicknell demanded strict adherence to deadlines.

It was a good thing Bicknell was in charge because it was all the Joint Publishing Board and the JANIS contributors could do to keep up with the demands of a new campaign plan for the Pacific released by Admiral Nimitz in January 1944. Campaign Plan Granite outlined a tentative schedule of future combat operations in the Central Pacific based on guidance from the Joint Chiefs Sextant Conference the preceding December.

With the Japanese on the defensive after the success of the early invasions, it was time to wade further into the heart of the amphibious campaign, advancing through Japanese-held islands in the Central Pacific. The direction was along a path similar to the one that Major Earl Ellis originally envisioned in the 1920s when he first outlined a combat strategy to "island hop" across the Pacific. Although Ellis's plotted course and the weaponry utilized had changed, the general concept endured, as spelled out in Campaign Plan Granite: "To obtain positions from which the ultimate surrender of Japan can be forced by intensive air bombardment, by sea and air blockade, and by invasion if necessary."

There were two principal routes to Japan, and the path ultimately chosen depended on a number of conditions. One route ran through Formosa (now known as Taiwan) and up the eastern coast of China. Another route veered more to the north, straight through the Bonins and Ryukyus and into Okinawa, only 320 miles southwest of Japan, and well within heavy bomber range. Whichever route the Americans took, they would initially have to fight their way through what were known as the Mandated Islands—the Marshalls, Carolines, Marianas, and Palau islands.

After Campaign Plan Granite was released, the planning meetings for the next three JANIS reports on the Caroline Islands, the Marianas, and the Palaus rapidly followed in January and February of 1944. The Oceanographic Unit was still compiling data for the New Guinea JANIS when these new reports were assigned. With the three new reports all due in April, an already tight timetable had just become punishing for the oceanographers.

Sears was now racing up and down Constitution Avenue, attending several meetings a week in the "tempo" buildings on the Mall in Washington, D.C. She also made stops at the United States Coast and Geodetic Survey to pick up tide tables to take back to Suitland.

After attending presentations for upcoming JANIS projects at the Munitions Building in the afternoon, Sears would often walk next door to Main Navy for impromptu meetings with Lt. Roger Revelle, her counterpart from Scripps, in his office at the Bureau of Ships. Drawn together by their mutual interests of oceanography and the war, they had become friends, and would remain so long after Revelle headed back to Scripps and Sears to Woods Hole.

"Roger moved slowly," she later related. "And he was often late." Sears walked fast and was the furthest thing from a procrastinator. To occupy herself while waiting for him she would sort through some of his mail that had piled up, which he kept in the bottom drawer of his desk and, answer Revelle's correspondence. Later, when Revelle finally showed up they might go out for a late dinner, occasionally joined by his wife, who had moved with their children to D.C.

With deadlines looming, Sears had to trust that Mary Grier would be able to locate a wide range of critical references. She had performed brilliantly for the New Guinea report and in record time. For the next wave Grier had to be out of the office most days, tracking down references in the Library of Congress or the Smithsonian and traveling to New York or other states when necessary to peruse references in military libraries. It would be up to Sears, Dora Henry, and Fenner Chace to put the information together, construct diagrams, figures, and tables, and to edit for accuracy. The pressure was intense, but Sears was determined that the team would finish the reports on time and supply enough information to the navy to avoid another amphibious disaster.

Meeting that standard would pose challenges for Sears and her team for the next target—the remote, inaccessible, heavily defended and mountainous Mariana Islands, in the Central Pacific Ocean—slotted for attack in the summer of 1944.

The Marianas, along with the Marshalls, the Carolines, and Palau were handed over to Japan under a mandate from the League of Nations after World War I. As a condition of custodianship, the Japanese had agreed not to establish bases or fortify the islands with defenses. Yet there was little evidence they had abided by the terms and plenty that they had not.

The total land area of the Mandated Islands was a thousand square miles, but their range extended even farther, up to fourteen hundred miles in an east-to-west direction and over five hundred miles north to south across the ocean. With this amount of centrally located real estate under Japanese control, if war broke out, Japanese naval and air forces could easily take control of the entire Western Pacific. The Philippines would be cut off from American protection, Guam would be surrounded, and Wake Island would be within easy striking distance.

Once they acquired the Mandated Islands, Japan restricted shipping and, after 1935, banned foreign vessels of any kind from docking there. A veil of secrecy allowed the Japanese to fortify island defenses and build airstrips, ports, and fuel depots. By the time the Japanese attacked Pearl Harbor in 1941, there were already eight fully outfitted bases with troops in the Mandates. Their strategic location positioned Japan to attack the United States at Pearl Harbor and continue their island-grabbing hot streak throughout the Western Pacific. And in the hours and days after Pearl Harbor, the Japanese carried out Major Ellis's worst nightmare. They seized Guam, invaded Wake, and attacked the Philippines.

Roosevelt and Churchill had been itching to take those islands out of Japanese hands and to avenge Pearl Harbor as soon as it made sense to do so. The Joint Chiefs directed Nimitz to get on with it.

Invading the Marianas, however, meant treading into Japan's Absolute Defense Sphere, a perimeter designated by the Japanese late in 1943 after they had suffered major defeats at Guadalcanal and Tarawa. The southern perimeter extended from Western New Guinea through the Caroline Islands and all the way to the Marianas, exactly the areas the Americans intended to target next. The "absolute defense" designation meant that the Japanese would fight viciously to hold on to their territory.

The Marianas were a long way from friendly shores—thirty-three hundred miles from Pearl Harbor and thirteen hundred miles from the nearest American base, the recently captured Kwajalein in the Marshalls— which would limit aerial support to carrier-based aircraft only. With access to multiple airfields in the Marianas, the Japanese had the strategic advantage. On the other hand, capturing the Marianas would fuel the remainder of the Pacific Campaign and serve as a moral victory by restoring Guam to American control.

As Admiral Nimitz planned the invasion of the Mandated Islands, the nation's leaders were focused not just on the next operation in the Pacific, a huge one at that, but also on preparations for another critical amphibious assault across the Atlantic. Operation Overlord, the Allied Invasion of western Europe at Normandy planned for early June 1944, would precede the invasion of the Marianas by just over a week and would understandably command the majority of the army's attention. Allied hopes in Europe rested on the success of this massive invasion, in which 156,000 American, British, and Canadian troops would land on five beaches along a fifty-mile stretch of beach in northern France.

As the Allies planned Overlord, the Germans were at work constructing the Atlantic Wall, a twenty-four-hundred-mile obstacle course on France's western coast to defend their perimeter. They had erected six-foot iron bars crossed at right angles like giant jacks. Steel frames jutted out of the sand alongside rows of sharpened, half-buried logs armed with land mines. Just inland, thousands of concrete pillboxes protected machine guns, artillery, and antiaircraft guns.

German Field Marshal Rommel was hoping to use the twenty-foot tidal range off the coast of Normandy to his advantage. At low tide, a wide section of landing beach would be exposed, which would leave amphibious troops vulnerable to intense fire. Rommel believed that the Allies would instead attack at high tide to minimize casualties. He configured the obstacles to be submerged at high tide and in prime position to tear into the hulls of unsuspecting Allied ships.

The Allies' air reconnaissance, however, had spotted the obstacles. Eisenhower adjusted his plan. The Allies would land at low tide and employ demolition teams to blast channels through the forest of iron and wood that blanketed the beach. To pull off this plan, however, they would have to predict when low tide would occur on the beaches between Le Havre to the east and Cherbourg to the west, areas about which there was little existing oceanographic data. And, because the Allied forces wanted to surprise the Germans by arriving under the cover of darkness, they would need to coordinate the landing time with dawn. They would have to identify the handful of days a month when both conditions would be met.

During World War II, the British were fortunate to have on their side the world's leading authority on tide prediction, oceanographer Arthur Thomas Doodson, at the Liverpool Tidal Institute at Bidston Observatory. Doodson used two large tide-predicting machines outfitted with gears and pulleys to generate tide tables, one that was built in 1872 and the other in 1906. The machines were of such great value to the British that they were kept in two separate rooms of a two-story sandstone building to minimize the chance that both would be destroyed by German aerial bombardment. At peak demand, Doodson kept them running from early morning to late at night, seven days a week.

The Americans also had a version of the early tide-predicting machines, known as "Old Brass Brains," which was housed at the United States Coast and Geodetic Survey (USCG) in Washington. Like the British machines, Old Brass Brains could produce accurate tide predictions for all major ports of the world. Sears frequently visited the USCG to pick up tide tables generated by Old Brass Brains to include in her reports.

Before a tide-predicting machine could calculate tide tables, though, a harmonic constant for the shore area in question had to be calculated from water-level measurements manually collected at the beach over a period of several weeks. The Admiralty had already calculated harmonic constants for major ports and harbors around the globe and kept these and tide-prediction tables confidential. The tides at subordinate locations, where no harmonic constants were available, could then be extrapolated from the reference station tide tables if ocean measurements had been collected in advance. These were the types of calculations that Sears would be called on to make on short notice once a definitive landing site had been selected in the Pacific.

British teams deployed in small boats and two-man submarines in several midnight reconnaissance missions to obtain water level and current measurements, measure beach gradients, and collect sand samples. Doodson received the tide and current data and calculated the harmonic constants for a location so secret that not even he was told where the measurements had been taken.

Because Allied forces needed to cross the English Channel in darkness, then land at first light and at low tide, the British Hydrographic Office constructed a tidal illumination diagram that superimposed low and high tides with visibility (moonlight, sunrise, sunset, and twilight). Based on Doodson's analysis, June 5, 6, and 7 were selected as potential D-Days on which all the landing conditions would be met. General Eisenhower picked June 5.

When the forecasters predicted stormy weather for June 5, including high winds and rough seas, Eisenhower decided to postpone the operation. Late on the evening of June 5, while the howling storm was battering the coast, a British weather officer, Captain James Stagg, made the gutsy call that there would be a temporary break in the weather the next day. Eisenhower decided to "go."

On the morning of the invasion, the tide predictions proved to be accurate and demolition teams were able to clear most of the beaches. Rough seas did, as expected, cause some mishaps for the initial waves of invaders, but by noon the weather had cleared. As at Tarawa, the tides had proven to be crucial. The difference was that accurate tidal predictions had been supplied to military commanders for Normandy in advance, allowing for optimal timing of the landings.

During the war the British and Americans split responsibility for oceanographic analysis. The British collected information on the Atlantic, the North Sea and its tributaries, and the Mediterranean Sea. The Americans supplied data on the Pacific and Indian Oceans. Although Sears did not correspond directly with Doodson, she was regularly in touch with British oceanographer, Dr. J. N. (James Norman) Carruthers, who prepared nearly one hundred reports on French beaches as possible landing sites for the Normandy invasion. Carruthers, Sears's British counterpart, had been pressed into service at the British Hydrographic Office in 1937, on the eve of the European War. Like Sears, Carruthers had a comprehensive bibliographical knowledge of oceanography. He produced oceanographic reports for use in naval operations, very similar to "Chapter III, Oceanography" that Sears compiled for JANIS reports.

On June 6, 1944, Americans woke up to news from Normandy with giant headlines proclaiming simply "INVASION!" Church bells rang out along with factory whistles, car horns, air raid sirens, and foghorns, anything that could make a gleeful noise to welcome the long-anticipated offensive and, hopefully, the imminent defeat of Hitler. In New York City crowds swarmed Times Square, where the electronic ticker overhead scrolled the latest news updates. Mayor La Guardia thrilled a crowd in Madison Square with a rousing speech. Americans took to local town squares or parking lots, anyplace where they could greet their neighbors and celebrate in unison. The jubilation was tempered by a good dose of fear for the safety of the troops and the success of the mission. When the flare of excitement had faded, citizens joined friends and neighbors to pray in churches and synagogues, most of which stayed open for twenty-four hours to accommodate demand.

In Washington, D.C., however, the nerve center of the war, the streets were calm and people went to work as usual, knowing more than ever how important it was to keep working and doing everything possible to bring the troops home as fast as possible. D-Day was especially somber at the Hydrographic Office, where Admiral Bryan made an exception to his "no radio" rule, allowing the staff to listen to actual battle dispatches on the radio. Those with brothers and fiancés in Europe teared up from time to time as they waited for news about which divisions were involved in the initial assault waves and whether loved ones had landed on the beaches. There was a lot riding on Normandy, the largest amphibious invasion to date. It was a milestone, a predicate to the end of the war and enlivened the hope that Hitler would one day be defeated.

With so much secrecy surrounding the Mandated Islands, the question for the Oceanographic Unit was whether they would be able to find any recent information for the next wave of landings. The Marianas had been totally isolated for decades with the exception of Guam, which had been an American territory until captured by the Japanese. If oceanographic information on islands so distant from Japan was available at all, it was most likely because the Japanese were avid ocean explorers and their ruler, Emperor Hirohito, had trained as a marine biologist.

Mary Grier did her usual sleuthing in the regional libraries, hoping to find Japanese publications on the secretive island holds. Even though she found only three references published in Tokyo, one was a key survey of the western part of the North Pacific Ocean carried out by the Japanese Navy on the HIJMS (His Imperial Japanese Majesty's Ship) *Mansyu* from 1925 to 1928. The *Mansyu* was a workhorse of her time. First commissioned as a warship in 1900, she had served as a submarine depot ship initially but was deployed as a survey ship when the Japanese began collecting more data from the surrounding seas. It just so happened that the *Mansyu* had collected data around the Mandated Islands that could not be obtained anywhere else—measurements of subsurface temperatures of the Pacific, ocean depths, and currents, and salinity samples that were later analyzed at the emperor's Imperial Fisheries Institute.

If not for the *Manysu*'s remarkable three-year voyage, Sears and her cohorts at the Oceanographic Unit would have fallen short of their goals for the Marianas. Grier would return to this valuable reference again and again, gathering data for strategic targets for future JANIS reports. Even though it was one of numerous articles published in Japanese, the Ocean-ographic Unit had access to translators and made good use of them when necessary.

The WAVES "enlisted girls" were able to gather nautical charts on other parts of the Pacific with currents, surface temperature, sea and swell, and sound-ranging data from Hydro. The United States Coast and Geodetic Survey contributed tide tables and charts on Guam and the Mar-ianas. J. N. Carruthers shared tide tables from the British Hydrographic Department. He also provided data from the voyage of HMS *Challenger*, a British vessel that sailed over sixty-eight thousand nautical miles from 1872 to 1876, collecting data on temperature, currents, sediments, and salinity from 362 stations and published in fifty volumes. This voyage was said to have "laid the foundation of the science of oceanography," in what many considered the first true oceanographic expedition.

Through Roger Revelle's connections at Scripps, Sears obtained un-published data collected by the *Carnegie* on its seventh and final global voyage from 1928 to 1929, an ill-fated trip that ended tragically when bar-rels of gasoline exploded, killing the captain and a cabin boy. Revelle knew of the data because he had analyzed deep sea sediments from that voyage.

Despite the tight security around the Marianas, Sears, Chace, and Henry reviewed eighteen references and sorted them into groups to fill in the oceanography topics for "Chapter III Oceanography." They then dis-tilled the reams of data into a report that contained relevant information for war planners. Chace designed the surface current drawings showing direction and speed of flow and oversaw the production of detailed bot-tom sediment drawings demonstrating the coral reef formations around Saipan, Guam, and Tinian.

Because the Marshalls offensive had concluded earlier than expected, the deadline for the report was moved up by four and a half months to mid-June. To get the most relevant information out as soon as possible, the Joint Publishing Board put out the JANIS on the Mariana Islands early, in April 1944, as an abbreviated provisional edition. Its two chap-ters, rather than the customary twelve, were what the planners needed soonest—fifteen pages on oceanography and twenty-two pages on climate and weather. Hydro advised readers to consult JICPOA Bulletin No. 7–44 and ONI-99 Strategic Study of Guam for further information on the Marianas to supplement the thin JANIS 102. With the Saipan offensive being moved up and reports on the Palaus and Carolines coming due, there was surely a shortage of both expertise and time to complete a full report.

The targets for the Marianas offensive—Saipan, Tinian, and Guam— were the only southern islands large enough to use as naval and air bases, something the Americans desperately needed in their push across the Pacific. At fourteen by five miles wide, Saipan was home to the Japanese Aslito Airfield, which the Americans would need to seize early to prevent its use in air operations against the assault. The central part of the island was marked by rugged, mountainous terrain, cliffs, and a central extinct volcano that rose to fifteen hundred feet.

Tinian, across a channel from Saipan, was a smaller twelve by three miles. Taking Tinian was crucial to prevent Japanese attacks from there against Saipan as the invasion progressed. It would also provide an ideal site for a future airfield. The third target was the former United States territory Guam, which had been seized by the Japanese soon after the attack on Pearl Harbor. The largest island of the Marianas at thirty-four miles long and seven miles wide, it also featured rugged terrain, volcanic hills, and high cliffs. Winning back this American island would boost morale and also provide a forward naval base in the war against Japan.

The oceanographers had several concerns about these islands. All of the Marianas were steep-sided volcanic peaks with narrow shelves, a configuration that could result in strong surf on landing beaches. Wave heights due to sea and swell for the month of June were expected to be low to moderate. On the western side of Saipan an extensive and complex formation of rock and reef stood between the sea and the shore. It would have to be traversed by landing craft if this side of the island was chosen as a landing site.

Not unexpectedly, operational concerns drove selection of landing sites for the assault. While Magicienne Bay, on the eastern side of Saipan, might have made for a calmer landing, planners chose the southwest coast in an attempt to avoid enemy defenses. The western approach also allowed a more direct route to Aslito Field, which the Americans wanted to neutralize as early as possible, but the offshore coral reef and underwater rock formation lurked offshore. Plunging waves, some forceful, could be swirling around the reefs, causing landing craft to broach and capsize. Still, the marines hoped to escape these dangers by once again relying on the amphibious tractors (LVTs) instead of on Higgins boats.

The marines had learned many lessons from Tarawa. For instance, it would take better amphibious tractors and a lot more of them to ensure the safe movement of troops across a barrier reef in the Pacific. For Saipan, the first of the three targets in the Marianas, the marines received 732 updated LVT-As (Landing Vehicle Tracked, Armored), specifically designed to transport troops in combat and configured for assault missions with ramps and hatch covers. The new LVT-As were armored to withstand bullets, a feature that had been sorely lacking at Tarawa, and were equipped with mounted cannons. The hope was that by landing the first waves of troops aboard LVT-As the marines would be able to roll across the shore and farther inland, allowing them to set up a defensive perimeter to protect the beachhead while reinforcements landed.

Operation Forager would be led by Admiral Raymond A. Spruance commanding the Fifth Fleet along with Vice Admiral Marc Mitscher, commander of Task Force 58. Vice Admiral Richmond Kelly Turner, Commander Amphibious Forces, Pacific, would lead the assault force with General Holland Smith of the Marine Corps. As the date for the invasion of Saipan neared, the next large-scale, long-range assault after Tarawa, naval commanders, feeling the pressure, began to recheck their intelligence for the area.

"We don't want another blunder like the one at Tarawa," Vice Admiral Turner told Lt. Commander Draper Kauffman, the head of a new underwater demolition team (UDT), when he called him in to discuss the formidable coral reef a mile off the shore of Saipan. The UDTs, forerunners to the navy's current SEAL teams, were a new undercover weapon in the never-ending quest to gain the latest oceanographic intelligence. Some landing conditions couldn't be studied in advance and would never be known without a last-minute look and a hands-on assessment, even though the unarmed men who carried out these missions faced a high risk of death or injury as they approached the enemy's shore.

Turner had asked Kauffman to meet with him in Pearl Harbor in April 1944 for a very good reason. Before he sent thousands of troops across another reef in the Pacific, he wanted to know if the water depth in the shallows would be sufficient to prevent landing craft from going aground but not so high that tank engines would flood and stall. He also wanted Kauffman's frogmen to make note of any underwater obstacles the Japanese might have constructed in the lagoon and to return to clear them if warranted. Kauffman was confident of success until Turner added that he wanted the UDTs to go in at nine in the morning the day before the landing.

The UDTs had been trained in the surreptitious tactics known as "sneak and peak" warfare. They usually entered enemy waters on boats at night with the goal of damaging or disabling enemy boats and weaponry, and slipping out again unnoticed. By scheduling a daytime mission Turner was asking Kauffman to expose his team to unnecessary risk. Turner reassured Kauffman that the navy would be shelling the shore and providing cover, but Kauffman had serious reservations nevertheless.

Kauffman started preparing for the mission, which entailed developing new training and techniques. The frogmen were used to rowing all the way to shore under the cover of darkness. This mission, executed in daylight, would call for a distant drop-off point from which the men would need to swim at least a mile to the target. The UDTs would have to start training right away for longer distances.

Kauffman instructed the frogmen to paint black stripes around their torsos and arms spaced a foot apart so they could use their bodies as yardsticks to measure water depth. They would employ a "string reconnaissance" technique, using a large reel of fishing line knotted at twenty-five-yard intervals, to approximate the location of each depth reading. A frogman would fasten one end of the string to an offshore buoy and swim toward the beach with the reel in tow, checking the depth at designated intervals and writing the measurements down with a wax pencil onto a plastic tablet he wore around his neck.

Just before the sun came up on D-1, the day before the assault, the frogmen set out, not in protective wetsuits, but in swimming trunks and tennis shoes with optional knee pads for crawling over jagged coral. Like Russian nesting dolls, they started out on converted destroyers and then transferred into smaller and smaller craft—from destroyer to landing boat, from landing boat to rubber raft, from the raft directly into the water. In the light of day, the Japanese could readily spot the boats and fire on the team. The frogmen also had to watch out for underwater mines, penetrating obstacles, sharks, and slashing coral.

Not surprisingly, the Japanese spotted the men transferring to smaller boats, a mile outside the reef. Right away, one man was shot and killed and another was wounded but the team continued on until just outside the reef, where they transferred to the rubber rafts. At that point the men started rolling into the water at fifty-feet intervals. Under fire the entire time, they still managed to complete the mission, albeit at the cost of two dead and several other casualties.

Upon returning to the command ship, worn out and shivering with hypothermia, Kauffman's men were immediately debriefed by intelligence officers concerned about the one question that mattered above all others. *Could the troops get through?*

Or would they be stuck on a reef like at Tarawa, or blocked by some other barrier, and have to wade into the relentless fire of Japanese infantry? The frogmen relayed their measurements and gave assurances that water depth would not be an issue. There were no mines or other underwater obstructions, but the UDTs still had work to do for the invasion. Undaunted, they returned on D-Day and followed the landing craft in, once again without protective gear, dragging pounds of explosives to blast channels in the reef so that bigger boats and equipment could get through.

• • •

On June 15, 1944, PFC J. T. "Slick" Rutherford, traveling in the first wave of the assault on Saipan and manning a .30-caliber machine gun on an LVT-2 Water Buffalo, witnessed what the combination of breaking waves and coral reef could do. He watched as plunging waves caught the stern of a nearby amphibious tractor and flipped it "ass over teakettle." Under heavy fire and fighting for their lives, Rutherford's crew could not stop to help the marines trapped underneath.

As soon as Rutherford's tractor hit shore his driver was shot in the head and his troop commander was killed by mortar fire. The concussion knocked Rutherford to the cold metal floor. With half the crew wounded or dead, the vessel retreated back out to the ocean. This was not the landing the marines had planned, but the Japanese had been expecting them to hit the beach and, as anticipated, they were dug in, trying to hold on to their territory. Heavy surf was every bit the enemy too. This was a different tactical problem than that encountered at Tarawa, where the tides around the coral reefs were too shallow for the boats to cross. The marines had no answer.

After John Graves, a battery officer with the marines, was launched in the fourth wave in a Higgins boat he was greeted by a scene of absolute chaos. "A whole bunch of the LVTs, got smashed right away in the landings," taken down by a combination of high surf and enemy fire. "I ran around out there trying to find some way to get in over the reef. It was all along the landing beaches. And I couldn't find any."

After getting fired upon, turning around, and going back out to sea, Graves came upon a couple of tractors and was able to load up his crew and land ashore.

Difficulties maneuvering the LVTs thwarted the plan of the troops moving farther inland immediately after landing. The combination of intense Japanese resistance, the fringing reef, a steep landing beach, and high surf complicated everything the marines tried to do, but they persisted and made it to shore.

• • •

The coral reefs that rim the shores of volcanic islands in the Pacific, would bedevil the navy for much of the war as they tried to find the best way to cross them. These formations could extend miles out to sea and sometimes completely encircle an island's shore. The reefs might be totally submerged at high tide, but at low tide they could rise above the water level, forming a rock-hard barrier to passage.

James Dana, a Yale geologist, explored Pacific island regions from 1838 to 1842 as part of the Wilkes Exploration Expedition and encountered the same dangers posed by the coral reefs that the Americans navigated almost a century later. Dana described lines of heavy breakers "miles in length" and plunging waves near coral reefs, and how his boat wound up "grinding over the coral masses, then thumping heavily at short intervals." Ultimately his boat landed "helpless on the coral reef," where the strength of the waves alternately lifted and dropped the vessel until it was completely destroyed.

Now the marines were learning that same lesson. Crossing an obstructing reef even at high tide could be fraught with disaster from the battering effects of plunging waves. All they could do at those moments was hope that their boats stayed intact while they looked for a channel across. Even then the narrow passage would have to be carefully navigated, as it too could be intermittently obstructed by coral outcroppings.

More challenges lay ahead once the marines had landed. The Japanese launched nightly counterattacks in the quasi-jungle terrain. Then the Japanese decided to attack American aircraft carriers supporting the amphibious task force in the nearby Philippine Sea. Naval aviation blunted that counterattack. The marines also outlasted a nighttime banzai attack of four thousand Japanese troops, though not without severe casualties. After twenty-four days of combat, American losses came to sixteen thousand versus twenty thousand Japanese killed.

The event that created the most horrific and lasting memory of Saipan was a mass suicide. Japanese propaganda had instilled a fear of torture by the Americans, prompting hundreds of Japanese and native civilians to jump from the cliffs of Marpi Point to rocks below. When Nimitz toured the scene days later he saw the aftermath and a preview of the civilian carnage that might ensue if the Americans invaded Japan. He vowed to find some other way to force Japan to surrender that would spare the lives of its citizens.

Saipan was also where the first African American marines of World War II, the Montford Point Marines, made their debut in an amphibious invasion. At the outset of the war, the navy accepted only small numbers of African Americans and only as cooks or stewards. The Marine Corps adamantly refused to admit them.

Only when Black leaders exerted pressure on President Roosevelt did the military began to change its ways. In April 1942, Secretary of the Navy Frank Knox mandated that Black service members be accepted for general service in the navy, marines, and coast guard. The marines agreed to accept them but only at Montford Point Camp, a segregated boot camp located on the outer edge of their main boot camp at Camp Lejeune, North Carolina. The all-white drill sergeants put the men through the standard rigors of one of the toughest military trainings imaginable, but that wasn't the end of the punishment they endured to wear their country's uniform.

"It was unreal, absolutely unreal. Like a bad dream," Steven Robinson recalled of the endemic racism he encountered after taking a train from Pittsburgh, Pennsylvania, to camp.

First he was put off the train a mile from the station and made to walk the rest of the way. Upon arriving at the train depot, he found signs he had never before seen for white-only waiting areas. He was told to join the rest of the African American recruits in a small, crowded room. Robinson had stumbled into some kind of alternative universe, one in which he saw, for the first time, hate in people's faces because of the color of his skin. In his youthful optimism he kept hoping that "maybe it would go away," but the entire time he was in the service, it never did.

"We were fighting the war against the bigotry at home and fighting the war against the bigotry overseas. And we were fighting the war to liberate people who had more liberty than we had," Robinson said.

Even though they withstood the identical boot camp training as the white marines, the Black marines were relegated to lesser, supporting roles. Only the white and brown marines were allowed to serve as front-line combatants. But being in the rear did not mean the Black marines would entirely escape the risks of combat.

At Saipan, the Montford Point Marines served in depot and ammunition companies, tasked with distributing food, water supplies, and ammunition to the front lines. After moving staggeringly heavy crates from supply ships to landing craft, they stood in waist-deep water unloading under heavy fire from the beaches. They drove trucks packed with explosives, fuel, and ammunition through the shelling and on up the beaches, knowing that if their cargo was struck their lives would end in a ball of flame. The men were more than able to hold their own in combat, as they demonstrated time after time when the Japanese doubled back and tried to infiltrate the rear. More than one Montford Point Marine was killed or wounded in the line of duty.

The marines could not have functioned without the supplies the Montford Point Marines delivered, but they did more. With no special training and without anyone asking, they picked up the wounded, carried them across the beaches, and loaded them into the DUKW amphibious trucks waiting to evacuate them to ships.

At Saipan, the Montford Marines drew the praise of Lieutenant General Alexander A. Vandegrift. "The Negro Marines are no longer on trial. They are Marines, period," he said.

The Montford Marines went on to serve at all three invasions in the Mariana Islands and at Peleliu. Approximately seven to nine hundred served at Iwo Jima and another two thousand helped capture Okinawa, taking part in the largest amphibious landing in the Pacific theater. A total of twenty thousand African Americans trained at Montford Point and served in the marines during World War II, but not a single one would become a commissioned officer. Segregation in the military would continue until 1948 when President Harry Truman signed an order that ended it.

• • •

Sears described the shoreline at Guam, the second target in the Marianas, as "mostly rough and broken with patches of coral and many ledges and blocks which have eroded from the shoreline dotted with cliffs." Troops arrived in landing craft that could not traverse the rocky reef and had to transfer into the dwindling supply of amphibious tractors. Just as at Tarawa, some troops had no option but to wade ashore under enemy fire. Luckily, Japanese resistance had ebbed and the Americans prevailed, despite delays caused by the substantial barrier reef and rugged terrain.

The landing at Tinian, the third target in the Marianas, was remarkably easier than at Saipan, partly because of favorable offshore geography. Five hundred LVT-As and 130 DUKW amphibious trucks deployed easily across the reef and penetrated the Japanese shore defenses. In nine days, Tinian fell, with a minimum of U.S. casualties. The result was a model amphibious assault that yielded the largest B-29 base in the world, one that would play a major part in ending the war. The Americans had prevailed in capturing the Marianas, exacting a heartbreaking price in human life and losing unimaginable amounts of armament. The payoff was a string of strategic bases that boosted their island-hopping strategy and a victory free of the taint of Tarawa.

The provisional JANIS report for the Marianas, prepared in haste with minimal and, in some cases, outdated information, still gave planners notice about the one feature that would prove to hamper operations— the extensive coral reefs ringing Saipan and Guam and the need for large numbers of tractors. Although the oceanographers had warned of the narrow shelves around the islands and the possibility of strong surf, they had not specifically highlighted the possibility of plunging waves around the reefs that impeded the path to shore. The oceanographers would have to drill down further to ferret out these hidden dangers.

There were many more amphibious battles ahead, and already the Oceanographic Unit was onto its next mission. The scientists had swept their desks clean of data and charts on the Marianas, the way the Pacific Ocean would sweep clean American bodies and boats from the beaches.

CHAPTER 13

The Oceanographic Unit Digs In

— *Washington, D.C., 1944* —

As the Pacific Campaign unspooled, getting the troops to shore presented a range of problems, confirming what Sears had said about the navy's lack of preparation. They had gone to war knowing very little about the ocean, at least about the offshore challenges of launching amphibious landings. But there was no stopping the action so American forces could rehearse and get better. The march to Japan would not wait.

The Americans had not fought this way or at this pace before. In World War I troops had sailed across the Atlantic into welcoming harbors, docked at piers, and unloaded without enemy resistance. Those operations were easily achieved without oceanographic information. The Allies rarely had such advantages in World War II. Harbors, if they existed at all at island targets, were not welcoming. There were no piers at which to dock. There was nothing simple about dropping marines into boats and tractors bucking in the grasp of heaving waves and sending them over jagged coral reefs, under a barrage of machine-gun fire and artillery shells toward plunging waves. The problem was, there didn't appear to be any other way to win the war in the Pacific.

The success of the Pacific Campaign mandated capturing one island after another in far-reaching locales, as the military worked its way toward

Japan. Mary Sears and Dora Henry were both experienced sailors—Sears in Peru and Henry in Puget Sound—and they had both worked in oceanography for over a decade. They knew that a navy skipper might be able to navigate a course to a distant island using a hundred-year-old nautical chart, but there were still unknowns in sailing those waters and landing on unfamiliar shores for the first time, unknowns that created havoc for the amphibious forces. It was these unknowns offshore and on the landing beaches that the oceanographers homed in on. This is where they could make a difference.

The oceanographers' number one priority was to warn of every possible danger to the troops risking their lives to go ashore in hazardous waters. Reminders of the costs of war appeared in every issue of Hydro's newsletter, particularly those that personally touched the staff.

The *Scuttlebutt*, so named because in bygone days, a ship's crew would gather to hear the daily gossip around a cask that held fresh drinking water, published news items, jokes, cartoons, and sports scores. Over twenty-two hundred copies a week were distributed not only to Hydro employees but also to "fighting forces all over the world."

"*Scuttlebutt* extends its deepest sympathies to Mr. George W. Shaw of Air Navigation on the death of his only son Pvt. Gorham C. Shaw who was killed in action May 12 on Luzon while serving with the 158th Combat Group. Pvt. Shaw is survived by his widow and two-and-one-half-year-old son of Washington, D.C."

"Our deepest regrets and sincere sympathy to Commander Patterson [officer-in-charge of the Division of Research] for the loss of his brother Lt. Bruce Patterson who was killed last week in an aeroplane crash."

"We wish we could omit this paragraph: it is particularly heavy and close to home this week, but our deepest sympathies to Sam Glovinsky and Charles Kirchner whose brothers are reported missing in action in Germany and to Lt. Bickford whose cousin was killed in action off the Philippines."

As the action heated up on the two major fronts of the war—Normandy and the Pacific—the death toll rose. If the oceanography team working in Suitland needed any extra motivation to dig deep in finding the most accurate data to prepare the very best tables and charts, they found it in these sad but powerful reminders of what was at stake.

The *Scuttlebutt* also printed updates on deployed former coworkers, which underscored the ongoing risks of active duty. Specialist Len Brown, a former Hydro employee, sent a letter to the *Scuttlebutt* editors from the front lines in Germany describing the perils of combat.

"A few times I knew my number was up," he wrote. "I was crossing an open field when a machine gun opened up on me. Fortunately, the first burst missed and I hit the ground. He then laid in on me, and I had one bullet tick against the top of my helmet. His burst[s] were so close, I couldn't even raise an inch to crawl out from under the fire. I had to just sweat it out until one of the tanks came up and put him out of business."

Another employee had been called up for survey duty, a risky assignment during wartime on open seas patrolled by enemy submarines.

"Our very popular and veteran Chief Rogers has up and left us for duty on board one of our Survey ships. Rogers is one of the oldest in service at the H.O. and will be missed by many of our crew who have had the pleasure and comradeship of his company for these past years. Best of luck, Chief."

The survey ship Chief Rogers had deployed aboard collected oceanographic data like the temperature at varying water depths, the slope of a landing beach, the type of bottom sediment, and the presence of underwater obstacles, information that could only be obtained by surveying a particular area. Survey ship missions were especially crucial to support the amphibious landings.

Chief Rogers well understood there were risks to being on a survey ship during wartime. On the eve of the war, the navy's only survey ship, the USS *Sumner*, had been outfitted with four three-inch guns, four mounted machine guns, and a five-inch broadside gun and dispatched to Pearl Harbor to await further orders. Early on December 7, 1941, a quartermaster on the bridge of the *Sumner* spotted ten Japanese dive bombers marked with red discs attacking the Navy Yard. The *Sumner* was the first ship in the vicinity to open fire with all its weapons and was credited for destroying at least one torpedo plane, helping to disable others, and firing on kamikazes.

With the advent of World War II, the *Sumner*'s new mission became surveying the waters around potential invasion targets in the Pacific, eventually being joined in the task by a second survey ship, *Pathfinder*. It too was regularly attacked, and on April 7, 1943, when 187 Japanese planes attacked Tulagi Harbor, the *Pathfinder* shot down two dive bombers, assisted in downing two others, and narrowly escaped crippling damage to its rudder. Hydro's survey ships would be a ubiquitous presence during the Pacific Campaign, venturing into hostile territories to perform surveys in advance of landings, and printing updated maps at sea to deliver to commanders.

The oceanographers appreciated the fact that Chief Rogers, a married colleague with a family, had swapped the safety of a desk job for the dangers of navigating enemy waters. It was up to them to make sure that the information the Chief was risking his life for was put to good use in planning combat missions.

Hydro's workload had continued to climb astronomically as the military intensified its operations in the Pacific during 1943. The once small agency, initially manned by just two hundred personnel, kept expanding to keep up. The move to Suitland in early 1942 had more than doubled the square footage of the cramped office to 134,000, but within a couple of months the agency had requested the construction of an additional wing. After this filled up, Hydro overflowed into two floors of the adjacent Census Building, raising the space allocated to over 200,000 square feet, roughly the same area as three and a half football fields.

Part of the space was taken up by the many charts that had to be kept in stock for the Fleet and merchant shipping. The variety of charts included wide-area ocean charts, harbors and special plans, wind and weather charts, magnetic variation charts, position plotting sheets, bathymetric charts and silk handkerchief maps. Hydro also had to store the huge number of aeronautical charts for aircraft navigation that had never before been needed and navigation bulletins and pamphlets.

On top of the heavy workload, the oceanographers had been frustrated by their perception that they were wasting valuable time and resources toiling away on meaningless reports. The first three JANIS reports had done little to move the needle in the war against the Japanese. The first JANIS on Bulgaria had taken way too long to finish and had no direct relevance to the Pacific Campaign. The second report on New Guinea, published only weeks before the invasion, was too late to be of much assistance in war planning and had no chance of getting out to the field in time. And then, because of an accelerated schedule, the third report on the Marianas had been hastily assembled and published with only two chapters that issued general warnings but failed to specifically highlight the dangers of plunging waves around the reefs.

This oversight stuck in everyone's craw, not because Colonel Bicknell or anyone else called the oceanographers out on it. It bothered them because of their own high standards. They knew they could do better. Sears was already at work one morning when a haggard and heavy-lidded Fenner Chace came in.

"I stayed up all last night because it was the last night for the invasion, and it never came off," he told her.

Chace had worked late, flipping through files and Hydro publications, hastily assembling everything he could find about an area for a top secret mission only to have it cancel at the last minute.

Understandably, the war planners had their own reasons for making the decisions they did, and not surprisingly, they did not share them outside their inner circle or with the researchers working on JANIS reports. But the constant change of plans meant the small staff had to research and compile reports on several different targets at the same time, dividing their time and attention from what they saw as more pressing matters. Inevitably, they started to wonder about the value of their efforts.

Had they given up their families and left their careers for three years only to churn out reports that no one was paying attention to? What about the missed opportunities, like Tarawa? Was anybody even reading their reports?

Sears sympathized with Chace. "You could never tell whether they were going to do it or not," she said, meaning an operation they had worked hard to support might or might not take place as scheduled. "It went off into the blue and you never knew."

Just like her cohorts, Sears had come from the more orderly world of academia, where scientists conducted experiments, accumulated data, and carefully analyzed results with the hope that when the work was published it would be well received and highly praised. But Chace and Sears weren't in the hallowed halls of academia anymore. They were in the navy, where battle plans changed every time Churchill and Roosevelt got together, which they did at least seven times throughout the war at Combined Chiefs Conferences.

Those meetings frequently convened in remote locales, the times and places kept secret until the last minute, lest the Axis Powers plan an attack. Once the meetings were over, however, Roosevelt would release a statement or brief the press or Congress issuing general comments about what had been discussed.

In the aftermath of a Combined Chiefs Conference, a flurry of requests would start flooding Sears's desk, requesting new data on proposed targets. Then Sears would know: the two powerful world leaders had been at it again, tweaking the battle plans for the Pacific and generating assignments for her team. Reports that the team had sweated over around the clock, striving to meet urgent deadlines, would be suddenly rendered irrelevant. False starts, incomplete data, a change of plans with no notice, searches for information that did not exist, all of it was built into the job description of being a naval oceanographer, and they had to get used to it.

"As we came to know only too well during the war, military necessity does not wait for explorers and scientists to accumulate sufficient information, but many problems can be answered by an understanding of the factors that control conditions in the sea . . . and by the skillful interpretation of such knowledge as we have," Sears later wrote.

She understood that the team had to keep looking forward to the next mission, not backward, regretting what had been missed or couldn't be found in time. They were also going to have to make educated guesses, an approach scientists abhorred. But they weren't scientists now; they were military intelligence experts. There was no achieving "an impossible standard of perfection." The team would have to live with the fact that there was only so much information available about these remote islands.

Looking ahead to the remainder of the schedule, Sears still wondered just how well the JANIS reports were fulfilling their intended role of assisting war planners on a strategic level. The Joint Chiefs weren't known for offering feedback, but one indicator that they were hitting their marks was that the Joint War Planners had started requesting the JANIS reports for upcoming Pacific targets as soon as the individual chapters were ready.

The war planners were now leaning on the Joint Publication Board to prioritize the publication of the JANIS on Palau. They wanted the report five months in advance of the assault on Peleliu. This would give them plenty of time to review the information for planning military operations and also allow time to dispatch critical intelligence out to the theaters of command. With that much lead time, Sears knew the JANIS on Palau could be a difference maker. She hoped it would contribute the kind of intel that made for smooth landings on distant shores.

With several reports under their belts, the oceanography team was starting to settle into a routine. For the Palau report, Sears had attended the JANIS meetings in Washington, D.C., where she learned the geographic boundaries for the islands and noted potential problem areas that would need further investigation. When she brought the specifications back to Suitland she called a meeting with the team to discuss assignments. She instructed Dora Henry to keep applying her red pen to the Marianas reports so they would be ready in time for a fast-approaching deadline. Mary Grier was to head out the door to start tracking down references in the

Library of Congress. The enlisted WAVES would comb through the Hydrographic Office files and pull any pertinent charts or sailing directions.

Considered by Sears to be the only "true" oceanographic librarian in the country, Grier was not just a gopher for the Oceanographic Unit. Librarians did more than pull articles and shelve books during the war. They became intelligence specialists with the know-how to track down obscure facts and data. The government found this out when they initially sent Office of Strategic Services (OSS) agents overseas to retrieve foreign publications that could no longer be mailed to the United States because of security concerns. The OSS agents, lacking specific training, couldn't find the references they were sent to get.

The government had to recruit librarians to join the Interdepartmental Committee for the Acquisition of Foreign Publications to help the OSS. In 1943, the women traveled to Lisbon, Portugal, to acquire newspapers, scientific periodicals, and technical manuals from bookstores, under the guise of collecting them for the Library of Congress for general interest. They were able to find a wide range of references, including some published directly from Axis and occupied countries, with descriptions of enemy troop strength, weaponry, and manufacturing activities, all of which proved to be quite valuable to the OSS. Whether it came from a library book or captured enemy documents, this kind of intelligence would help win the war.

Sears found Grier to be a "marvelous" member of the team, and one who was irreplaceable. If not for Grier, Sears later acknowledged, she didn't know where they would have found all the oceanographic publications they needed to compile reports about enemy-held islands in the Pacific.

Disappointed in what she had found on the Marianas, Grier turned to her own bibliography *Oceanography of the North Pacific Ocean, Bering Sea and Bering Strait*, which she had published in 1941, to guide her next search on the Palaus. Grier read German, French, and Dano-Norwegian and could, with the help of a dictionary, parse Russian, Italian, Spanish, and Dutch titles. She had cataloged every publication, in every language, that had been published in the physical oceanography and marine biology literature, all 2,929 of them.

The bibliography included articles like "A Brief Note on the Submarine Geology of the Pacific Ocean between the Tokyo Bay and the Bonin Islands," published in the *Journal of the Geological Society of Tokyo* in 1908 and "On the Annual Changes of the Surface Temperatures and Salinities between Nagasaki and Shanghai," published in 1932 in the Japanese journal *Umi to Sora (Sea and Sky)*. Such references might very well contain the minutiae of oceanographic data that could affect military operations for distant islands in the Pacific Ocean. Grier not only knew of their existence, but also knew how to find them in the libraries in and around Washington, D.C.

One reference proved to be particularly helpful, *Records of Oceanographic Works in Japan*, compiled annually since 1928 by the Committee on Pacific Oceanography of the National Research Council of Japan. This one journal included articles that described the physical and chemical characteristics, marine biology, and fisheries technology in Japanese waters. It came into existence around the time that the Japanese Hydrographic Department set up an extensive network of marine biological research stations and sent out ninety-five vessels to conduct extensive surveys of Japanese waters.

With his marine biology background, Emperor Hirohito indulged his passion for expeditions and spurred much of the oceanographic exploration in Japan. Hirohito had taken part in numerous excursions to collect specimens. He had a marine laboratory built on the palace grounds, where he spent at least two days a week studying slime molds and hydrozoa, small predatory animals that lived in salt water.

In 1942 the Japanese suspended publication of *Records of Oceanographic Works in Japan* for national security reasons but Grier still had access to issues published before the war. She used those to gather data on water depth, temperature, salinity, and bottom sediments on the waters in and around Japan. Grier also sourced papers from *The Catalog of Scientific Papers of the Royal Society of London*, *The Zoological Record*, *The*

Current Bibliography of the International Council for the Study of the Sea, as well as card catalogs and reference books in multiple languages.

She would scurry around the stacks in the Orientalia section of the Library of Congress, pulling her own books and journals from the shelves. For security reasons, she sought only minimal assistance from research librarians. She would quickly scan the articles herself for applicable data. Then she would carry the references back to her assigned reading room at the Library of Congress and copy relevant parts by hand or typewriter, a labor-intensive effort that could take hours. Grier was used to working until closing time, when she boarded the Constitution Avenue bus for the thirty-minute ride back to Suitland, laden with notebooks filled with data that she hoped would bring a smile to Sears's face.

When Grier delivered the Palau materials to the Suitland office, she brought back data from eight articles published in Tokyo and one from Berlin, an impressive haul compared to the handful available for the Marianas. Sears again tapped J. N. Carruthers at the British Hydrographic Office to provide tide tables, salinity, surface temperature charts, and monthly meteorological charts of the Western Pacific. She had also stopped by the United States Coast and Geodetic Survey in D.C. to get data on tides and currents near the western Pacific islands.

The enlisted WAVES had found a cornucopia of relevant publications in the library at the Hydrographic Office including *Sailing Directions for the Pacific Islands, Current Charts of the Northwest Pacific Ocean, Palau Harbor and Approaches, Sea and Swell Charts Northwestern Pacific Ocean, Sea Surface Temperature Charts Western Pacific Ocean and Palau Islands Central Part*, with surveys as recent as 1938.

With all this material on the Palaus, Fenner Chace was going to be busy sorting the articles, notes, and books into stacks corresponding to the sections in the chapter on oceanography. Sears, Henry, and Chace then divvied these up with the goal of translating complex scientific concepts into everyday language, tables, and diagrams that a nonscientist could easily comprehend. WAVES working as draftsmen turned them into print quality drawings.

• • •

Palau, a critical target in the two-prong Pacific Campaign, was scheduled to be the site of the next major amphibious landing in September 1944. While Admiral Nimitz's forces had been battling across the Central Pacific, General MacArthur had been moving northwest toward the Philippines. Operation Stalemate to capture the Palau Islands would divert the amphibious forces from their more direct path to Japan, but it would knock out enemy installations that could threaten MacArthur's advance and provide a much-needed air base to support his drive into the southern Philippines.

The Palaus, an arc of islands about eighty miles long situated along the western rim of the Caroline Islands are located 450 miles east of Mindanao, the southernmost tip of the Philippines. As with almost every island target in the Pacific, the Americans would once again have to cross an extensive coral reef, up to eight hundred yards wide at some points. The Palau Islands, in fact, were almost entirely encircled by coral reef. Barrier reefs, shoals, and narrow passes stood squarely between the Americans and the Palau beaches. Only the low limestone islands, like Peleliu, were considered approachable from the open sea.

Peleliu, a small coral-limestone island shaped like a lobster claw, measuring six miles long by two miles wide, was the site of an important airfield and the offensive's initial target. With well-defined objectives, the marines expected a quick "get in, get out" operation lasting only a few days. This thinking was reflected in the remarks of Major General William H. Rupertus, commander of the First Marine Division, after the last rehearsal for the invasion. "We're going to have some casualties, but let me assure you this is going to be a short one, a quickie. Rough but fast. We'll be through in three days. It might take only two." He would later have occasion to regret that prediction.

Unlike the JANIS for the Marianas that had been hastily compiled and short of key details, the JANIS on the Palaus was a well-researched tome.

A report of over four hundred pages with a massive amount of data, tables, charts, and illustrations, this JANIS would provide more than enough information for war planners to pick optimal landing sites.

Though there were many different oceanographic factors to analyze, two weighed heaviest on Sears. She was concerned about the possibility of rough waves and that the coral reef encircling the islands would once again complicate the landing. As Sears explained in her report, "The data on sea and swell apply to offshore conditions. Information of this type is desirable in planning operations requiring aircraft carriers as well as those requiring the transfer of personnel and heavy equipment from large to small vessels." In other words, the magnitude of the waves could greatly hamper amphibious maneuvers and everyone involved in planning this operation had better pay attention to them.

Powerful waves could be treacherous no matter how well the navy and marines prepared. By late 1944, amphibious operations were well supplied with LVTs, the tracked landing vehicles that could cross coral reefs even at low tide, but there was no landing craft on earth that could safely mitigate the swells caused by a rough sea. Accurate predictions about wave height and surf were crucial to operational success.

Sears studied historical data on the amount of sea (waves generated by local winds) and swell (waves generated by distant weather systems) to get an idea of the range of conditions near the Palau Islands on landing day. She analyzed the percentage of calm seas, those with waves less than a foot; low seas, with waves up to two feet; medium seas, with waves from two to nine feet high; and high seas with waves greater than nine feet. She then plotted the frequency of each wave height by months of the year. Low and medium sea and swell predominated in September, the month when the invasion was planned, meaning the marines would likely avoid rough seas.

The news on the encircling reef was not as favorable. All the islands in the Palaus, except one, were surrounded by fringing or barrier reefs. The east side of the islands had a narrower fringing reef, but farther inland was a large mangrove swamp that would have slowed the assault. An extensive barrier reef, up to a half a mile wide, flanked the western coasts.

The oceanographers were waving a hazard flag: the marines must come prepared for trouble on the coral reefs once again.

The warnings and advisories from the Oceanographic Unit did not stop with the waves and reefs. This exhaustive report covered every aspect of ocean characteristics, including cutting-edge concepts addressing submarine warfare. Sears had become proficient at analyzing undersea conditions, explaining features that could affect submarine operations, including surface current, sonar performance, and diving maneuvers.

"Sub-surface temperature gradients in the open sea are the chief factors in determining the paths of sound rays and thus delimit the effectiveness of underwater sound-ranging equipment," she wrote in the JANIS on the Palaus. "Familiarity with these conditions will therefore aid a submarine to avoid detection by diving to the optimum depth, and it will conversely inform surface vessels concerning ranges and depths at which enemy submarines are likely to be encountered.

"On the rare occasions when there is diurnal surface heating or 'afternoon effect,' a submarine may be able to avoid detection by remaining at periscope depth, but usually it will be necessary to dive to depths greater than 200 feet," Sears further advised.

Sears had been receiving bathythermograph data throughout the war with temperature readings taken at various depths in the ocean. The data arrived from Scripps and Woods Hole in the form of index cards that listed readings from the glass slides that had been inscribed at sea for various longitudes and latitudes. It was her job to compile and disseminate the information as quickly as possible to the submarine fleet in the form of *Submarine Supplements to the Sailing Directions*.

Sears would also include observations from submarine patrols:

"Sound conditions in general were poor. During both attacks the targets were not heard until the range was 100 yards. The large freighter we tracked was never heard by sound.

"Listening conditions are very poor due to loud background noise attributed to current over an uneven, rocky bottom.

"On the deep submergence following the fourth attack another most welcome decrease in temperature was found. Temperature decreased from 84 degrees F to 72 degrees F between 110 feet and 250 feet. Ship evaded at 275 feet, gradually growing heavier, due to water leaking into the boat."

These were the kind of play-by-play descriptions that submarine commanders found exceedingly valuable when traveling through nearby waters, specific clues of what to expect in the great Pacific unknown, and information they could not obtain any other way.

Sears had come quite a long way from the day that Roger Revelle had first tapped her to serve at Hydro for an ill-defined role of sitting at a desk in the Hydrographic Office. She had settled into the role of being chief naval oceanographer. The more experience she accumulated responding to requests and compiling reports, the more assured she grew in interpreting the data and suggesting how it might be used in military operations.

In addition to advising submarine commanders about where to seek refuge from enemy ships, she also issued advisories on underwater acoustic conditions. "Echo ranging conditions are usually good throughout the area at all times of the year, except when the background noise level is high. Echo ranges greater than 2,500 yards may therefore be expected away from the islands. The average distance at which screw noises can be heard is about 6,000 yards, with a maximum recorded distance of 12,000 yards."

Sears went on to explain why background noise levels might be high, particularly near the islands. "The high noise level caused by reef-dwelling organisms is usually the limiting factor to sound-ranging near the islands and reefs. These reef noises may be troublesome to distances of three miles or more. Even in the open sea fish noises are often prevalent, and rain squalls and high seas may drown out all other sounds. Surf noises may be troublesome within 2,000 to 3,000 yards of reefs. When the water is sufficiently deep near reefs the high noise level and echoes produced there will assist submarines in avoiding detection."

Chace added intricate bottom sediment drawings depicting the locations of mud, sand, coral, and a mud/sand mix in the harbor areas because, as Sears noted, "knowledge of the distribution of bottom sediments in water shallower than 100 fathoms is important in predicting underwater sound conditions, in mine warfare, and in planning landing operations." The navy preferentially placed mines in locations with firm bottom surfaces composed of either sand or a mixture of sand and mud. They avoided mud alone because the mine could sink and fail to deploy.

Sears also noted a problem with bioluminescence in the region. "Night detection or concealment of PT boats, submarines, and other craft are seriously affected by the luminescence of their wakes and bow waves due to small light-producing organisms." The risk of a vessel being detected by an enemy plane as it moved through the water at night was therefore high in the Palaus and to be avoided if at all possible.

Well in advance of the invasion, the JANIS report on Palau made its way to the Joint Pacific Intelligence Center, Pacific Ocean Areas (JICPOA) in Hawaii, the naval intelligence office that issued bulletins for the Pacific Campaign. Admiral Nimitz had seen the need for JICPOA after the attack on Pearl Harbor, but it was not fully formed until 1944, when it was housed in a new complex in Pearl Harbor. A full-service intelligence agency for Pacific operations, JICPOA included sections for army and navy radio intelligence, photographic interpretation, troop estimates, and mapping and tracking of naval activity in the Pacific. Nimitz headquartered there most of the war.

JICPOA incorporated data from the JANIS reports in its own bulletins. Operations planners for the Pacific Campaign consulted the JANIS on Palau when choosing a 2,600-yard stretch of southwestern beaches for the landing. Despite an extensive reef, they were determined to land on the western beaches. They knew going in that the reef was formidable, but they believed it could be crossed with a full complement of LVTs. Admiral William F. "Bull" Halsey led the Third Fleet into battle accompanied by troops under the direction of Marine Major General Roy S. Geiger.

Unfortunately, because Peleliu was expected to be a quick operation and because there were so few "profitable targets" to eliminate, the preinvasion naval bombardment had been limited. This judgment, made on the basis of spotty aerial reconnaissance, would prove to be shortsighted, especially to the marines who had to contend with the resulting intense enemy fire on the ground.

George Peto had boarded the LST-227, a slow-moving troop and vehicle transport, and sailed from Pavuvu to Guadalcanal to rehearse a mock landing for the upcoming invasion. On September 3, 1944, he got back on board the LST and headed for combat. In one briefing along the way superiors delivered the news that the operation would be over in less than a week.

It took eleven days to get to Peleliu. On September 12 at 0730 hours, Peto climbed down a ladder inside the LST and loaded his equipment into an armored tractor known as a "water buffalo" because it was "big and bulky, and looked like buffalo slowly going through the water." Men waited in the cargo hold amid the deafening drone of two dozen tractor engines, struggling to breathe in a haze of blue exhaust. Finally, LST-227 lowered its heavy forward ramp and the LVTs began to crawl out, one at a time, into a calm Pacific Ocean, just as Sears had predicted.

As the tractors neared the island, Peto could see white waves crashing into and over the coral reef. The LVTs started to grind over the limestone surface, which Sears had cited as a potential problem, and that's when the trouble began as heavy enemy fire peppered the landing vehicles, disabling many. The Japanese were sniping at the tractors from a ridgeline that overlooked the beaches, a potential threat that preinvasion reconnaissance had failed to detect because thick jungle foliage blocked the view.

Enemy fire whizzed around Peto's head, causing him to duck down farther. When his LVT hit the coral reef, Peto felt like they were "ramming a brick wall." The men fell forward into each other and then hung on as the treads of the tractor slowly dug into the reef. The vehicle inched forward. As Sears had predicted, the coral reef was wide and dense, and it looked to Peto like even the tractors couldn't get across the obstruction.

As the LVT climbed the men began to fall backward until seawater was splashing over the back of the vehicle. After interminable minutes, the amtrack finally cleared the reef, lurched forward and began the final run to the beach. Upon landing, the men climbed over the side and dropped eight feet onto jagged coral projections that tore through their pants and jabbed their legs.

All around Peto enemy fire pelted his fellow marines. He looked behind and saw bodies floating in the surf and more scattered on the beach mixed in with mines and artillery shells. The shore was supposed to be a safe haven but, instead, heavy fire was raining down from a point of land to his left. The marines were pinned down, struggling to move inland. Twenty-six LVTs and numerous DUKWs were hit, exploded and burned, slowing the arrival of reinforcements.

When Marine Private Eugene B. Sledge arrived on the beach he saw a Peleliu beach that was a "wall of flame."

"We piled out of our amtrac amid blue-white Japanese machine-gun tracers and raced inland," Sledge later wrote. "Back on the reef I saw burning amtracs and struggling marines. . . . A DUKW came in and stopped, to be hit almost immediately by a large shell. . . . I didn't see anyone get out."

Once again, the navy and Marine Corps had underestimated the ocean and the enemy, a deadly combination of oversights for an assaulting force. The horror of the landing foreshadowed the rest of the operation. For those in later waves, who did not have the benefit of landing in an LVT, the barrier reef lived up to its name, creating chaos as the Higgins boats tried to maneuver across.

Oris Brehmer was a twenty-year-old medical corpsman from Luckenbach, Texas, who came in late on the first day of the offensive. His Higgins boat could not get across the fringing reef, so his battalion unloaded into the ocean. "They just dropped the ramp and you walked off the front, hoping that the water wasn't deep enough that you would drown," Brehmer later recalled. "I remember jumping off with all my gear on. I had all the gear that a marine carried, plus the two medical packs, and in other words we were just loaded, all we could carry. I jumped off and went down and then I hit solid ground, whatever it was: coral, and my mouth was just above water. . . . It was a terrible, terrible landing."

Giles McCoy, an eighteen-year-old sniper from St. Louis, Missouri, came in on a Higgins boat in one of the early waves. When the ramp went down, he jumped into water waist high and started wading toward the beach, machine-gun fire "popping all around us."

"There was a young marine on the side of me that got hit by a machine-gun bullet that blew his right arm off, and he was squirting blood about twenty feet and I knew he was going to faint, so I got him over and got him up on my hip . . . and I reached around and got a hold of the blood vessel that was blown off and I pinched it till my fingers cramped," McCoy later recounted. When he got to shore, still dragging the wounded marine, McCoy called for a corpsman to come over and said, "You got to tie this guy off. He's going to bleed to death."

"Son, he's already gone," the corpsman said. "He's dead. Turn him loose."

The grisly scene was just a sample of the cataclysmic casualties ahead on "bloody Peleliu," where things would not get better. The landing took much longer than expected as the hours turned into days and then weeks of fighting. Worse yet, the Japanese had brought in engineers to direct construction of a network of over five hundred caves, some equipped with sliding steel doors, to shield their weapons. They had dug in, prepared for the long haul.

The vicious, bloody fight to take Peleliu lasted ten weeks. While the Americans eventually prevailed, two operational failures dogged the mission: an intelligence lapse that left troops vulnerable to withering attacks and an abbreviated preinvasion bombardment that failed to knock out Japanese defenses. The cost was ninety-six hundred casualties, including twelve hundred killed.

Peleliu marked a new phase in the amphibious campaign. The Japanese, drawing on lessons learned in earlier amphibious invasions, began to adjust their tactics to counteract the Americans' effectiveness. They had recognized the need to create a "defense-in-depth," a complex of positions from which they could counterattack, instead of expending excessive resources opposing the initial landing forces at the shoreline. Their engineers designed intricate defensive systems using the natural terrain to their advantage.

The Palau offensive also marked a turning point for the utility of the JANIS reports. Finally, a report had reached field planners several months in advance and had provided critical information that had been incorporated into a theater operations plan. The dense, expansive reef had proven to be formidable on the western side where the marines decided to launch the assault for tactical reasons, but at least they were not caught off guard and knew in advance to employ as many amphibious tractors as they could muster for the operation.

One aspect of the oceanographers' role took some getting used to. However much information they provided, however many obstacles they identified or dangers they flagged, operational planners had the final word. Their plans had to take into account many considerations other than just the oceanographic factors, not least of which were the size, strength, location, and capability of enemy defenses. While it was frustrating to learn that marines had stalled and died on reefs that the oceanographers had clearly identified, Sears and her team learned to accept their role as providers of information, not war planners or commanders.

Despite the mixed outcome in the Palaus, news that experienced oceanographers were producing reports for amphibious invasions spread further increasing demand. No other reference like the oceanography chapter of JANIS 103, the most extensive and detailed assessment of the conditions at a marine-based combat mission, had ever been compiled. The JANIS reports were on time; they were relevant; and they drew notice as the most detailed target coverage under one cover, making them an essential resource for the planning and execution of combat missions. Almost overnight the Joint Topographic Committee requested advance copies in draft form and intelligence agencies started asking that reports be shipped directly from the printer.

The chief of the Weather Division of the Army Air Force requested three hundred copies of "Chapter III, Oceanography." OSS requested extra copies. Admiral Nimitz requested one hundred copies each of JANIS reports on the Celebes Sea and the Philippines for JICPOA.

Nimitz's chief strategist, Admiral Forrest P. Sherman, deputy chief of staff, CINCPAC, sent a memo on December 18, 1944, to Captain C. G. Moore, chair of the Joint Topographical Committee, citing the JANIS reports as an "indispensable basic reference work" and one that was more popular with shore-based planners and intel organizations than skippers. "They are much admired out here and have proved very useful." Now that the reports were in sync with the schedule of operations, the Oceanographic Unit's work was having the kind of impact Sears had envisioned from the moment she had first donned her uniform. She and her team were using their scientific expertise to save American lives.

After passing many a long night checking and rechecking ocean currents, tide tables, bottom sediments, and wave observations, their heads nodding over open books at their desks, while laundry spilled onto floors and dirty dishes crowded sinks in their neglected apartments, the exhausted oceanographers deserved to let off some steam. Dora Henry, always eager to host an impromptu cocktail party, would whip up a pitcher of martinis at her place, where she could smoke a few cigarettes and let her hair down. Mary Grier might have been a teetotaler but not Mary Sears. She had learned to drink Johnnie Walker Black with the sailors and scientists at Woods Hole. Fenner Chace could finally loosen his tie, put up his feet, and puff away on his pipe. One can imagine it would be the perfect time for the team to swap stories about how they had managed to pull off the impossible—a thirty-three-item oceanography report on a group of obscure islands in the middle of the western Pacific Ocean.

But any break from the pressing duty at hand was only a brief respite. With the dawning of the next day more requests would flow in to the tight-knit Oceanographic Unit for reports on places unknown. The team would have to start searching, calculating, writing, and sketching all over again. They would have to check and recheck all their numbers and make tough calls about what to include and what to leave out. But for one night they could allow themselves a small celebration and look forward to the day when the war's end would bring a much bigger one.

CHAPTER 14

Narrowing the Path to Victory

— Washington, D.C., 1944 —

After two and a half years sacrificing for the war, ration fatigue started to creep into Washington, D.C., and temper the enthusiasm of residents. Everyone wanted to do their part, but what had begun with restrictions on the sale of gas and rubber had bled even further into the staples of everyday life. Soon the government was controlling access to sugar, flour, meat, and even cigarettes, issuing the coupons required to purchase them in limited numbers. The effort to conserve materials deemed essential to the war effort expanded so much that the newly formed Office of Price Administration ultimately hired an army of sixty thousand workers to oversee the nation's rationing program.

Rationing snuck into everyday life in odd ways. Who could have imagined that going to war would strain the supply of wool, cotton, and fabric dyes? But over the course of World War II, sixteen million men and women left their old wardrobes and identities behind to join the armed forces and wear their country's uniform. The demand for fabric caused a scarcity of bolts of material on store shelves. Access to Japanese silk was cut off entirely, and blue and brown clothing dyes were reserved exclusively for the military.

The War Production Board even influenced fashion, issuing "Order

L-85," directing manufacturers to limit skirt lengths and widths with the goal of reducing the amount of material used in women's wear by 15 percent. They banned any design feature that required extra fabric including pleats, ruffles, turned-back cuffs, sashes, scarves, and hoods, although the board made exceptions for wedding gowns, maternity clothes, and religious vestments.

In the world of men's fashion, wide lapels and cuffed trousers gave way to a new "Victory Suit" with narrow lapels and straight-hemmed pants. Designers went all in on the new directives and beyond, creating suits that projected a "shoestring silhouette," which required even less fabric than L-85 had prescribed.

Conserving for war production changed daily life in D.C. in other ways. An influx of government workers from rural America planted victory gardens in vacant lots, esplanades, and backyards. Long lines persisted at grocery stores and gas stations. All over town huge piles of donated scrap metal and rubber tires edged up to the streets. Because the Japanese had gained control of rubber production in Malaya and Indonesia, the nation's tire production had been strangled, creating a situation so dire that the government prohibited the sale of new tires altogether at first, later allowing purchases by coupon only.

Gasoline rationing followed tire rationing, not because gas was in short supply, but because it helped deter rubber use. Rationing fuel—five gallons a week for the average citizen—along with drastic restrictions in automobile and tire production, jump-started a carpooling craze throughout the nation's capital. Instead of waiting in long lines just to catch a bus one way, a rider could sign up for a guaranteed roundtrip to and from work in the company of fellow workers. The American Automobile Association (AAA) helped stoke the trend, starting a "Share A Ride" program to match drivers with riders.

The carpooling boom caught on at the Hydrographic Office in Suitland, especially for workers who lived in D.C. proper fifteen miles away. Employees advertised in the *Scuttlebutt*'s new weekly "Rider" column: "Mary and Helen Buchak, 612 Sheridan St., N.W., Ex 132 want rider from there or downtown area," "Ride wanted to vicinity of 12th Penn. Ave.,

N.W.," "2 riders wanted—vicinity of Rittenhouse and Tennyson Streets, N.W. (Pinehurst Circle) Mrs. Ferris-Census 285."

As if rationing weren't stressful enough, constant reminders of the enemy threat hung over the nation's capital. Forty-millimeter gun crews were stationed on rooftops within sight of the Washington and Lincoln Memorials. The shriek of regular air raid sirens sent everyone, from schoolchildren to factory workers, rushing to nearby shelters. The city conducted regular blackout drills in preparation for nocturnal bombing raids. At 10:00 p.m., outside lights would darken and streets would empty as citizens dutifully stayed indoors with window shades pulled down or lights off. Even the White House could not escape the pall of long blackout curtains, "gloomy in winter and hot in the summer," much to the displeasure of Eleanor Roosevelt.

The president's wife may not have been a fan of her new window dressings, but it didn't deter her from inviting a lucky group of twenty-five WAVES from the Hydrographic Office to the White House on April 4, 1944, including Specialist Lucy Berkey.

"We stood in a circle in the blue room and Mrs. Roosevelt shook hands with each of us," she wrote home to her parents. Then the first lady led her guests into the formal dining room for punch and cookies where they were greeted by FDR's Scottie dog, Fala, the highlight of the trip.

By the spring of 1944 the Joint Publishing Board was scrambling to meet the demands of a military that was desperate for details and data. Colonel Bicknell traveled to Philadelphia to prod the printers to speed up production. The board started looking for four thousand square feet of additional space to house a staff that had grown from three support personnel to thirty-three, including nine editors as production ramped up. At least half of the staff were now women, mostly civilians, who worked as cartographers, draftsmen, editors, file clerks, and typists. The program had expanded beyond anything Bicknell had envisioned when he took over the production of topographic intelligence reports for the Joint Chiefs. He was on a merry-go-round that was spinning faster and faster—hanging on and trying to keep the operation going as smoothly as possible.

The Oceanographic Unit had settled into a routine, albeit a demanding one. They were cranking out a staggering three JANIS reports almost simultaneously while also compiling data for other Hydrographic Office publications on foreign areas and answering urgent queries. Coordinating it all was a nightmare for the officer-in-charge, but Sears persisted, spurring Fenner Chace to review the mass of data smothering his desktop and reminding Dora Henry to submit her revised copy so Sears could push the reports out the door on time. One person Sears did not have to prod was the robotic Mary Grier, who was wearing out the heels on her pumps walking up and down the five floors of the Library of Congress and to every government agency with a library. She ended her workday at a bus stop, hugging the nation's secrets tightly to her chest as she waited for the bus back to Suitland.

There was still no end in sight for the war, especially in the Pacific, where beleaguered troops were steadily island-hopping their way to Japan, but only halfway there. Sears was attending yet another JANIS planning meeting on March 15, 1944, when she first learned that the war planners had Formosa (the present-day Taiwan) in their sights. Like most in the room, she knew very little about the region, but as she listened to Colonel Bicknell describe the location and expanse of the massive island, one thing was clear—the oceanography report on this behemoth was going to be a heck of a lot of work.

Bicknell turned up the heat on the contributors even further with his final directive: anything completed prior to the deadline should be submitted "immediately." The demand for intelligence in distant, unfamiliar Pacific areas had pushed the board to publish individual chapters as soon as they were received, highlighting the urgency to get information out to war planners as quickly as possible.

There was no such thing as a relaxed pace in wartime. The Oceanographic Unit would once again feel the pressure to deliver ahead of schedule. As Sears rode the bus back to Suitland, she knew there could not have been a worse time to announce such an extensive project. As the oceanographers pulled their straight-backed chairs around maps to go over the specifications on Formosa, she could almost hear a collective sigh rippling around the large wooden table. She too wondered how many hundreds of landing beaches they would have to analyze for the enormous island and when they would find the time to do it.

Looking at a map of the North Pacific region, it was easy to see why Formosa was an enticing target. The large, mountainous island jutting into the Pacific between the Philippines and Japan measured 240 miles long and 90 miles wide, dwarfing other island targets of the amphibious campaign. Along with its imposing land mass came a well-developed infrastructure of highways, telecommunication networks, and manufacturing facilities. A part of the Japanese Inner Defense Zone, Formosa was only 575 miles from Kyushu at the southern tip of Japan. The Japanese had constructed extensive air, ground, and naval installations on the island. To American war planners, Formosa presented as a perfect base of operations for an assault against Japan, *if* they could pull off such an invasion.

But to fully describe the waters and beaches of this mammoth area to military commanders would require the oceanographers to spend countless hours reviewing data, making calculations, drawing diagrams, and writing up their findings. That burden would fall particularly hard on Grier, who could look forward to long days searching foreign journals, hoping that the Japanese had included Formosa in their surveys of the waters around Japan.

An urgent request for oceanographic data could land on Sears's desk at any time of the day. When it did the team would set aside the articles they were reviewing, put down drafts Dora Henry had marked up, and clear a space for a brainstorming session about the newest problem. The query might be from a naval operational planner, wanting to know about offshore currents for an amphibious assault not yet covered in any published reports. It might be from a marine planner seeking specific tidal data or a submarine skipper shipping out to unchartered waters. Whatever it was, the team would have anywhere from a few hours to a day or two to scrape together the best possible data, depending on the mission deadline.

Sometimes the request came to Hydro in the middle of the night via Teletype. Minutes later a courier would knock on Sears's Suitland Manor front door, which she would answer in bathrobe and slippers. She would reach out her hand for the piece of paper with a request for updated tidal tables on locations so secret only Sears, the officer-in-charge, could be entrusted with the exact coordinates. Whatever combination of strategy, tactics, and conditions had dictated the final landing spot it was now up to Sears to make adjustments.

She would have to get dressed, go into the office, rummage through the Hydro library, looking for tide tables for the closest location and use those to extrapolate tides for the new obscure target. Of course, she worried about the accuracy of her calculations. Her sleep had been interrupted after piling one exhausted day on top of another and there was no one to check her work in the middle of the night. But it wasn't as if she was new at this, and as the head oceanographer at the Hydrographic Office, the navy was depending on her.

By mid-1944, those urgent requests had become more common. The oceanographers might not have the references ready at hand to find the needed data. They might need to contact Grier, who would be out for the day, having taken the early morning bus into D.C. Sears and Grier worked out a system to stay in touch. Several times a day, Sears's office phone would ring and it would be Grier, calling in to see if she needed to look up something for a "quickie." Speaking on a nonsecure line, they avoided using names or identifying details. Instead, they spoke in code.

"Do you remember Number 302? Well, you go up northeast of that," Sears had said on one occasion, referring to the number of a past report, to provide a clue.

"Oh, yeah, yeah," Grier would answer if she knew the location Sears was referring to, but if the location wasn't clear, Sears would keep dropping hints, steering clear of any mention of the exact location.

Grier was well aware that spies could be watching her as she moved about the Library of Congress. To avoid inadvertently disclosing military targets to the enemy she made every effort to cover her tracks and leave no traces of the topics she was pursuing while searching through the stacks at the Library of Congress. When reshelving books or using the card catalog she was careful to place everything back in its original location out of concern that someone would come behind her and be able to detect what region she had been researching.

Others were not so careful. Grier discovered more than once that she could discern the locations others were investigating when she came across cards that were out of place. Sometimes when she got a new assignment for a particular region, she was not at all surprised because she had been tipped off by what she had observed in the card catalog and on bookshelves.

With her experience as a librarian and her network of contacts among other librarians, Grier was granted special privileges at the libraries she frequented, especially the Library of Congress, the largest library in the world. She had found a special home in the Adams Annex.

To alleviate overcrowding in the main building, the Library of Congress had opened its new five-story extension in 1939, just in time to meet the research needs of an information-hungry government. Described in Washington's *Sunday Star* as a "handsome box . . . faced with white Georgia marble," the Adams Annex proudly displayed its 250 miles of shelving situated within twenty acres of floor space. The new building had the capacity to house ten million books in addition to the five million volumes already shelved in the main building. The Adams Annex's "solid mass of shelving, encircled with work spaces," was perfect for Grier and researchers from other government agencies who needed a private space in which to review references.

It was no accident that the Library of Congress served as the central receptacle of valuable information for war-related research. In 1939, Franklin Roosevelt had appointed Archibald MacLeish, a poet and a lawyer, as the Librarian of Congress because FDR entrusted his friend not only to safeguard America's most precious artifacts but also to ensure that the library collection would expand to meet the needs of a government at war.

In 1940, MacLeish instructed staff to survey the collections to determine which materials should be removed to more secure locations outside the city, which could be stored within the building in a bomb-proof shelter, and which resources should be kept on-site to meet the needs of Congress, federal agencies, and library patrons. MacLeish also spurred the acquisition of "materials useful to the conduct of the war," including topographies, gazetteers, dictionaries, official documents, maps, surveys, and military studies. He also subscribed to periodicals from "far-off places" that described the lives of other peoples and their customs, "the ideologies of our Allies and our enemies," and "all of those materials which contribute to an understanding of ourselves, our heritage and our democratic purpose."

Acquiring these resources during wartime wasn't easy. Already, the regular channels of international communication, particularly with enemy-occupied countries, had been disrupted. Outbound shipments had been slowed or canceled altogether. The library placed special emphasis on obtaining historical, social, and geographic resources relating to the Far East, which included Thailand, Indochina, Burma, Ceylon, and India. They acquired works on European philosophy, Judaism, Nazism, and anti-Nazi periodicals and pamphlets.

As the war wore on, the number and type of readers visiting the library shifted toward those engaged in gathering information to aid the war effort. The Adams Annex offered study rooms, which over twelve hundred investigators from 127 government agencies used during the war. At the request of Admiral Bryan, the library assigned one fifth-floor room to the Oceanographic Unit, where Grier could hide her work from prying eyes. The Orientalia collection, which included Japanese language publications, and the Science and Technology section, were conveniently located on the same floor.

Given her security consciousness, it was highly ironic that Grier was investigated more than once as a suspected member of the Communist Party. In the 1940s, such an affiliation would have raised suspicions that she could compromise national security. Grier had a brother-in-law in Seattle who, as a known member of the Communist Party in the 1930s, had lost his job at the Office of Civilian Defense. Grier had allegedly supported Communist Party candidates while living in Seattle and sympathized with Communist causes by signing petitions. The FBI alleged she had joined an underground "government" cell of the Communist Party when she moved to D.C.

As a condition of her employment, she had been required to sign a loyalty oath, and to answer "yes" or "no" regarding whether she was a member of a Communist organization or any party or organization which advocated overthrowing the government. Grier had answered "no."

She was interviewed in January 1945 while working under Sears at Hydro about her alleged Communist Party activities. Grier stated she was not a member of the Communist Party. As her supervising officer, Sears must have been aware of the investigation and perhaps had even been questioned about Grier. Yet this episode did not diminish her high regard for her star researcher. As Sears later indicated, she was contacted by the FBI about many people throughout the war, including other coworkers. She took the questions about Grier in stride.

The issue arose again on April 16, 1953, when Grier appeared under subpoena before the House of Representatives Committee on Un-American Activities (HUAC). Grier refused to answer any questions regarding past Communist Party affiliations, including during the war, but she firmly denied ever transferring classified material or information to the Communist Party or a foreign government.

"As I understand it, is it correct that you compiled material or as a researcher got material together and that that material was used officially by the armed services of the United States?" Robert Kunzig, an attorney for HUAC asked Grier.

"For the people who compiled it, who wrote it, who prepared these intelligence reports, I went to the library to hunt for what they might need. . . . In compiling in oceanography they need data and the data has not been organized in this country to the point where you do not need somebody who knows something about libraries to hunt for it. I went and hunted for the material and the people used it and they won the war with it," Grier explained.

"You say this material has not been organized in this country?" Congressman Gordon Scherer asked.

"Library materials have not been organized in this country around the science of oceanography in such a way as to be easily obtained. Intensive research was required in order to get the material together. . . . I feel that librarians are quite important in this world, that when we started in fighting this war we had to use them at last because we had to dig the stuff out of the libraries in order for us to know what we were doing in parts of the world before. There had not been depth data made by this government or even the British Government since the middle of the nineteenth century, in certain sections of the South Pacific," Grier answered, pointing out just how complicated and essential her job had been.

Grier accurately categorized the disorganized state of the oceanographic literature. When World War II began, aside from Grier's own bibliography of marine life in the Western Pacific Ocean, oceanographic indexes and journals of oceanography published in English were scarce. This lack made her job more difficult, but it also explained why Grier, a librarian and not an intelligence officer, had been entrusted with the task of gathering confidential oceanographic intelligence in the first place. An experienced oceanographic librarian was one of the few people who had the training and expertise to "dig the stuff out of the libraries."

The other aspect of the job that had complicated Grier's mission was the need for secrecy, something she had taken very seriously throughout the war.

"We only would discuss it, sir, in the office. I never discussed it with anyone outside of the office, nor in any other way handled it . . . that is an important thing for people working, not only in time of war but in time of peace, with American military matters. Not only must one be careful in regard to conversation or otherwise about certain aspects of it but in military campaigns you've got to be very careful even in hunting this material not—for people not to know what you are hunting about, as you can—as you probably well know."

Grier must have satisfied the committee's concerns with her heartfelt testimony. Afterwards she returned to her job at the American Geologic Society of America and never heard from investigators again.

On the morning she set out to tackle Formosa, Grier knew where to go first. The Orientalia collection at the Library of Congress was a rich source of oceanographic data on the islands in and around Japan. Unlike the oceanography literature in the United States, which had not been collected and organized so it could be easily found, Japanese oceanographers, funded by the government, had published extensively in oceanography journals and indexed these materials.

Grier found numerous publications by marine geologist Hisikatsu Yabe (Tohoku Imperial University) who had analyzed the coral reefs around Japan and neighboring islands, including Formosa. Given the difficulties the Americans had encountered in getting across coral reefs in almost every island assault, Yabe's studies would not only serve to warn the troops of offshore obstructions but would also identify channels and passageways through the reefs. Grier was also able to find useful data on Formosa from the *Bulletin of the Hydrographic Department of Tokyo*, again pulling the survey of the western North Pacific Ocean by the HIJMS *Mansyu*, sailing directions from Taiwan and Nansei-Shoto, and tide tables from a third article.

Sears's contacts at Scripps provided other salient details in the form of unpublished reports from 1943 through 1944 on surface currents, isotherm charts, and temperature and salinity tables. The Oceanographic Unit drafted "Study 27" on the transparency of the water off Japan by using data collected from contacts in the scientific community and the Coast and Geodetic Survey computed tide tables for the region.

Altogether seventeen major textual sources from across the country and seven additional maps and charts, mainly from the Hydrographic Office, provided enough details to render a fairly accurate portrayal of what to expect in the waters off the thousand-mile coastline of Formosa. Only

"Chapter III Oceanography" and "Chapter IV Climate and Weather" were published on time in June 1944, but those were the most important chapters for war planning purposes, especially for predicting the optimal time frame for an amphibious invasion.

The oceanographers had highlighted several major areas of concern about Formosa. First, the tides around the island varied considerably, from eight to twelve feet high along the northern half of the West Coast to one and a half to two feet on the southwest coast. There were wide variations according to the phase of the moon and time of day. High sea and swell were also frequent in the area, although the seas tended to be calmer from April through September. Any amphibious landing from fall to early spring risked highly variable tides and raucous waves with similar results to those already seen throughout the war. Since the Formosa invasion plan called for a target date of "early 1945," the landing site would have to be carefully chosen to avoid catastrophe or perhaps be reconsidered altogether.

Roosevelt, Churchill, and the Combined Chiefs met again at the Octagon Conference in Quebec in September 1944 where the Joint Chiefs openly deliberated whether American forces should take Formosa on the way to Japan, or bypass Formosa in favor of Luzon and hop to the Bonin Islands.

Formosa was the more desirable target, but it was also the more difficult to successfully invade. Formosa was within the Japanese Inner Defense Zone, which meant that Japanese troops would defend it with extra reinforcements. Attacking from the sea, the Americans would need at least three times the estimated number of troops they would be up against to ensure victory—an invasion force of up to five hundred thousand men. With the war in Europe ongoing, there were not enough combat units available in the Pacific theater to pull off an invasion of Formosa.

After much debate, the Joint Chiefs scrubbed the plan to invade Formosa because they were not willing to delay progress in the Pacific until

Germany had fallen. On October 3, 1944, they announced their decision to attack Luzon instead and bypass Formosa. American amphibious forces would be taking a more direct path to Japan through Iwo Jima and Okinawa.

When word filtered back to Sears and her team, they might have concluded that all the time spent on Formosa had once again been a terrific waste of time. After almost two years on the job, though, they had learned there was nothing definite about strategic plans. Numerous factors had come into play in mapping out the path to Tokyo, and changes had been made as necessary to expedite victory. Yet the reports had still fulfilled their purpose, playing a valuable role in informing the Joint Chiefs' war planning as well as others down the chain of command.

Even though plans to invade the large island had been shelved, naval intelligence in Hawaii requested thirty-five additional copies of JANIS 87 on Formosa to be dispatched as soon as possible. Everyone knew that plans could change with little notice and the need to invade Formosa might arise in the future. Other ongoing operations in the area could also be informed by data included in the Formosa report.

Pacific commanders not only kept the JANIS reports on file but also sent them out to their lower echelons to use as they saw fit. By September 1944 the JANIS Publishing Board had distributed nine complete JANIS reports, seventeen short studies, and an untold number of secret "quickies" to the various military commands in all theaters of war, select government agencies, and the White House map room.

As it would turn out, JANIS 87 on Formosa, as well as other JANIS reports on areas that were not directly targeted in the Pacific Campaign, would help save lives in unexpected ways as the war wound down. They would be needed to help plan amphibious landings to disarm Japanese forces and implement the occupation of Japan immediately after the war. They would also be used to help locate the hundreds of prisoner of war camps hidden across Japanese territory in China, Formosa, and Korea. Every JANIS report would eventually play an essential role in the months ahead, and in ways their authors never expected.

• • •

Since December 22, 1941, when the Japanese had routed a mix of American and Filipino troops to capture Lingayen Gulf on the island of Luzon, it had been in enemy hands. The next day MacArthur had reluctantly ordered a retreat from Luzon, and the subsequent disastrous withdrawal of troops to Bataan followed. Three years later the United States Army had returned to take back Lingayen Gulf and Luzon, the largest, island in the Philippines.

The amphibious forces initially planned to land on the southern coast in January 1945. These were not the optimal landing beaches. They were backed by fish ponds and rice paddies, features that limited troop movement, but they were weakly defended and closer to a targeted airstrip. Planners also wanted to land on the eastern beaches that provided better routes for the troops to move inland. The question arose whether it would be safe to attempt to land on the eastern beaches where the waves were known to be higher than on the western side. As the previous landings had demonstrated, the combination of high waves and small landing craft was a recipe for disaster.

The JANIS report on the Philippines indicated that high sea and swell were frequent especially on the coasts bordering the Pacific Ocean. Although the seas in the Lingayen Gulf region were, in general, roughest from November through February, the average percentage of high sea and swell in January had been observed to be lower than the seasonal mean.

Although wave prediction was still in the experimental stage, Sears was able to make general prognostications with the aid of historical wave data and knowledge of the expected winds. She estimated that the surf would be less than six feet on the eastern side on the day of landing and therefore safe for an amphibious operation.

Almost always the Japanese had their best defenses situated near the optimal landing beaches, which deterred the Americans from landing there. One of the prime uses of the JANIS reports throughout the war was to identify safe alternative landing sites, beaches that the Japanese did not typically use but where the risks of landing would be acceptable and might keep troops out of harm's way. In the end, the operation planners decided to land on a broad front made up of the southern Luzon beaches to attempt tactical surprise, and the eastern beaches for their better inland routes.

In December 1944, while the military had been preparing to invade Luzon, the Hydrographic Office celebrated the holidays with a caroling party hosted by the WAVES of Air Navigation and an office decoration competition that the Survey Section won. Mistletoe hung throughout the office, and "Smitty" was congratulated for having kissed 321 "hydroettes." Smitty's behavior, real or imagined, was emblematic of the banter that took place at Hydro when it came to male–female interactions. Despite the fact that the women were more than pulling their weight by keeping the agency afloat in a time of crisis, they could not escape the undercurrent of sexism that permeated the office environment. The *Scuttlebutt* regularly published off-color jokes, risqué cartoons, scantily clad pinups, and remarks about the WAVES' attire.

One full-page cartoon in particular carried the sarcasm to a new level. "Important Warning to All Men!! Beware of the Man-Hungry SHE WOLF!" the headline read. "This new breed of an already deadly species is a wartime development. Her savagery increases as more men leave the home front. She may be wearing WACS', WAVES', WAR WORKER's or SHEEP's clothing. No man is safe from this ferocious female!"

It is well known that the navy was considered a "macho" organization before the arrival of women and that some "old-timers" didn't want women in the Hydrographic Office in the first place. While the sexist remarks published in the newsletter were likely intended as humor they could also be offensive to fellow workers. For the WAVES who preferred a workplace free of this annoyance, though, there was no possibility of complaining about the *Scuttlebutt*'s mischaracterizations without appearing "unpatriotic." WAVES were expected to serve alongside their male colleagues in silence and put up with the sexual harassment and blatant sexism that came with the job.

The *Scuttlebutt* published a "What I Want Santa to Bring Me for Christmas," column poking fun at employees. "Twinkle" Trinkle asked for "noiseless IBM machines," George Means asked for "noiseless WAVES." Phil Watt wanted to see "hula skirts with zippers." In a spoof of her highly technical role, Mary Sears wished for a mythical "self-propelling ectocardiograph with a bi-sectional armature."

Sears might have wished for the impossible in the *Scuttlebutt* column, but within her extended family she was known more for giving than for receiving, especially around the Christmas holidays. Each year she would turn one bedroom of her house in Woods Hole into a makeshift Santa's workshop with rolls of wrapping paper and ribbon and stacks of books taking over every available inch of bed and floor. Her niece Leslie Sears Karpp recalled that Sears gifted as many as ten books per child in her family during the yuletide season, earning their aunt the nickname "Christmas Mary." Sears was so generous that her siblings had to place limits on the number of presents she was allowed to bring. Sears would also send books around the world to the children of her friends in oceanography and would even drop them anonymously on doorsteps for neighborhood children.

The Christmas celebrations at Hydro included a dance that over three hundred employees and their guests attended. Entertainment was provided by the "Hydro Hotshots," a coed combo, complete with xylophone, upright bass, saxophone, and guitar, with a male officer and a WAVE providing vocals. Ted Egri, a former employee now stationed in the Pacific as a combat artist, sent two hand-drawn Christmas cards to the editors at *Scuttlebutt*. The card he drew "For the boys" featured two scantily clad females under a palm tree. "For the girls" he drew a Santa Claus sporting a pair of swimming trunks riding in a rowboat packed with presents, harnessed to a whale.

"Palm trees don't help create a[n] Xmas mood, but we are celebrating anyway," he wrote. "We took part in the Philippine invasion as you must know, and now feel we have something to celebrate about. We hope to be able to celebrate the next year in the States. Scenes of battle at the Philippines were so abundant that I am still painting battle scenes. I wish you a happy celebration and New Year."

Despite the holiday celebrations and remembrances, there was a busy slate of operations planned for early 1945, and the oceanographers worked through the holidays on the next round of reports. Fenner Chace was finishing charts for Japan while Dora Henry edited the narrative sections. Grier was gathering references for a series of reports on China due after the first of the year, and Sears attended organizational meetings at the end of December to focus on an upcoming target, Borneo.

"The wheels of war will not stop this Christmas," wrote the editors of *Scuttlebutt*. "Men working, fighting and dying—that is the picture this holiday season. Allied infantrymen braving the worst possible elements of Nature as nothing compared to the enemy positions that must be taken. Allied artillerymen, mortar crews, tank men, supply men, medical men— all driving slowly, terribly onward."

The "wheels of war" did not stop turning for the holidays and neither did the presses staffed by the dedicated workers at Hydro.

On the morning of January 9, 1945, an armada of Allied ships found the sea was calm in Lingayen Gulf off the coast of Luzon. As Sears had predicted, gentle swells and a mild surf in the eastern gulf promised a smooth ride to the beach. At 0900 hours, LVTs and armored LVT-As led the first assault waves to the beach, arriving forty minutes later. There had been little opposition to the landing and, in fact, a Filipino welcoming party began to assemble onshore ready to offer assistance to their American liberators.

"With good weather data and adequate charts, invasions can be planned as at Lingayen Gulf," Sears later wrote, clearly scoring the landing as a much-needed win. The Sixth Army, flanked by the marines, had safely landed on Luzon. The navy could now direct its full might back to the Central Pacific and the next strategic target standing between the United States and Japan, the island of Iwo Jima.

CHAPTER 15

Flying Blind in Iwo Jima

— Iwo Jima, 1945 —

For the first few years of World War II, planners had intentionally left Iwo Jima, a rocky, barren, pork chop–shaped heap of lava, off the list of invasion targets. The value of the Japanese "Sulphur Island" had been obscured by the blinding allure of the larger jewel of Formosa, stocked with military bases, highways, and beaches, a war planner's ideal base of operations from which to launch an invasion of Japan. But as the Pacific Campaign rolled along and the Joint Chiefs digested the staggering number of troops necessary to attack the heavily defended dreamscape, they decided that snagging Iwo Jima and Okinawa would be an infinitely more manageable course on the march to Japan.

Iwo Jima might have been an ugly duckling, with its rocky terrain and rotten egg smell, but the compact island, ideally situated midway between Tokyo and American-held airfields in the Marianas, made the perfect launch pad for the Okinawa invasion and could support the Americans' long-range bombing campaign against Japan. The newly developed Boeing B-29 Superfortress, based in Saipan and Tinian, could easily cover the thirteen hundred miles to Japan to launch airstrikes, but the shorter-range American fighter planes could not protect them from Japanese fighters launched from Iwo Jima. Capturing the island would neutralize this threat as well as provide airstrips from which to launch American fighter planes and refuel bombers. It would also knock out an early-warning radar station that gave Japan advance notice of incoming American bombers.

There was no killer coral reef to cross at Iwo Jima and no neap tides to drag down the landing boats, but there were other dangers to consider. Because Iwo Jima was a volcanic island, it had only slivers of beaches that dropped off sharply into deep water, creating a vicious surf zone. Instead of firmly packed golden sand, beaches were covered with a porous, black mixture of lava and ash spewed from volcanos. Both vehicles and humans sunk into this loose, structureless sand, slowing the rush of an offensive. The combination of dangerous surf and sinking sand had the potential to produce a new variety of landing nightmare for the marines.

These were just the type of topographic features that Sears and her, by now, seasoned team of oceanographers would have exposed in a JANIS report. But the decision to abandon Formosa and substitute Iwo Jima and Okinawa at the last minute meant that a long-range strategic report, where all the topographic data on Iwo Jima could be reviewed under one cover, would never be completed. Instead, military planners had to make do with reports published by different agencies to prepare for this important mission, the same patchwork system that JANIS had been established to replace.

Early on, Commander Bailey had instructed Sears and the other JANIS contributors to start on a preliminary "second-phase" study on the Bonin Islands that encompassed Iwo Jima, but in the fall of 1944 the study was put on hold. When Colonel Bicknell announced the change of plans, he told the JANIS members that "MID [Army intelligence] will attempt to keep the study up to date." Military intelligence had to pick up the slack on Iwo Jima, even though relying on them alone turned the clock back to a time when oceanographers did not contribute to the analysis.

The Oceanographic Unit did prepare limited reports on Iwo Jima, although not with its customary thirty-three item intensity. In October 1943, they produced "Study No. 14: Oceanography of the Waters Surrounding the Bonin and Volcano Islands," which included data on tides, currents, and waves. The relevant features from this study were likely incorporated into a special edition of *Sailing Directions for Nanpo Shoto*, published in January 1945 by the Hydrographic Office, one month before the operation.

Hydro's report included frank warnings of "sheer and forbidding cliffs" and "narrow rocky beaches." It advised of steep slopes along with the possibility of high winds and dangerous landing conditions in southeastern anchorages off the village of Minami near Iwo Jima. "During winds from west, through north, to northeast, landings become difficult if the wind becomes greater than force 4, and *landing is impossible in a swell*." The picture painted by the oceanographers was one of a coastline that ranged from difficult to dangerous for a landing force, and its complement of equipment and vehicles, to navigate to shore.

The Office of Naval Intelligence (ONI) had also weighed in with an earlier report published in September 1942. A brief hydrography section noted the possibility of difficult winds in the area and again included the ominous statement "*With a swell, landing is impossible*." There was no further explanation of what might be done to mitigate the danger.

Most Pacific islands were well outside the orbit of the United States armed forces, especially regions as distant and unknown as Iwo Jima. Inevitable intelligence gaps spelled chaos for an assault force that needed to ship supplies and equipment to prepare for contingencies weeks in advance. Moreover, the Iwo Jima mission had been sandwiched between two other major offensives, Luzon in January 1945 and Okinawa in April. By the time Luzon was wrapping up, there was only one month left to concentrate on the rugged pork chop in the sea, only thirty days to review intelligence and the game plan for any dangerous conditions that might threaten a landing.

Still, in the weeks leading up to the operation, American military commanders were feeling confident about their amphibious experience and about the intel on the landing beaches on the southeastern shore of Iwo Jima. A submarine, the USS *Spearfish*, had provided excellent periscope photography and soundings of the area. Underwater demolition teams had assessed the landing beaches and one commander judged aerial reconnaissance to be "unusually good."

The JICPOA intelligence staff at Pearl Harbor published an updated bulletin one month prior to the assault that described the nearshore slope off the beaches as "mild to gentle." But the report did raise red flags about the beaches by further noting, "The trafficability of this beach soil is low for wheeled vehicles, especially when it is dry. . . . It also would be difficult and tiring to move over it rapidly by foot. Movement for tracked vehicles should be easier." The report advised the use of Marston mats, ten-foot stainless steel planks that could be joined together to provide a firm surface for vehicles to drive across. The steel sections were perforated to allow drainage and to help reduce their weight to a manageable sixty-six pounds per section.

The CINCPAC-CINCPOA intelligence bulletin on Iwo Jima failed to highlight the steep and narrow beaches mentioned in Hydro's *Sailing Directions for Nanpo Shoto*, possibly overlooked due to a tight schedule.

Intelligence, or the lack thereof, was at the forefront of Lt. Art Anderson's mind in the days before the Battle of Iwo Jima. Anderson, part of the Seabees, a naval construction unit, reviewed a captured Japanese map and discovered that the beaches on the southeastern side of the island, targeted for the landing, had a steep slope that ended where the waves broke, just as Hydro's sailing directions had advised. Anderson, a military engineer, knew enough to worry that these conditions could cause a strong undertow that would endanger landing craft.

"I told our skipper that was the wrong beach for us to be going in on, because of the tremendous slope of the beach," Anderson later recalled. He thought it would be safer to land on the western beaches, which had more gradual slopes. His commanding officer passed the information along to the marines, but by then operations planners had made the decision to attack from the east.

Anderson had also pointed out to his superiors that the Japanese maps

described beaches covered with volcanic ash. He knew from prior training exercises that it would be nearly impossible for vehicles to gain any
traction on the soft, black sand, hampering the delivery of supplies and
heavy equipment.

Because Anderson's analysis conflicted with aerial reconnaissance,
the marines sent in frogmen to assess the beaches. They packed samples
of black sand into tobacco cans for analysis by navy experts. The frogmen also checked the firmness of the beaches by hand, but because they
were under enemy fire, they couldn't go in very far. They reported back
that the surface was as "hard as iron." While marine commanders were
reassured by this information, it did little to allay Anderson's concerns.
He suspected that the frogmen had misjudged the ground conditions because, as the Japanese documents had noted, while the beaches did firm
up immediately after ebb tide for a period of up to two hours, when they
dried out, they would "become just dust again."

On the morning of the offensive the weather was clear and winds were
favorable. Marines disembarked from forty-six troop transport vessels and
loaded into LSTs headed to shore. Around nine o'clock the LSTs disgorged
several hundred amphibian tractors loaded with the first waves of marines. Within ninety minutes, over eight thousand Marines had landed.
The operation to this point had been flawless, with negligible opposition
from the Japanese, but as troops disembarked, instead of racing across
firmly packed sand they sank knee-deep into the muck of volcanic ash.

Bud Nardecchia, a nineteen-year-old marine from Austin, Texas, carried ammunition for a gunner at Iwo Jima. "It was almost impossible
to run on it. You would run; take two steps forward and one back," he
later recalled. "We didn't do much running. We did more crawling than
anything else."

Not only did the ash and sludge slow progress, but it also damaged
wheeled vehicles that sunk into it and mired. Exhausted marines crawled
on all fours to get across the sand. To make matters worse steep stone
terraces lay behind the landing beach that even tracked vehicles could not

surmount. The few tanks that managed to get ashore bogged down in the ash or were incapacitated by mines. The end result was a pileup of men, vehicles, and equipment on the beach. The Japanese watched and waited for disorder to dissolve into chaos, then unleashed a barrage of artillery and mortar fire. Stuck and pinned down, the marines were unable to flee or dig foxholes for cover. Hundreds died and many more were wounded, totaling an appalling twenty-four hundred casualties on the first day.

Marine Arthur Talmage, a runner for Third Battalion commander Lt. Colonel Archie Vandegrift, came ashore in the third wave and encountered dead marines "all over the beach" as soon as he stepped out of a Higgins boat. Then he started sinking into the volcanic sand. ". . . you'd slide back, you'd go up and you'd slide back, just, well, it's like a bunch of BB's under your feet it's terrible." All the while he was trying to get across the ash and up the steep slope of beach, he was also taking fire.

Veteran correspondent Robert Sherrod (who had also reported from Tarawa) noted, "Nowhere in the Pacific War had I seen such badly mangled bodies. Many were cut squarely in half. Legs and arms lay fifty feet from the nearest cluster of dead."

Anderson's construction battalion tried to cross the beach with the marines but lost all their equipment. "It all went into this mush of volcanic sand which had no binder in it. It just disintegrated under you," Anderson later recalled.

After the first waves came in on tracked vehicles, the landing boats launched.

Anderson watched as they tried to come ashore. "The minute that [the landing craft] hit the beach of course the door's supposed to go down and everybody run out. Well about the time the door would hit, a wave would hit from behind from this tremendous undertow, and the whole back end of this barge would drop . . . when the next wave came in it would lift the thing up and throw it sideways and just throw it up on the beach like kindling wood."

The steep gradient of the landing beaches created waves of up to ten feet, then caused them to break directly on the narrow strip of beach. And just as Anderson had feared, the breakers thrust downward on the plywood Higgins boats. When combined with a strong undertow, this pressure resulted in landing craft "broaching" or capsizing. Then, the violent surf shattered them, splintering wood across the beach. Over two hundred smaller landing craft were lost. The beach looked like a salvage yard.

The Seabees stayed on the beaches to clear obstructions and lay down Marston mats. They too suffered high casualties. Marine engineers, like Anderson, working with a determined crew of Seabees, ultimately cleared the beach of obstructions by towing some vehicles and blasting through others. They cut paths through the lower stone terrace, all while taking intense fire from Japanese snipers ensconced on Mount Suribachi. Despite the horrendous beginning, thirty thousand marines ultimately made it ashore that first brutal day.

In his after-action report, Vice Admiral Kelly Turner, commander of Amphibious Forces, United States, Pacific Fleet summarized the chaotic scene on D-Day: "The adverse beach conditions soon became apparent. With a steep gradient such as this, the surf breaks directly upon the beach. It was impossible with the heavy swells to prevent the landing craft from broaching. With each wave, boats were picked up bodily and thrown broadside to the beach where succeeding waves swamped and wrecked them. . . . The resultant accumulation of wreckage piled progressively higher, and extended seaward into the beach approaches to form underwater obstacles which damaged propellers and even gutted a few of the landing ships."

Turner blamed a lack of warning about beach conditions for the calamity. "The scarcity of reports, and uncertainty of the analysis of the weather map in this area made accurate and dependable forecasts of swell impossible," he said. Turner was in part correct. No one could have predicted the exact height of the swells on D-Day, but Anderson and others had raised serious concerns, and these had not led to alterations in the battle plan.

The preliminary observations of the underwater demolition team might have been more complete but for the fact that the only officer with oceanographic expertise took ill and had been evacuated to the rear. Similarly, three weather officers who had prior training in the study of waves and surf at Scripps also missed the breaking swells.

These intelligence "misses" were eerily similar to those at Tarawa and, like that ill-fated landing, resulted in an unnecessary loss of life, equipment, and support vehicles when the operation bogged down. In the discrete snapshots that a reconnaissance mission provided, oceanographic features that were predictable components of the landscape had been missed.

Even more frustrating for everyone in the Oceanographic Unit was the knowledge that this was just the type of information that a dogged Mary Grier might have unearthed while combing through Japanese publications in the Library of Congress. After the war, Grier compiled a bibliography on the Western Pacific Ocean that included numerous citations for the Nanpo Shoto region. She had found the information in the Library of Congress along with data contributed by other government agencies. An experienced team of oceanographers with numerous JANIS reports under their belts could have reviewed Grier's references, analyzed the information, and provided specific warnings to military commanders well in advance of operations planning that might have saved lives and boats.

Had Sears been able to review Anderson's captured Japanese documents, she too might have raised concerns about the southeastern beaches. And if her findings had been published in a JANIS report well in advance of the operation, they might have carried more weight with war planners. Still, the outcome might very well have been the same. As in all military missions, the location of an operational objective, such as an airfield that needed to be neutralized early, might have taken precedence in deciding where to land.

Unfortunately, things didn't get a lot better for ground troops after the less-than-stellar landing. Marines painstakingly penetrated an intricate system of Japanese "defenses in depth" and encountered the best fortifications to date. The Japanese were determined to defend Iwo Jima, an island firmly within their territory and deeply cherished. When the

Japanese intuited that the Americans were coming to take their highly coveted bomber strip, they sent in their best civil engineers to design a web of hillside caves in the island's interior connected by tunnels to outlying positions. They stashed artillery and troops underground out of sight, allowing them to move around the island undetected. They hoped to inflict enough casualties to deny the Americans Iwo Jima and ultimately to deter them from attacking Japan.

The plan succeeded in part, as Iwo Jima proved to be the bloodiest battle in the history of the United States Marine Corps and the only major Pacific battle where American forces sustained more casualties than the Japanese. In thirty-six days of combat, 22,000 Japanese were killed but the Americans sustained 25,800 American casualties, a third of the 76,000-man fighting force, including 6,800 killed in action. The butcher's bill again shocked the American public and no one felt it more than the man in charge of the Pacific Fleet, Admiral Chester Nimitz.

"Among the Americans who served on Iwo Island uncommon valor was a common virtue," Nimitz stated in a victory message.

Afterward he wrote to his wife, "I am delighted with the news that Iwo has finally been conquered and I hope that I will not get too many letters cursing me because of heavy casualties. I am receiving two or three a day signed 'a Marine Mother' and calling me all sorts of names."

Despite the exacting price, from a strategic standpoint the operation was an overwhelming success. With airfields 750 miles from Japan, long-range B-29 bombers had an unimpeded, direct approach to the home islands with the security of long-range fighter escorts. Disabled aircraft now had a safe haven on which to land in case of engine trouble or bad weather and, for the first time, all Japanese islands were within bomber range.

The marines also managed to snag a public relations feat out of Iwo Jima. They had raised a flag on Iwo Jima's Mount Suribachi on the fifth day of fighting, an event captured by Associated Press photographer Joe Rosenthal, whose photo of the event ran in every major newspaper in the United States. It became one of the most famous images of World War II. Of the six men in the photo, three were later killed in the ongoing battle to win the island. The surviving three marines went home on Roosevelt's orders. They participated in a war bond drive that raised an incredible sum of 26.3 billion dollars and provided an immeasurable boost to the Marine Corps image for decades to come.

The Battle of Iwo Jima added a new page to the history of amphibious warfare. The broaching of over two hundred landing craft and the resulting pileup of wreckage and damaged equipment was yet another in a long list of unforced errors.

Once the battle ended there was little time to waste, with the next major offensive only a month away. The assault on Okinawa promised to be a massive undertaking and one of signal importance, the last island on the road to Japan. With this huge battle ahead, the navy was going to need its oceanographers' best intelligence to avoid the dire consequences of another landing surprise.

CHAPTER 16

Penetrating the Zone of Safety

— Okinawa, 1945 —

Spring brings new hope to the world," the *Scuttlebutt* declared in March 1945. "From here, Hitler looks like a washed-up paperhanger and it won't be too long before Tojo goes down for the count. Maybe next spring we'll be cruising through the park decked out in sports jackets again, watching the wind blow those skirts a little higher.

"It's spring here in your old U.S.A. The birds are singing, the flowers and trees are starting to bloom, the veteran ball players are loosening up their rusty joints, the curfew in some places has been extended to one A.M. . . . and thank God, you men are bringing this war ever closer to victory and to an end," the editors opined in the "Our Men Overseas" column.

Three long years of war had derailed educations, diverted career plans, and separated loved ones. WAVES, servicemen, and civilians had worked shoulder to shoulder, around the clock, to supply a military with an insatiable appetite for nautical charts and oceanographic data. Now that the Allies had liberated France and penetrated Germany, a victory in Europe appeared close at hand. An air of optimism permeated the Hydro hallways as the staff dared hope that the war would be over by year's end.

The wartime economy still imposed strains on day-to-day life, like shortages of fresh vegetables, which motivated amateur gardeners. Workers from Hydro and the nearby Census Bureau raked out the victory garden for the third year in a row and planted tomatoes, corn, and sweet potatoes. Employees were still carpooling to get from D.C. to Suitland. And the shortages of fabric for clothing, nylon for hosiery, and even cigarettes, continued as the vast war machine gobbled up raw materials, but with the end at least imaginable, doing without seemed a little more tolerable.

The *Scuttlebutt* urged the staff to keep up their strong tradition of contributing to the Red Cross War Fund and participating in blood drives. They asked employees to further support the troops by collecting buckles, small hinges, beads, and yarn for the Red Cross occupational therapy program so that convalescing soldiers could learn crafts. Spring also brought the revival of outdoor sports, particularly the reemergence of the highly popular Hydro softball league, where each division fielded a team.

The WAVES had "scooped the spring season for hats" with their new garrison caps, known as "side caps," that could be folded flat when not worn. The caps, available in both navy blue wool and gray seersucker, added a jauntier, more casual look to the tailored uniforms and were cooler in the summer.

Recently, *The Fighting Lady*, a documentary produced by Twentieth Century-Fox in 1944 about an "anonymous aircraft carrier" in the Pacific, had been aired to 1,365 Hydro personnel who crowded the Wave Recreation Hall over several showings. The featured carrier was the USS *Yorktown*, a workhorse of the Pacific Campaign, whose fighter planes and bombers performed numerous air raids to support amphibious assaults from mid-1943 until the end of the war. The *Yorktown*, a product of Roosevelt's massive naval construction program, was a behemoth on the water—two city blocks long, the width of four freight trains abreast with an elevator "as big as a tennis court" that operated between the hangar and flight deck.

With a complement of twenty-six hundred men, the carrier housed a sick bay for the wounded, a full-scale galley, including butcher and bakery shops, capable of serving meals around the clock, along with a laundry and a cobbler shop. The Supply Department also operated a ship's store, barbershop, and a soda fountain. The massive ship provided every service necessary to support the population of a small town for months. When under attack, the sailors who provided those support services ripped off their aprons and ran to their assigned battle stations, eager to break away from their domestic roles and spring into action.

Hydro employees had been producing the thousands of naval and aeronautical charts that made it possible for aircraft carriers like the *Yorktown* to navigate the outer reaches of the Pacific. They watched with pride as their work came to life before their eyes, particularly Sears, who had issued specific warnings about turbulent waves that affected operations for aircraft carriers in the Pacific. The audience perched on the edge of their seats as fighter planes took off for missions to bomb and strafe enemy airfields, fuel depots, and ships, realizing that each mission carried the risk of injury, death, or capture.

Many were already familiar with distant targets in the Pacific like Kwajalein, Truk, and the Mariana Islands, but few knew those areas as did Sears and her team. As planes swooped down over Saipan, Tinian, and Guam, the oceanographers couldn't help but recall the long hours they had spent analyzing tides and waves for JANIS 102 on the Marianas, their third JANIS report, prepared a lifetime ago. This is why they had dug so hard for each detail. They couldn't do much about enemy attacks but they could verify the accuracy of every word to warn the fighting forces of the hazards at sea.

No doubt a few chuckles greeted the sight of the ship's dog "Scrappy" running across the flight deck in a yellow life vest. But the mood certainly grew more sober as damaged planes lurched back to the *Yorktown*, their shattered windshields covered in blood after both fuselage and crew had been sprayed by enemy fire. Some planes crashed on impact, others caught fire and skidded helplessly into barriers and some never made it back at all.

A final hush fell over the room when sailors clad in dress whites loaded body bags draped with American flags onto platforms and saluted as they slid into the sea. *The Fighting Lady* had pulled the staff away from their desks for a precious hour they couldn't afford to lose, but the boost in morale left by the film's vivid reportage lasted much longer and helped carry them through the rest of the war.

Morale climbed even further when an excerpt from a letter Admiral Nimitz had written to Hydro personnel was printed on posters and displayed throughout the building:

"The efficiency and promptness with which the Hydrographic Office has filled my needs has been, and is an important contribution in offensive action against the Japanese forces."

There wasn't a soul at Hydro who didn't cherish these words from the commander in chief of the Pacific Forces.

After two years of urgent deadlines, last-minute requests, and a grueling pace, the Oceanographic Unit had just completed its sixteenth JANIS report in April 1945. They were putting together intelligence for two more locations, on the south coasts of China and Korea, huge reports that would come due before the summer. Allied Powers had crossed the Rhine and lifted everyone's mood, but their progress didn't alter the work schedule at Hydro at all. As long as the Pacific theater was in full swing, with the invasion of Okinawa fast approaching and Japan after that, Sears and company could not let up for one minute.

Okinawa was a hilly, terraced island, in the Ryukyus, a part of the Nansei-Shoto complex of two hundred islands stretched across an eight-hundred-mile arc between Kyushu (Southern Japan) and Formosa. On Japan's doorstep, just 485 miles away from Kyushu, Okinawa's capture would afford access to air bases within easy striking distance of Japan's industrial center, nine hundred miles away. Unsurprisingly, the Japanese marshalled over one hundred thousand of their best troops to defend Okinawa. The Japanese always entered battle with a firm resolve to fight to the death, the more honorable option than returning home defeated, but Okinawa provided the extra motivation of defending the last remaining barrier to the homeland. If the Ryukyus fell, Japan was next.

American planners expected to encounter defenses in depth, especially cave defenses like the ones introduced at Peleliu and honed at Iwo Jima. But at Okinawa the Japanese expanded these to a new level. This time engineers had six months to design, build, and fortify hundreds of caves, along with blockhouses and pillboxes in the natural hilly terrain. Multiroom caves frequently rose higher than one story and included multiple exits and tunnels so the Japanese could maneuver stealthily underground. Engineers designed specialized rooms for barracks, mess halls, radio operations, and a hospital. They purposefully built cave entrances that would escape notice and camouflaged them well.

The marines would need to get onshore quickly and do everything possible to avoid the costly mishaps that seemed to plague every amphibious mission, mistakes that weakened their fighting forces and wrecked essential equipment. But to make a smooth landing, they would need to rely on accurate intel about the conditions of the waters and beaches near Okinawa. If ever there was a time for the Oceanographic Unit to deliver their best intelligence, this was it.

Almost a year earlier, Sears and her team had completed a preliminary report on Nansei-Shoto, well before Okinawa had been designated as a target. With Okinawa under Japanese rule and isolated from the rest of the world since 1879, gathering intelligence on the island had been difficult, with only sparse and dated information available. Aerial reconnaissance was limited then because the island had long been twelve hundred miles from the closest American air base and under frequent cloud cover. But, in mid-1944, when American forces had captured sixty Japanese charts, including one covering Okinawa, Nimitz had set a two-month deadline for Hydro to reproduce and distribute them to the Fleet. Sears had access to these in compiling her report.

Because of a dearth of English-language sources on Okinawa, Mary Grier had combed through Japanese-language publications in the Library of Congress's Orientalia collection. She hit the motherlode when she discovered a prewar report from the Imperial Fisheries Institute in Japan that recorded ocean temperature and depth around the islands, along with bottom sediments, the transparency and color of the water, and salinity. The eagle-eyed librarian also found reports on the Ryukyus' coral reef written by well-known Japanese oceanographers Hisikatsu Yabe and Toshio Sugiyama. This was the kind of information that the fleet landing forces craved. WAVE assistants at Hydro located even more data in the *Sailing Directions for Japan Volume II*, published by the Hydrographic Office. Sears secured additional reports from her contacts in the British Hydrographic Department.

The oceanographers narrowed their focus to forty-eight of three hundred and thirty-three available beaches they deemed the most suitable landing sites that were also close to operational targets in the Ryukyus. Sixty-mile-long Okinawa, because of its large size and air bases, was the leading choice, but anchorages on neighboring islands would also need to be captured before and after the main assault. They too demanded study.

In her preliminary report, Sears highlighted two major concerns. First, Okinawa was almost entirely encircled by coral reefs. The other hazard to the fleet, especially at the landing, was the potential for high waves, particularly on the western coast. As the date for Operation Iceberg to attack Okinawa approached, war planners revisited these issues because of what Sears reported. Naval commanders favored landing on the beaches of Hagushi on western Okinawa, which offered nine thousand continuous yards of flat coral sand that could be separated into sixteen landing areas for the various assault divisions. No mines had been detected directly offshore, and the individual landing areas were adjacent to major roads.

While operationally preferable, the western beaches were susceptible to strong gales, particularly in the winter. For the planned invasion date of April 1 there was only a low to moderate risk of high waves along the shore, but there were other downsides to landing on the West Coast. A squadron commander who had reviewed a preliminary survey of the beaches learned that "each was fringed with a coral reef extending approximately 300 yards to seaward, dry at low water and covered to a depth varying from 3 to 5 feet at high water." The survey further advised that because there were no channels through the reef, all small craft would have to unload outside it, on the ocean side.

Believing that improved amphibious tractors could surmount any obstacle, planners still wanted to attack from the west. However, in case strong westerly winds were likely, they designated Nakagusuku Bay, on the eastern coast of Okinawa, as an alternate landing site.

The military sought input from numerous experts, including Sears, who had described Okinawa's baseline conditions almost a year earlier before real-time conditions could possibly be known. She performed her own analysis based on more recent data and concluded that if the marines landed on the western coast, the waves would likely be uneventful. She gave a thumbs-up to undertake landings on the Hagushi beaches. Sears's last-minute calculation gave the amphibious forces more confidence in their operations plan. Troops had already experienced the dire consequences of not consulting experienced oceanographers at Tarawa. They had lost lives, landing craft, and tractors to predictable hazards along the long march to Okinawa. Those travails made Sears's opinion all the more valuable to them.

In 1938, the United States Army had started training exercises with more horses than tanks and ammunition for Springfield bolt-action rifles left over from World War I. Interwar neglect and underfunding had left the army and navy outmatched by the aggressive growth of the German war machine and a Japanese military that had been secretly building naval bases and airstrips on distant islands in the Pacific. Luckily President Roosevelt, who had toured army camps before the United States entered the war, mobilized private industry and a reluctant Congress to meet his goal of making America the "arsenal of democracy."

Roosevelt expanded the armed forces from fewer than five hundred thousand prewar troops to over four million by 1943. Between 1940 and 1945 the United States produced three hundred thousand planes, more than two million trucks, over a hundred thousand tanks, 87,620 warships, five thousand cargo ships, twenty million rifles, machine guns, and pistols, and forty-four billion rounds of ammunition.

Nowhere were the effects of this mobilization felt more acutely than in the amphibious forces that, with the exception of a handful of training exercises launched in improvised landing boats, had existed mostly only on paper before the war. Now, on the eve of the Battle of Okinawa, a series of ships specifically designed for troop and equipment transport had arrived, and new vehicles like the armored amphibious tractor had been developed. Innovative weapons like the flamethrower, especially useful to flush the enemy from caves, were ready for action.

Admiral Nimitz was taking no chances with the pivotal Okinawa offensive, placing his most experienced commanders in charge of Operation Iceberg. Admiral Raymond Spruance would lead the U.S. Fifth Fleet with Admiral Richmond Kelly Turner directing the amphibious forces. Army Lieutenant General Simon Bolivar Buckner, Jr., commanded the U.S. Tenth Army. Unlike previous amphibious operations that had gotten by with less experienced troops, Okinawa would have the benefit of eight veteran combat divisions made up of marines and soldiers.

A massive logistical enterprise, the battle for Okinawa exceeded all others in the numbers of men and tonnage shipped. The entire offensive was a testament to the success of the American war machine. The initial assault alone required transporting 182,821 troops, 129,917 tons of vehicles, and 156,718 tons of weapons, ammunition, rations, medical supplies, and other necessary equipment. Four hundred and fifty-eight ships moved this load of men and materials across the Pacific Ocean from ports that stretched from San Francisco to Leyte in the Philippines, a distance of six thousand miles.

The Americans had fought their way across thirty-five hundred miles in three and a half years to get to this point, a journey that had been fraught with unexpectedly high casualties, deaths from inopportune tides, plunging waves that splintered landing craft, and beaches that bogged down trucks and tanks. But if everything went according to plan, Okinawa would serve as the coronation of the amphibious forces, a much-needed demonstration of their evolution from a hastily thrown together assault group, in over their heads in the ocean, to a premier fighting force well suited to the mission.

On the night before Love-Day of the Battle of Okinawa, so named to avoid confusion with Iwo Jima's D-Day, war correspondent Ernie Pyle rocked back and forth in his bunk aboard a troop transport, contemplating what lay ahead. Pyle had already spent twenty-nine months abroad covering battles in Africa, Britain, Italy, and France, experiences that wore on him until he just "gave out" and returned home to New Mexico. But adjusting to civilian life wasn't easy for the incurable newshound. World War II was as much a part of his DNA as the color of his eyes and the shape of his nose. Pyle pushed through his dread of another round of combat and arranged to embed with the marines to get a taste of the "other war," the Pacific Campaign.

And now, he was once again headed into battle alongside marines and soldiers, in what was sure to be another long, bloody siege. The Americans had proven they could overcome any defense the Japanese designed, but each victory came at an enormous cost. Even the veteran Pyle could not escape the tension of an imminent attack. "We would take Okinawa," he jotted in his notebook. "But we knew we would have to pay for it. Some on the ship would not be alive in twenty-four hours."

Pyle had waded through American bodies in the surf at Normandy and trudged through sand sticky with the blood of GIs too young to vote. He fully expected that he would once again land at a beach "littered with mangled bodies." The spotty record of amphibious landings in the Pacific only served to magnify his misgivings. The amphibious forces had become more skillful with each outing and were better equipped, but each landing carried enormous risk.

Marine Sargent William Wellman, a twenty-one-year-old radar technician from Valparaiso, Indiana, was also jittery on the eve of battle. He'd had brushes with danger on the way to Okinawa, on board an LST that encountered a typhoon. In high winds, anchoring chains that secured three heavy trucks to the deck snapped, dumping the trucks and the six soldiers asleep inside them into the raging seas. It was a bad omen and one that set Wellman on edge. But his greatest fear was disembarking from the "real little landing craft" and dropping into deep water carrying a fifty-pound pack that would pull him down and pin him to the ocean floor. Even though his unit had rehearsed in rough conditions to prepare for this very scenario, he still feared drowning.

On April 1, 1945, as he attended an Easter morning service before going ashore, one bright spot appeared, a sign that everything might work out after all. A press boat sailed by with Ernie Pyle, smiling and waving to Wellman and his fellow marines. Catching a glimpse of Pyle was like seeing an old friend. The troops admired Pyle for his straight talk about the deprivations of war, his consistent advocacy for the men on the front lines, and the way he dared to name individual service members in his articles. The military frowned on his methods but he never changed them.

Pyle lived with the troops. He went weeks without a decent meal or a shower and took fire in foxholes. He'd exposed himself to the same risks as the men he covered just so he could write of their courage in battle. His resiliency was inspiring, but it also sent a reassuring message: *if Ernie Pyle can survive maybe I have a chance too.*

At dawn the largest convoy of marines and soldiers launched in the Pacific during World War II sailed toward Okinawa. Visibility of up to six miles worsened as the ships approached shore, not because of the weather, but from heavy fire from destroyers and battleships preceding the troop transports. Smaller landing craft lined up in a column to receive men unloading from the LSTs. Naval ships launched mortar shells toward shore while rockets arced from the gunboats. Just outside the barrier reef, men transferred from landing craft to armored tractors. The gunboats ceased firing and allowed armored amtracks to pass through and head for shore.

As Sears predicted, the waves on the westerly shore were calm. By 1600 hours fifty thousand troops were ashore. This was the opus of the amphibious campaign, an orchestra tuned to perfection, performing at its best. This was the kind of landing that naval commanders had envisioned from the start of the Pacific Campaign and strived to roll out. Like a football team that struggles to make plays during the season and, in the final game, finally comes together to execute at a championship level, so too did the American amphibious forces perform at their best at Okinawa.

The Japanese Navy had suffered significant losses leading up to the battle, leaving the kamikaze corps as one of the last effective weapons with which to attack the United States Navy. As early as March 25, a week before Love-Day, kamikazes began attacking and hitting American ships. On that one day alone, kamikazes crashed into a destroyer, a light minesweeper, and a high-speed transport. The next day kamikazes hit eight more ships, inflicting significant damage. The Americans defended themselves by forming a defensive "picket" around the amphibious forces using destroyers and destroyer escorts. These defenders attempted to fend off the suicide planes with antiaircraft fire that would draw more direct attacks on the perimeter vessels and away from troop transports.

Lt. Cesar L. Barber, aboard the USS *Teton*, had come prepared to help protect Allied ships from the kamikazes. Barber had worked with scientist Alfred Woodcock at Woods Hole studying the behavior of smoke as a defensive weapon for use at sea. Their research had centered around finding the most effective means of laying down a long-lasting smokescreen that would not dissipate in the wind or rain.

Woodcock had spent years observing the flight patterns of seabirds and had deduced the presence of invisible currents running through the air, just as currents run through the sea. When the air was warmer than the ocean, or stable, there was no convection and the seagulls spent a lot of time just sitting on the water, because they had to work too hard to fly. When the air was cooler than the sea, or unstable, the gulls took off and soared with ease, held aloft by a thermal layer.

Woodcock found that smoke generated by fog-oil generators behaved similar to the birds. Wind direction and speed affected not only smoke but also the temperature of the air relative to the surface of the sea. If the air was thermally stable a smoke screen would tend to "hug" the water, like a lazy seagull, and not dissipate.

Landing ships typically anchored along the beach after they unloaded the first waves of Higgins boats into the ocean, leaving the transports exposed to the risk of kamikaze attacks. Lt. Barber used Woodcock's methods to direct the laying of smokescreens to hide them.

"The unusual aspect in the employment of smoke at Okinawa," he later said, "was its constant use, hour after hour, over the anchorage. Smoke packed itself into every corner of the ships. People lived in it, slept in it."

The deck logs of the LST-227, a cargo transport vessel, confirmed the ubiquitous smokescreens employed at Okinawa. "Smoke was made at sunset, and every morning and evening thereafter while operating in the area. The smoke was effective in keeping suicide planes from attacking shipping hidden in the smoke."

Even so, there was no way to hide from all the kamikazes. They still sunk twenty-six ships, damaged another one hundred and sixty-four, and were responsible for the deaths of approximately five thousand naval personnel at Okinawa.

The Japanese also deployed suicide boats—eighteen-footers made of plywood, powered by Chevy automobile engines, loaded with a 250-pound depth charge—designed to be rammed straight into the hulls of American ships. However, few of them ever got the chance to inflict damage. Underwater demolition teams destroyed more than 350 Japanese suicide boats, effectively neutralizing the threat.

When Ernie Pyle landed on Hagushi Beach he was pleasantly surprised. He saw no dead bodies, no wounded, not even the wreckage of an errant landing craft. "The carnage that is almost inevitable on an invasion was wonderfully and beautifully not there," he wrote. The usual cacophony of gunfire, anguished cries, and an air of desperation were strangely absent, replaced by stillness that for a moment felt like peace.

Rather than contest the beach, a move that had proved futile in all previous amphibious invasions, the Japanese waited in their caves for the Americans to come ashore before unleashing their firepower. Troops in the initial assault waves pushed quickly inland. Pyle and his crew practically had the beach to themselves.

After hurling his body into the water, Sergeant Wellman, the radar operator, found the waves calm and the surf tame. He never came close to drowning. The old horror stories about landings did not apply to Okinawa because of a combination of calm seas, cooperative weather, and a Japanese strategy that shifted their defenses to an intricate network of caves farther inland. There would be further trouble ahead, but for now, for these few hours, the marines, who had grown to expect abject "butchery" on the beaches, savored a brief bullet-free interlude.

Sergeant Wellman survived his five-week stay at Okinawa—the kamikazes that bombed the harbor every night, the Japanese snipers sheltered in caves, booby-trapped corpses, and banzai attacks by desperate, suicidal opponents. Five of the original twelve marines in his radar unit were not so fortunate. Nor was Ernie Pyle, who was shot in the left temple, just below the brim of his helmet, on April 17, 1945, on the nearby island of Ie Shima. Pyle had covered the Battle of Britain, D-Day at Normandy, and countless other World War II battles. He had filed stories for over four hundred major newspapers in the country over three long years of war, but he did not survive Okinawa.

"It was a bad day for us. He was one of us," Wellman later recalled after returning home from Okinawa with a florid case of malaria, but he long remembered Pyle.

The troop landings escaped both high waves and armed opposition but there were more difficulties ahead. Over the next several days during the cargo unloading phase of the invasion a strong front moved in on April 4. Winds increased to twenty knots and gusted to thirty-five (equivalent to forty miles per hour on land), causing choppy seas and moderate to large swells. The Task Force commander directed sailors to secure ships and barges and hoist in small craft. Despite these precautions, ships still sustained significant damage. After action reports documented the scene: "reef punctured holes in ballast tanks and engine room of LST-756. Main engine room, forward bilge, control room badly holed and completely flooded. . . . Skin of ship punctured and bulkhead buckling in various places."

As the storm progressed over April 5 and 6, all unloading on the beach ceased. Overall, twenty-one landing ships and small craft were damaged, including twelve LSTs and the complete loss of one medium landing ship. It was yet another reminder that there was no way to entirely escape danger during operations at sea. With scant warning, conditions had deteriorated and placed ships, men, and equipment at risk.

The amphibious landing had been executed to near perfection. Yet Okinawa would be remembered as one of the bloodiest battles of the war— eighty-two days of close combat, 49,000 casualties and over 12,000 deaths, including those lost in kamikaze attacks. The Japanese damaged three hundred and sixty-eight ships and sunk another thirty-six, including twelve destroyers.

The Americans were now in an ideal position to finish the fight the Japanese had started three and a half years earlier. Preparations for that decisive contest, Operation Olympic, had long been underway even while the Battle of Okinawa continued to rage. That an invasion of Japan would be necessary was a foregone conclusion, at least to the boots on the ground who had no idea that the war could possibly end any other way.

CHAPTER 17

Closing in on Victory

— Japan, 1945 —

As the Battle of Okinawa wore on the United States suffered a severe blow on the domestic front. On the afternoon of April 12, 1945, while signing documents and sitting for a portrait at his cabin in Warm Springs, Georgia, FDR put his hand to his temple and said, "I have a terrific pain in the back of my head," and collapsed. FDR's physician, Dr. Harold Bruenn, had been traveling with the president because of his congestive heart failure but could not revive him. The president had succumbed to a massive cerebral hemorrhage at the age of sixty-three.

Bruenn called Eleanor Roosevelt with the news of her husband's death. It would fall to her to contact Harry Truman who, having just joined the ticket for FDR's last run the previous November, was still new to the role of vice president. Truman was as shocked as anyone when Eleanor summoned him to her sitting room at the White House and delivered the news. When Truman asked the first lady what he could do for her, she responded in her characteristic pragmatic style, "Is there anything *we* can do for *you*? For you're the one in trouble now."

Truman was sworn in and convened his first cabinet meeting that night. He had served as vice president for three months, had seldom met with the president and had not been included in any of FDR's war planning meetings. After the brief gathering, Secretary of War Henry Stimson insisted on an urgent private meeting. He had to brief Truman on the top-secret Manhattan project, which was on the cusp of producing an atomic weapon.

With so much hitting him at once, Truman felt like he had been "struck by a bolt of lightning." He told reporters it was as if, "the moon, the stars, and the planets had all fallen on me."

The next day, newspapers across the country ran some variation of the banner headline: "ROOSEVELT DEAD!" As news of FDR's death spread through Washington, the city ground to a halt. Performances were canceled. Sporting events were postponed. Employees were given the day off. A half million people crowded the streets to greet the funeral train that rolled at twenty-five miles per hour from Warm Springs to the Capitol so that grieving Americans lining the tracks could catch a glimpse of the president's flag-draped coffin.

A sense of shock settled over the staff at Hydro. Roosevelt had led the country through some of its most difficult times, guiding the nation through the Great Depression and pushing it to muster its resources to fight a global war.

"All of Washington is so upset over the president's death that things are very glum this weekend," Hydro WAVE Lucy Berkey wrote home to her family in Indiana. "None of the shows are open, and radio programs are canceled. . . . We got yesterday, Saturday, afternoon off and some of the kids went down to see what they could see at the White House. It seems so hard for everyone to believe—that Roosevelt is dead. It all happened so suddenly."

The editors of the *Scuttlebutt* ran a special edition the following day. Roosevelt's death "was so sudden and unexpected that it seems beyond apprehension. . . . To the very end, our President was a leader, an example for all of us to follow and God grant we have the spirit to do so and to fight on now not only to ultimate victory, and to a lasting peace as he so ardently fought for . . . Not only the Roosevelt family, but the whole world has lost and mourns a great man."

• • •

The Germans surrendered on May 7, 1945, ending the war in Europe. In New York City, a half million people flooded the streets. Yet everything remained calm in D.C. Government employees had been instructed to report to their jobs "to set an example" that the work must continue. At Hydro, Lucy Berkey and other excited WAVES who had faithfully reported for duty, were "overcome with joy and ran around cheering and hugging each other. They huddled around the radio and listened to a speech by President Truman, the "Accidental President," who had been on the job just three weeks.

"This is a solemn but glorious hour . . . ," Truman said in his address to the nation. "If I could give you a single watchword for the coming months, that word is work—work and more work. We must work to finish the war. Our victory is only half won."

As King George and Churchill addressed the United Kingdom, the WAVES could hear the long-suffering British people cheering in the background. Like the oceanographers toiling away on massive, detailed reports for the planned invasion of Japan, they knew they had to keep cranking out the charts that were keeping the fleet in action. Still, the news from Europe boosted everyone's spirits and fueled hopes that normal life was close at hand.

On June 18, 1945, as the Okinawa operation was winding down, Harry Truman asked the Joint Chiefs to brief him on Operation Downfall—the invasion of Japan. The operation would require at least two phases— Operation Olympic, the seizure of Kyushu in southern Japan, planned for November 1945, and Operation Coronet to seize Tokyo in March 1946. The estimated troop requirement was more than five million. The Joint Chiefs estimated casualties of 250,000 to 1,000,000 American troops. Invading the Japanese homeland would entail a substantial loss of life— Allied troops, Japanese soldiers, and particularly sobering to ponder, an even greater number of civilians.

Hearing these figures, Truman, who had been sworn in during the thick of the Battle of Okinawa, when a combined nine hundred casualties a day were being reported from the Pacific and European theaters, hesitated to approve the operation.

"I don't want to conduct another Okinawa from one end of Japan to the other," he told the Joint Chiefs.

Sears had first learned about the intelligence need for Japan a year earlier when a memorandum from the Joint Publishing Board hit her desk in Suitland. The board had issued a new priority schedule for the Japanese Islands. JANIS 84 on southwestern Japan, including Kyushu, Shikoku, and southwestern Honshu, was due on August 1, 1944, less than three months away. Reports on Hokkaido and northeast Honshu had been moved up to September and October. With Japan taking priority, the contributors were instructed to delay JANIS publications covering South and East China until further notice. Fast-tracking a series of reports on Japan signaled to Sears and her team that the Allies were ahead of schedule in the island-hopping campaign and would be reaching Okinawa, the doorstep of Japan, sooner than expected.

While the success of the amphibious campaign was welcome news, the accelerated timetable for Japan pushed the oceanographers to the breaking point. Fenner Chace was still busy culling through stacks of articles Mary Grier was bringing back on high-profile targets in the Ryukyus (Okinawa) and Kuriles. Dora Henry was editing JANIS 155 on the Philippines. Sears was maintaining her usual frenetic schedule, attending meetings for two Joint Chiefs subcommittees in D.C., computing tide tables for secret locations, collating bathythermograph data for *Submarine Supplments*, and helping to analyze data for the JANIS reports.

The addition of three more high-priority studies on a region as large and complicated as Japan severely strained the tiny workforce. There were literally no spare oceanographers available in the country. Gordon Tucker and Joe Wohnus, two assistant oceanographers who split their time between the Hydrographic Office, Woods Hole, and Scripps, pitched in intermittently, but they were already stretched with underwater sound projects and testing new devices for the navy. WAVE specialists like Yeoman 3rd Class Loretta Funk, rotated through the Oceanographic Unit filling the gaps where she could, but all throughout the war, the unit remained short-staffed.

On June 2, 1944, Sears rode the bus from Suitland to Washington, D.C., for a JANIS planning meeting for southwest Japan in the conference room of the creaky Munitions Building. Colonel Bicknell hung up a base map of the area and passed out an outline of locations to serve as a guide for the upcoming report. More than one participant pushed back on the proposed August deadline, arguing that it would be "impossible" to meet because of other pressing projects. Some attendees suggested supplementing the assignment with existing studies that overlapped with Japan.

Sears just kept taking notes, declining to join in the protest bubbling up through the room. She could count on her team to work around the clock to get the reports out on time, even if she had to juggle her staff and cancel days off. As she expected, the deadlines stood. The Joint Chiefs had made the study on Japan high priority. Colonel Bicknell was not going to bend.

Sears returned to Suitland and handed over the specs for JANIS 84 to Mary Grier, who once again hit the libraries to search for references for the waters around Japan. From her research while on the staff of the University of Washington, she already had an inkling where she could find a slew of applicable articles. Of the forty-three sources Grier collected for the study, fourteen came from Japanese journals and government agencies. As Sears later remembered, the closer the invasions got to Japan, the greater the chance critical data would be found in Japanese publications.

Naval intelligence also sent captured Japanese documents to the Oceanographic Unit for review. More often than not, any oceanographic data present in these recently translated documents that arrived in manila envelopes stamped "SECRET" had already been discovered in a library by Grier. This coincidence would always get a chuckle out of the team because the "SECRET" articles had been sitting out on their desks.

The oceanography chapter for the first JANIS on Japan ultimately expanded to 168 pages. For an invasion of such massive importance, Sears and her team scoured available sources and included all pertinent data they could find, never knowing which nugget of detail would make a difference in a combat mission.

In the summer of 1945, even though everyone sensed the impending end of the war, the nation was on edge as casualties continued. At Hydro, the *Scuttlebutt* reminded the staff daily of the ongoing costs of war. The June 2, 1945, edition included "Lest We Forget," an editorial written by John S. Knight, publisher of the *Detroit Free Press*. His son, John S. Knight, Jr., had been killed in combat in Germany on March 29, 1945. He had been awarded the Bronze Star for gallantry.

"We hear the war is 'practically over,' that 'losses are light,'" he wrote. "But every second of every hour it continues, some fine young American boy is being slaughtered by a maniacal foe indoctrinated with cruelty and hate. Nearly 300,000 Johnnies are gone."

"Let's give 'em out there that extra push to hasten victory," the *Scuttlebutt* editors wrote.

In the summer of 1945, the *Scuttlebutt* shed some light on the Oceanographic Unit's work while recognizing Vice Admiral C. A. Lockwood, Jr., U.S.N., Commander, Submarines Pacific. "For the last three years he guided the destiny of our underseas fleet in the Pacific. . . . Incidentally, the Hydrographic Office is the center for all oceanographic research of the Army and Navy, and in this role renders invaluable service to the submarine fleet, furnishing them vital information concerning the medium in which they operate."

Lockwood, who had assumed command of "the Silent Service" in the Pacific in 1943, was credited for revamping tactics and energizing the United States' submarine warfare capability. With Japan so dependent on sea routes and a strong merchant marine, Lockwood's efforts had crippled the Japanese economy and cut off its fuel supply and raw materials for weapons production.

The *Scuttlebutt* editors no doubt had an inkling that Sears was the person helping Lockwood's submarines find safe harbors in the ocean depths. Not only was she widely respected for her expertise, but Sears also had minor celebrity status at Hydro. As one of the highest ranking WAVES officers and one of the few female directors of any program in the navy, she was someone her more junior colleagues admired.

Even if the Americans had wanted to take the fight directly to Japan after Okinawa, even if there were a way to magically refresh and resupply the beleaguered troops and scrape together enough of them to storm across the southern coast of the island, they were going to have to wait. July through December was typhoon season, and after getting a taste of just how rough the waters near the Japanese home islands could be in a storm, there was no way they were going to risk it.

There were other issues to consider as well. As spelled out in JANIS 84, on southwest Japan, the terrain of the most logical invasion point, Kyushu, the southernmost island, would not be easy to traverse in the warmer months, even with the improved rugged version of tracked landing vehicles that could roll over the most menacing of coral reefs. Rice paddies ringed the lowlands of Kyushu. Landing boats could not easily cut across these swampy interfaces, and the tractors were likely to sink into the boggy terrain.

If conditions did permit smaller vehicles to make it to dry land, they would be able to travel along footpaths. Larger trucks and tanks, though, would have no chance of making it through these small, muddy trails and would have to stick to main roads. After crossing this messy landscape, the troops would run into mountains farther inland and encounter a region of "disconnected rugged plateaus, many parts of which have been subjected to intense volcanic activity which added ash, lava and volcanic cones to an already complex topography." Moving men, heavy equipment, artillery, and supplies through Kyushu was going to be hell.

The first edition of the oceanography chapter on southwest Japan, published in August 1944, disclosed the team's extensive use of Japanese data and noted that even though these data might include spotty errors, "there is no evidence of deliberate falsification of data by the Japanese." They attributed errors to faulty recording techniques.

The report warned of strong local currents that could affect small boats, placement of underwater mines and other coastal military operations. Some areas around Kyushu had a higher frequency of swells greater than six to eight feet, particularly in the winter months, which could pose a hazard to amphibious landings.

Throughout the region there were fish noises, similar to "the sound of screws," that might confuse sound operators attempting to detect submarines. In shallow water, especially near reefs, crackling noises could be heard from up to eight thousand yards away, capable of drowning out all other underwater sound.

Snapping shrimp, just one of many noisemakers in the ocean, were known to emit a loud crackling sound that caught the attention of sonar operators. Martin Johnson, a zoologist at Scripps, had studied the underwater chorus in the summer of 1942 by dangling a hydrophone over a San Diego pier. His observations, along with those of other marine zoologists, had been published in navy manuals to help sonographers identify underwater sounds in various localities in the Pacific.

In the summer of 1945, the Americans assembled troops, ships, and equipment for Operation Olympic while intensifying the bombing of Tokyo and continuing a submarine blockade of shipments to Japan. The Japanese were shoring up defenses on Kyushu, while training and deploying troops to construct fortifications, including artillery casements and machine-gun pillboxes with walls up to ten feet thick. They were also preparing massive kamikaze air strikes and thousands of suicide boats and torpedoes. Whatever happened at the invasion of Kyushu, the Japanese intended to fight to the death, ensuring a staggering number of casualties on both sides.

In Los Alamos, New Mexico, Robert Oppenheimer, the head of the Manhattan Project, was making preparations to test the first atomic bomb. That test took place on July 16, 1945, in a remote area near Alamogordo, New Mexico.

"The test was successful beyond the most optimistic expectations of anyone," Major General Leslie R. Groves wrote to Secretary of War Henry L. Stimson. "I estimate the energy generated to be in excess of the equivalent of 15,000 to 20,000 tons of TNT; and this is a conservative estimate."

Harry Truman now had new options to consider. He didn't have to order a series of dangerous amphibious landings followed by long and bloody battles to defeat Japan. He could instead leverage the threat of the atomic bomb to force the Japanese to surrender or order deployment used on a carefully selected target. Truman had been hesitant to okay Operation Downfall because of the number of American lives at stake. *Would he instead approve dropping a bomb that could injure and kill hundreds of thousands of civilians?*

Even though Truman had been briefed about the Manhattan Project shortly after taking office, he had become immersed in other pressing matters after Germany's surrender. Subsequently, Truman had begun preparing for an upcoming Combined Chiefs conference at Potsdam, Germany, where he would meet with Churchill and Stalin for the first time. Truman learned of the successful atomic test while flying to Europe. The bomb was ready and Truman decided to deploy it directly, although with conditions.

"I have told the secretary of war, Mr. Stimson, to use it so that military objectives and soldiers and sailors are the target and not women and children," Truman wrote in his diary on July 25, while still in Potsdam.

The United States would warn Japan and make one final demand for unconditional surrender. Only if and when the Japanese refused would the United States drop the bomb. This was in keeping with FDR's wishes. He had confided in Stimson that he would only use the weapon after issuing a stark warning to the Japanese or staging a demonstration of its power.

The United States, the Republic of China, and Great Britain sent the Potsdam Declaration to the Japanese government on July 26. The Allies were "poised to strike the final blows upon Japan," they said and asked for surrender. The declaration went unanswered.

On August 6, 1945, flying from a captured airbase on the island of Tinian in the Marianas, the *Enola Gay*, a Boeing B-29 Superfortress, dropped the atomic bomb, "Little Boy," on Hiroshima, an industrial center and military headquarters. The destruction was nearly total.

Afterward, American bombers dropped thousands of leaflets on Japanese cities encouraging civilians to evacuate to the countryside, both to save lives and to disrupt further war production in urban factories. The Japanese government did not surrender, and on August 9 a second atomic bomb, "Fat Man," fell on Nagasaki, a major military port and shipbuilding center. The combined deaths from Hiroshima and Nagasaki ranged between 100,000 and 130,000.

"The force from which the sun draws its power has been loosed against those who brought war to the Far East," Truman stated in a press release to the American public.

On August 14, 1945, Truman announced Japan's unconditional surrender, then walked out onto the front lawn of the White House, greeted by cheers from crowds lining Pennsylvania Avenue. WAVES from the Hydrographic Office took a bus into downtown Washington, D.C., and joined a mob of celebrants hugging, kissing, throwing confetti, and unfurling paper from rooftops into traffic jams below.

As *Yank* magazine put it: "This capital city . . . relaxed its worn nerves and celebrated the winning of the war with a screaming, drinking, paper-tearing, free-kissing demonstration which combined all the features of New Years and Mardi Gras."

Upon hearing that the Japanese had surrendered, the soldiers of the United States Sixth Army, who were preparing to invade Japan, felt nothing but relief. "We knelt in the sand and cried. For all our manhood, we cried. We were going to live. We were going to grow up to adulthood after all," one veteran later remembered.

After two and a half years of faithful service to the nation, the oceanographers could finally put down their pencils and push away from their desks. They were going home.

Epilogue

After Japan's agreement to an unconditional surrender, overt military hostilities ended, but the American military's job was far from over. At the same time that the Americans had rolled out plans for Operation Olympic in the summer of 1945, the military had also been making contingency plans to execute critical, time-sensitive missions in the event that the Japanese suddenly surrendered or the empire collapsed. Now came the monumental task of implementing Operation Blacklist, the American occupation of Japan.

A critical part of the mission was to locate prisoners of war and to air-drop food, clothing, and medicine to the men and evacuate them as quickly as possible. The operation plan stipulated that "the urgency of this mission is second only to military operations." There were approximately 140 prisoner of war camps in Japan, Korea, Formosa, Shanghai, Hong Kong, and Peking, holding an estimated thirty-six thousand prisoners—American, British, Canadian, Australian, Dutch, and East Indian soldiers and civilian internees. All were in poor physical shape after years of torture, starvation, demanding physical labor, and unsanitary living conditions. Some were suffering from dehydration, illness, and severe injuries. Without immediate intervention, many would die.

In the final act of World War II, JANIS reports took on a new purpose in addition to helping win the war. Without them, the job of landing troops and equipment for the occupation and for the difficult undertaking of locating and rescuing tens of thousands of prisoners of war would have been nearly impossible. JANIS reports weren't just the best resource. In many cases, they were the *only* resource ready at hand. Fortunately, the Joint Chiefs distributed them down the chain of command as fast as they were published.

Even before the formal surrender ceremony on September 2, the Americans were moving forward with plans to occupy Tokyo, the seat of Imperial rule, as quickly as they could get in, before any organized military resistance could gain steam. But they still had to proceed with caution because they could not trust that enemy troops throughout Japan and the Pacific island outposts would entirely acquiesce to the emperor's order. An estimated three million Japanese troops in Japan, Korea, and parts of China had to be disarmed, possibly by force. This meant that the American military still needed to execute combat-ready amphibious landings on the coasts of Japan, Formosa, Korea, and the east coast of China.

Military commanders once again relied on oceanographic intelligence to plan amphibious operations and prepare for surprise attacks, insurgence, and sabotage. The clock was ticking. The lives of prisoners of war, innocent civilians, and American troops once again hung in the balance. They needed the best intelligence.

Lt. Col. Thomas L. Ridge was a marine intelligence officer who was in charge of reviewing intel for Operation Blacklist. CINCPAC Forward Echelon and the Twenty-First Bomber Command sent him several documents—a copy of JANIS 84 on southwestern Japan, "Strategic Engineer Study No. 124" from the Office of Naval Intelligence, port studies on Nagasaki and other areas and some U.S. Army Air Force target folders.

The JANIS on southwestern Japan proved to be "the superior reference" and, as Ridge pointed out, the only intelligence report that would have been available in time if "the original date of the landing had been carried out." Ridge's high praise of JANIS 84 reiterated just how valuable JANIS reports had become in the field. Beyond serving as a planning tool for the Joint Chiefs, these trusted reports provided essential details so that operations could be planned and battle plans drawn.

"JANIS has become an essential type of publication that should be maintained in times of peace and constantly improved as to quality, accuracy, completeness of coverage, scope, usability, and timeliness of the information contained therein," Ridge noted in a postwar memorandum to the Chief of Naval Operations. It was crucial to keep basic intelligence "ready to use, prior to the beginning of hostilities . . . because military plans can only be as sound as the intelligence upon which they are based," he added.

As Ridge and others pointed out, with the victory in the Pacific, the United States was entering a new era in foreign policy, one in which it would be assuming international responsibilities to help enforce treaties in distant lands. JANIS reports might be the only intelligence source available for many of these locales and, without question, the most comprehensive.

As the war was drawing to a close and military cutbacks loomed, the navy had to make decisions about the future of the Oceanographic Unit at the Hydrographic Office. Before the war, oceanography consisted of the minimum capabilities necessary to survey the ocean and produce navigation charts. During the war, the navy grew to depend on the oceanographers' assistance in waging war. Sears and her team of scientists, draftsmen, and "enlisted girls" had developed critical intelligence for numerous amphibious missions, prepared manuals for general use by sailors and navigators, assisted in creating survival maps for air-sea rescue, and collated bathythermograph data for use in submarine warfare, all while coordinating and compiling research between Woods Hole and Scripps. It was an astounding growth in capability under wartime duress achieved in a remarkably short time.

On October 19, 1945, Sears, her male cohorts in the navy, and civilian scientists attended a meeting at the Hydrographic Office convened by Rear Admiral Bryan to discuss the future of oceanography. Largely thanks to Sears, oceanography had improved combat readiness and made the navy a more capable fighting force. The development of oceanographic expertise and research had to continue. After that meeting Bryan made the recommendation that the Oceanographic Unit be expanded into a permanent Oceanographic Division with Sears as the officer-in-charge.

When Sears had shown up for duty as the first full-time oceanographer, she had occupied one desk in the Pilot Chart section of the Division of Maritime Security at the Hydrographic Office. From there she had transformed naval oceanography into a fifteen-person unit whose impact she could not have imagined when she started in April 1943. After the war, the new division continued to collect and coordinate basic research for the navy, the coast guard, the War Department, and other government agencies and carried out its own research program. The recently promoted Lieutenant Commander Sears continued to push through programs and improvements in oceanographic research until she left active duty, June 4, 1946.

Sears was a quiet American hero, more workhorse than show horse, toiling behind the scenes as long as the United States Navy needed her to help hide submarines and guide amphibious forces to shore. As Nimitz had intimated in his chance meeting with Sears's sister Leila, she had indeed played a critical role during the war. On May 20, 1946, Admiral Nimitz issued a postwar commendation to Sears noting:

"Your technical knowledge and administrative skill were instrumental in the selection, compilation, and publication of oceanographic data of great value to the armed forces of the United States. In your capacity of oceanographer you were frequently called upon by the Joint Chiefs of Staff to furnish critically valuable information for use in combat operations. Your performance of all these duties was at all times exceptional, and beyond the high standard normally expected."

Nimitz, who had served as commander in chief of the Pacific Ocean Areas and had since been promoted to Chief of Naval Operations, had summed up better than anyone Sears's many contributions during the war.

Secretary of the Navy Richard Danzig, who announced in 1999 that the USNS *Mary Sears* would become the navy's next oceanographic survey ship echoed Nimitz's praise:

"Commander Mary Sears, USNR (W) (1905–1997) established a small oceanographic unit in the Hydrographic Office during World War II and helped expand the role of applied oceanography within the navy. During the war, she studied and reported oceanographic conditions affecting naval operations. Her most important reports, 'submarine supplements to the sailing directions,' predicted the presence of thermoclines under which submarines could escape enemy detection."

While assisting submarines in identifying thermoclines was of critical importance, we know from the JANIS reports, Sears's oral histories, and the remarks made by those who reviewed other confidential reports that she achieved so much more. Because Sears served in naval intelligence, where much of her work product was classified, we may never know the true extent of her clandestine activities. The historical record for the Oceanographic Unit is thin. Like many who served in that time, Sears remained mindful of the classified nature of her work and spoke only in generalities, even after the war, about the many missions in which she was involved.

Mary Sears, a scientist who studied miniature marine life-forms, a woman who had first been rejected by the navy and then recruited to work in an office as a placeholder for a man, would never have expected the special honor of having a naval survey ship named in her honor. But, one can imagine that if the reserved oceanographer had been alive to hear the news, a sly smile might have escaped her lips and maybe she would have found a way to take pride in a job well done for just a minute before putting her head down and getting back to work.

MARY SEARS (1905–1997)

After retiring from active service on June 4, 1946, Mary Sears was still prohibited by the "men only" policy from boarding the research vessel *Atlantis*. She headed to Denmark for a year to visit colleagues and institutions overseas and also spent time on the Norwegian research vessel *Gunnar Knudsen*. When she returned she rejoined the staff at the Woods Hole Oceanographic Institution in 1947 as a senior scientist and served as a trustee of the Marine Biological Laboratory and clerk of the Woods Hole Oceanographic Institution Corporation.

She continued her research but also took on the roles of editor and organizer for the field of oceanography. In 1953 she became a founding coeditor of *Deep Sea Research*, the premier journal of oceanography, and held the post for twenty years. She also cofounded and edited *Progress in Oceanography*. Sears coordinated the First International Oceanographic Congress held in New York in 1959. In taking on these roles Sears helped to turn a loosely aggregated oceanography community into a recognized international science. "She was the conscience of oceanography who initiated and maintained an uncompromising standard of excellence in scientific publications about the ocean," Roger Revelle later recalled.

"She has done as much for the advancement of oceanography as anyone I know," Columbus O'Donnell Iselin wrote in his personal memoir.

Sears was a member of nine scientific and honorary societies and received many awards including a mention in the 1961 edition of *American Men in Science*, a fact that always amused her. She received honorary doctor of science degrees in 1962 from Mount Holyoke College (sharing the stage with author Harper Lee) and in 1974 from Southeastern Massachusetts University. She remained a member of the Naval Reserve until 1963, reaching the rank of commander. After retiring from WHOI in 1970, she traveled extensively, visiting oceanographers around the world who had become good friends. She learned to cross-country ski and sailed around the harbor on her sailboat, the *Piquero*, named after a species of guano bird.

Sears was a familiar sight around the village of Woods Hole, riding her bicycle, walking her dog, and swimming in Vineyard Sound. With her death came an outpouring of sentiment and remembrances and a stream of visitors to a grave marked with a simple headstone in a cemetery in Woods Hole.

FENNER A. CHACE, JR. (1908–2004)

After leaving the army in June 1946, Fenner Chace joined the staff of the National Museum of Natural History at the Smithsonian Institution as curator of crustaceans and stayed until his retirement in 1978. In the sixty-six years that he worked in the field of carcinology Chace, "one of the most influential carcinologists of the twentieth century," published ninety-four scientific works and identified over two hundred species and subspecies of crustaceans, including shrimp, crab, and lobster. Chace kept a pet hermit crab on his desk at the Smithsonian, feeding it lettuce daily for eleven years.

Throughout his career, Chace drew the illustrations for his own publications, which were meticulous, detailed, and highly readable. He was shy, afraid of heights, terrified of flying, and fainted at the sight of blood. Despite his timidity, Chace volunteered for the Army Air Force during World War II where he rose to the rank of captain over four years of service.

DORA PRIAULX HENRY (1904–1999)

Dora Henry resigned from the navy in October 1945 and returned to the University of Washington. She received a Certificate of Meritorious Civilian Service to the United States Navy for her contributions to the Hydrographic Office. She resumed what would become an almost seven-decade career in cirripedology (the study of barnacles) in the Oceanography Department of the University of Washington. Over the course of her career, Henry described eleven new species of barnacles, published extensively in the scientific literature, and was honored by the naming of a species of barnacle, *Arossia henryae* (Newman, 1982) after her. She continued to deploy her expert editorial skills for graduate students and colleagues.

Henry and her husband traveled extensively in the summers, particularly to the Pacific coasts of Central and South America, where she collected more barnacles, adding to one of the most complete collections of Pacific coast barnacles in existence. Even after retiring from teaching in

1988, Henry continued to be known as "The Barnacle Lady" and answered queries from around the world. In 1990, the navy selected Dora Henry to christen the oceanographic research vessel R/V *Thomas G. Thompson*, named after the oceanographer who had first hired her at the University of Washington. After her death in 1999, her ashes were spread at sea from the deck of the ship she christened. She left her extensive barnacle collection to the National Museum of Natural History of the Smithsonian Institution, where her colleague Fenner Chace had spent his postwar career.

MARY CATHARINE GRIER (1907–1988)

After the war, Mary Grier compiled the bibliography *References on the Physical Oceanography of the Western Pacific Ocean*, published in 1946 and left Hydro in 1947. She took a position as chief analyst on the project staff of the Arctic Institute of North America, collecting research materials at various libraries in Washington, D.C., and New York and helped to prepare the sixteen-volume *Arctic Bibliography*, published in 1953, under an Office of Naval Research contract.

In 1951, Grier put her bibliography skills to good use once again at the Geological Society of America (GSA) library in Washington, D.C., where she continued to work until retiring in 1969.

ROGER REVELLE (1909–1991)

Roger Revelle stayed in Washington after the war to organize the research program for the first atomic test on Bikini Atoll (Operation Crossroads), assisted by Sears. He then transferred to the Office of Naval Research, where he stayed until 1948. He returned to the Scripps Institution of Oceanography in La Jolla, California, to head up seagoing investigations and became director in 1951. In a 1957 landmark paper, with coauthor Hans Suess, Revelle posited that carbon dioxide from fossil fuels could be harmful to the atmosphere and oceans, potentially leading to global warming.

Revelle attended Mary Sears's eightieth birthday celebration at Woods Hole where he paid tribute to his former colleague. "Because the Federal Government has very little memory, it is generally forgotten that the first Oceanographer of the navy in modern times was a short, rather shy and prim WAVE lieutenant, j.g. . . . They underestimated the powerful natural force that is Mary Sears," he said.

THE OCEANOGRAPHIC UNIT

After the Oceanographic Unit was upgraded to the Division of Oceanography in 1946 with Lt. Commander Mary Sears as the first officer-in-charge, the role of oceanography in the navy continued to expand. In 1962, the United States Hydrographic Office was renamed the United States Naval Oceanographic Office (NAVOCEANO). In 1976, NAVOCEANO moved from Suitland, Maryland, to the John C. Stennis Space Center in southern Mississippi. It is responsible for providing oceanographic information, publications, and services to the Department of Defense and all branches of service. In 2017, the hydrographer of the navy, Rear Admiral Tim Gallaudet, attended a World Hydrography Day celebration and stated, "It's hard to believe that only five percent of the volume of the world's oceans has been explored. . . . There is still so much we don't know."

THE JOINT ARMY-NAVY INTELLIGENCE STUDIES

After the war, the Joint Topographical Subcommittee conducted a survey of JANIS users. JANIS reports were described as "the most widely used intelligence document produced by the American Government because they were in all theaters of war as well as in the State, Commerce and Treasury Departments and able to be utilized by war planners as well as in civil affairs."

Over the course of its existence, through July 1947, the JANIS program produced a total of thirty-four comprehensive studies, primarily related to the Far East. After the United States created the Central

Intelligence Agency (CIA) in 1947, the JANIS reports were subsumed into the CIA's National Intelligence Survey (NIS) program, which produced digests of basic intelligence for high-level operational planning in matters affecting national security. The United States would never again be in the position it was in at the outset of World War II, lacking basic information on regions of strategic importance.

Author's Note and Acknowledgments

After four years of researching and writing this book I know more now than I ever have about what my father experienced as a sailor in the United States Navy during World War II serving in the Pacific theater. He must have been one scared seventeen-year-old sitting in the gun tub at the top of the LST-227 moving through the waters around Okinawa when kamikazes started raining down from the skies. Five thousand sailors in the United States Navy were killed that day by suicide bombers. They should have been safe on their ships, delivering troops, tanks, and supplies to the battles onshore, but the Japanese had other plans—devastating attacks that earned my father and the men with him combat medals.

I had already started researching Mary Sears and the JANIS reports she prepared when I recorded Dad's oral history of his service in World War II. When he mentioned places like Peleliu and Okinawa, I knew I would have to write this story. Even though he did not live to see the finished book, he has been with me every step of this journey.

In telling the story of Mary Sears's many contributions I have concentrated on select amphibious landings in the Pacific Campaign, the "storm" landings, as defined by naval historian Joseph Alexander in his excellent book, *Storm Landings: Epic Amphibious Battles in the Central Pacific*. There were many more amphibious landings around the globe that I did not cover, but they each deserve a special place in history and recognition of the heroics of the men who fought and died on these complicated, aquatic battlefields.

It takes a lot of digging to write a book like this and I owe a debt of gratitude to the countless librarians and archivists across the country who dug with me, none more so than Dave Sherman, formerly of the Woods Hole Oceanographic Institution (WHOI) Archives who guided me through the Sears Papers and other collections. I am also grateful to Chris McDougal at the National Museum of the Pacific War and the Nimitz Foundation for access to an incredible array of oral histories and operations plans, Sarah Hutcheon from the Schlesinger Library, archivist Brett Freiburger of WHOI, Suzanne Willet of the Woods Hole Museum, Jennifer Harbster from the Library of Congress, Mary Sears (a distant relative of our hero) from the Museum of Comparative Zoology at Harvard, Margaret Warren of the Winsor School, John Olson at the Oral History Archives of Columbia University, the Wayland Historical Society, and the Maury Library of Oceanography.

Many thanks also go to the following individuals: military historian Chris Holmes, a genius at excavating key documents from the past, Mat Moten for providing a tutorial in military terminology and for reviewing the manuscript, Sam McGovern for reviewing battle scenes and naval terminology, Dr. Patricia Morse, for reviewing oceanographic concepts, Anita Whitney and Dr. Richard Sternberg for sharing historical details and photographs of Dora Henry, Liz Illg for memories of Mary Grier, Dr. Rafael Lemaitre for memories of fellow carcinologist, Fenner Chace, Karen Berkey Huntsberger for WAVES materials and her book *I'll Be Seeing You* about her aunt, Lucy Berkey, Wendy Nies of Woods Hole for the opportunity to review papers that Mary Sears left in her care, Leslie Sears Karpp for memories of her aunt Mary Sears, Priscilla Robinson for research materials, Dr. Jackie Kelly and Liza Mundy for words of wisdom, and John Oberg for going the extra mile.

My agent, Marcy Posner, believed in this project from the beginning and guided it to fruition. Editor Mauro DiPreta embraced Mary Sears and her quirky band of marine scientists and, with assistant editor, Vedika Khanna, helped bring them to life. Shelly Perron's copyediting added clarity to the final draft and Elina Cohen created an amazing design. I am most grateful to Anne Morgan, my first and last reader, who kept me afloat during the *Lethal Tide* years. Any factual errors are unintentional and entirely my own.

Endnotes

PROLOGUE

1   They had scoured online articles: "Top Ten Names Selected in Navy's Oceanographic Ship Naming Contest," Office of the Oceanographer of the Navy, May 4, 1998, https://man.fas.org/dod-101/sys/ship/docs/980504-topten.htm.

2   Upon informing Nimitz: "Leila Sears," Wayland Historical Society, May 13, 2018, https://www.waylandmuseum.org/leila-sears/ accessed May 8, 2019. For most of the war, Nimitz directed the Pacific Campaign from his CINCPAC headquarters in Hawaii. It is possible that Leila Sears met with Nimitz when he returned to the U.S. or that she met with another naval officer headquartered in Washington, D.C.

CHAPTER 1: CHASING PLANKTON ON THE EVE OF THE WAR

5   working in the warm waters off the western coast of South America in Pisco Bay: Sears, Mary, "The Beginnings of the Woods Hole Oceanographic Institution," undated, sixteen-page, handwritten history of WHOI, WHOI archives, Sears Papers, (hereafter "Beginnings"), 9.

6   Native Quechuan-speaking laborers: Durfee, Nell, "Holy Crap! A Trip to the World's Largest Guano-Producing Islands," *Audubon*, April 27, 2018, https://www.audubon.org/news/holy-crap-trip-worlds-largest-guano-producing-islands, accessed July 9, 2021.

7   If she could perform field research in Pisco Bay: Sears, Mary, five-page, handwritten memoir excerpt that begins "I am a victim of happenstance," [hereafter "Happenstance"] WHOI archives, Sears Papers, 2.

9   "it was not done in my day": Mary Sears interview by P. K. Smith, "Reminiscences of Mary Sears: oral history, 1982," December 1, 1981 (interview 1) January 26, 1982 (interview 2), Columbia University, Oral History Archives, typed transcript (interview no. 2, 49–50) [hereafter Sears interview, Smith, 1982], 2–56.

9   For hundreds of years: Bonatti, E., and K. Crane, "Oceanography and Women: Early Challenges," *Oceanography* 25, 2012, 32–39.

10   The captain could have thrown: "A Female Explorer Discovered on the High Seas," NPR staff, https://www.npr.org/2010/12/26/132265308/a-female-explorer-discovered -on-the-high-seas, December 26, 2010, accessed October 13, 2020.

10   And as she was quick to point out: Sears, Beginnings, 9.

10   When she was discovered: "Tradition Falls on Caryn; Woman Scientist 'Stows Away,'" *Falmouth Enterprise*, July 18, 1956.

10   Despite her sound argument: "Tradition Falls on Caryn."

11   "we have a woman who sincerely wanted to go to sea": Blanchard, Duncan, A. H. Wood-cock, Joanne S. Malkus, et al., "Women Oceanographers?" an undated letter to the WHOI administration signed by thirteen staff members regarding the Roberta Eike stowaway incident, circa 1956, Eike file, WHOI Archives.

11   "Notwithstanding the presence of a woman": Bonatti, E., and K. Crane, 25, 32–39, 2012.

12   the sexist restrictions had finally been forced into extinction: "Employee Portrait Gallery—Betty Bunce," Woods Hole Oceanographic Institution, https://webarchives .whoi.edu/75th-archive/gallery/week46-en.html, accessed May 18, 2019.

12   "I am so jealous of you,": Bunce, Elizabeth "Betty," interview by Kathleen Broome Williams, July 8, 1998, Woods Hole Oceanographic Institution (WHOI) Archives, Oral History Collection (AC-45), 1.

13   Sears would have a private moment with a pail: Mary Sears interview by Victoria Ka-harl, September 29, 1989, WHOI archives, typed transcript [hereafter Sears interview, Kaharl, 1989], 9.

14   She learned to sidestep the accumulated "skim": Meir, Mary, "Science Rewards Woman's High Aim," *The Boston Globe*, May 21, 1963, 32.

14   assessed ocean transparency with a Secchi disk: "Using a Secchi Disk or Transpar-ency Tube," United States Environmental Protection Agency, https://archive.epa .gov/water/archive/web/html/155.html, accessed May 6, 2020. "A Secchi disk is a black and white disk that is lowered by hand into the water to the depth at which it vanishes from sight." The distance to vanishing is then noted as a measurement of transparency.

14   "Birds coming in from the North": Sears's cruise book of the Expedition to Pisco Bay, September 5, 1941–December 17, 1941, Sears Papers, WHOI Archives.

14   Approximately two months into: Sears's cruise book of the Expedition to Pisco Bay, September 5, 1941–December 17, 1941, Sears Papers WHOI Archives.

15   Rather than lose her precious net: Sears Interview 1989, Kaharl, 8.

15   the Japanese were moving massive numbers of troops to Indochina: "Document

no. 5: Draft Memorandum, FDR to Secretary of State Cordell Hull and Under Secretary of State Sumner Welles," December 1, 1941, The Franklin D. Roosevelt Presidential Library and Museum Archives, http://www.fdrlibrary.marist.edu/archives/pdfs/pearlharbor.pdf, accessed September 13, 2019.

15   "No!" Roosevelt yelled: "Pearl Harbor: How FDR Responded to the 'Day of Infamy,'" https://www.cbsnews.com/news/pearl-harbor-how-fdr-responded-to-the-day-of-infamy/, December 4, 2016, accessed September 10, 2019.

16   When his commanding officer: Holmes, W. J., *Double-Edged Secrets: U.S. Naval Intelligence Operations in the Pacific during World War II* (Annapolis, MD: Naval Institute Press, 1979), 2–5.

16   gathering in the Marshall Island: Holmes, 26–28.

17   "For the moment, no guns were firing": Holmes, *Double-Edged Secrets*, 4.

17   Roosevelt addressed the nation: Goodwin, Doris Kearns, *No Ordinary Time, Franklin and Eleanor Roosevelt: The Home Front in World War II* (New York, NY: Simon & Schuster, 1994), 357.

19   The unpacking of her jars: Sears Interview, Kaharl, 1989, 6. After the war, when Sears finally sat down with a microscope to examine the plankton specimens, she could find very few intact structures. During the war, her specimens had been stored in an unheated room at the Marine Biologic Laboratory and they froze, which broke up the structures. She was able to produce only one paper from her trip to Peru in 1941, published well after the war in 1954.

CHAPTER 2: CHOOSING AN UNLIKELY PATH

20   Wayland, formerly East Sudbury: Wolfson, Evelyn, *Legendary Locals of Wayland*, Legendary Locals imprint (Charleston, SC: Arcadia Publishing, 2015), 7–8.

20   The Reverend Sears also wrote hymns—500 of them: Mace, Emily, "Sears, Edmund Hamilton (1810–1876)," *Harvard Square Library*, December 11, 2013, https://www.harvardsquarelibrary.org/biographies/edmund-hamilton-sears, accessed May 5, 2020.

22   Mary, the firstborn, arrived on July 18, 1905: "Edmund Hamilton 2nd Sears," undated notes furnished by the Wayland Historical Society, December 2019.

22   Their property abutted lush Heard Pond: Denton, Peter, "Mary Sears: Brief Life of an Oceanographer and Patriot: 1905–1997," *Harvard Magazine*, July–August, 2015.

22   Sears's idyllic upbringing was also interrupted by tragedy: "Sears," unsigned, undated document from the Wayland Historical Society, Wayland, MA, compiled by Jo Goeselt, from papers in the estate of Edwin B. Sears (1911–1987), March 1988. According to this account Edmund Sears hired Sophie Bennett to care for his three small children, however, she was also a full-time teacher from 1907–1917.

23   how much time Edmund spent out of the country: Ancestry.com passenger lists for Edmund H. Sears II from April 25, 1915, and August 25, 1916.

23   "Father forgot to send us to school.": Nies, Wendy, Conversation with the author in

Woods Hole, MA, September 2018, stating that Mary Sears mentioned her father leaving after the death of his wife and that he forgot to send them to school.

23   Mary Picard Winsor had opened: "Mission & History," https://www.winsor.edu /about/mission-and-history, accessed December 15, 2021.

24   During World War I, fifty-eight Winsor graduates: Haley, Dianne, *Generous-Minded Women: A History of the Winsor School*, (Beverly, MA: Memoirs Unlimited, 2012) 114.

25   "Mary Sears is a fine girl, upright, responsible and loyal": Ford, Katharine, "Estimate of the Candidate's Character," form included in academic files of Mary Sears, Radcliffe Archives.

26   "her family depend on her a great deal to look after her brothers and sisters": "Mary Sears," *The Lantern*, Winsor School yearbook, 1923, 32–33.

26   a source of embarrassment for someone of his social standing: Fanning, Patricia J. *Norwood: A History* (Mount Pleasant, SC: Arcadia Publishing, 2002), 89–101.

26   In her passport photo: Ancestry.com, United States of America Passport Application for Mary Sears, June 18, 1922, accessed August 15, 2021.

27   "Adamless Edens": Clemente, Deirdre, "'Prettier Than They Used to Be': Femininity, Fashion, and the Recasting of Radcliffe's Reputation, 1900–1950," *New England Quarterly* 81, 2009, 644.

28   years overlapped with the arrival of Ada Comstock: "Ada Louise Comstock (Radcliffe College President from 1923 to 1943)," Radcliffe Institute for Advanced Study Harvard University," https://www.radcliffe.harvard.edu/people/ada-louise-comstock, accessed May 6, 2020.

29   She grew into a strong, broad-shouldered young woman: "Mary Sears," *The Radcliffe Yard-Stick of 1926–1927*, Cambridge, MA, 94, https://iiif.lib.harvard.edu/manifests /view/drs:427987268$7i, accessed December 15, 2021.

CHAPTER 3: FINDING A MENTOR FOSTERS A CAREER

30   "I was a victim of happenstance": Sears, Mary, Happenstance, 1.

30   Elizabeth Cary Agassiz, the first president of Radcliffe: Tonn, Jenna, "Extralaboratory Life: Gender Politics and Experimental Biology at Radcliffe College 1894–1910," *Gender & History* 29, 2017, 332–34.

31   But the telltale smell: Sears, Mary "Oceanography—then and now," undated, five-page, typed document, Denton Papers, Woods Hole, MA, 1.

31   Bigelow had found his way: Bigelow, Henry B., *Memories of a Long and Active Life* (Cambridge, MA: The Cosmos Press, 1964), 3, reviewed at WHOI Archives, Bigelow Papers.

32   "We also had to haul our pots by hand": Bigelow, 4.

32   As he continued to engage: Bigelow, 5.

32   The next chance came: Bigelow, 9.

33   "Schools of brilliant red": Bigelow, 10.

34 It was as if she had her own private tutor: Sears, Mary, "Beginnings," 2.

34 "Too, over the years that I worked": Sears, Mary, "Beginnings," 3–4.

35 "In short, he was a one-man task force in oceanography operating off our east coast.": Sears, Mary "Oceanography—then and now," 2.

37 Sears's thesis for her Ph.D. from Radcliffe: Sears, Mary, "Responses of Deep-seated Melanophores in Fishes and Amphibians," *Summaries of Theses: Accepted in Partial Fulfillment of the Requirements for the Degree of Doctor of Philosophy, 1931–1934*, Radcliffe College Graduate School of Arts and Sciences, Cambridge, MA, 1935, 91–92.

37 Her examination for the doctor's degree: Mary Sears Academic Record, Radcliffe College Archives.

38 She spent the fall and spring semesters: Sears Interview 1989, Kaharl, 19.

38 they held the contents of fish stomachs: Williams, Kathleen Broome, *Improbable Warriors: Women Scientists and the U.S. Navy in World War II* (Annapolis, MD: Naval Institute Press, 2001), 34.

40 "He pushed me out": Sears Interview, Kaharl, 1989, 19.

40 "as scientists they were atypical women": Rossiter, Margaret W., *Women Scientists in America: Struggles and Strategies to 1940* (Baltimore, MD: Johns Hopkins University Press, 1982), xv.

40 they were subjected to a system of segregated employment: Dominus, Susan, "Sidelined," Smithsonian.com, October 2019, 44–49.

41 he was "an old-fashioned man": Mary Sears interview by Gary B. Weir, 22 June 1992, United States Navy History and Heritage Command, Washington D.C., (CD, no transcript available) [hereafter Sears interview, Weir, 1992].

CHAPTER 4: SMOKE SCREENS AND SUBMARINES

43 the establishment of the Woods Hole Oceanographic Institution in 1930: "Woods Hole: The Early Years," NOAA Fisheries, https://www.fisheries.noaa.gov/new-england -mid-atlantic/about-us/woods-hole-early-years, accessed November 10, 2020.

43 putting up an average of thirty buildings a day: "The Story of Camp Edwards, from Scrub Pines to Medical Center: 7. Cape Cod as the Cradle of Invasions," *Falmouth Enterprise*, June 22, 1945.

43 the influx of workers created a housing shortage: Turkington, Frederick T., "The War Years in Falmouth," *Spiritsail* 9, Winter 1995, 5.

44 Camp Edwards, adjacent to nearby islands like Martha's Vineyard: DUKW: amphibious vehicle, *Encyclopedia Britannica*, https://www.britannica.com/technology /DUKW, accessed July 1, 2020, stating that the DUKW, aka "duck," is a 2.5-ton six-wheel amphibious truck used in World War II.

44 the Navy Pigeon Loft, brought four pigeon fanciers and a flock of pigeons: "Navy Breeds and Trains Carrier Pigeons at Woods Hole Base," *Falmouth Enterprise*, April 9, 1943.

45   The value of the blackouts was literally brought home: "2 New Englanders Saved in U.S. Ship Torpedoing," *The Boston Globe*, August 6, 1942, 9.

45   Ten crew members were never found: Witzell, Susan Fletcher, "Life in Woods Hole Village During World War II," *Spiritsail* 9, Winter 1995, 26–27.

46   White wooden guard shacks had sprouted up: Miner, Jr., T. Richardson, "The Impact of World War II on Soldiers, Scientists, Civilians and the Town of Falmouth," *Spiritsail* 25, Winter 2011.

47   to journey to Woods Hole to do "real war work,": Sears, Mary, "Beginnings," WHOI Archives, Sears Papers, 13.

50   "motley mixture of scientists, yachtsmen, fishermen, and amateurs": Stommel, Henry M., "Columbus O'Donnell Iselin: 1904–1971, a Biographical Memoir," National Academy of Sciences, 1994, 170.

50   sixty-three of WHOI's employees left for active military service: Cullen, Vicky, *Down to the Sea for Science: 75 Years of Ocean Research, Education, and Exploration at the Woods Hole Oceanographic Institution* (Woods Hole, MA: Woods Hole Oceanographic Institution, 2005), 59.

51   "The meaning of the words 'ocean' and 'atmosphere'": Iselin, Columbus O., "WHOI History During War Years: 1941–1950," undated, WHOI Archives, Iselin Papers, 2.

51   Iselin had sailed south to Guantanamo Bay: Schlee, Susan, *The Edge of an Unfamiliar World*, (New York, NY: E.P. Dutton & Co., 1973) 287.

51   drafted a memo to the newly formed National Defense Research Committee: Iselin, Columbus O'Donnell, "Memorandum concerning the research facilities available at Woods Hole Oceanographic Institution," from "WHOI History During the War Years," Iselin Papers, WHOI Archives.

53   that led him to join research expeditions: Malone, R. F., E. D. Goldberg, and W. H. Munk, "Roger Randall Dougan Revelle: 1909–1991," National Academy of Sciences, Washington, D.C., 1998, http://www.nasonline.org/publications/biographical-memoirs/memoir-pdfs/revelle-roger.pdf, accessed October 16, 2020.

54   He described the Hydrographic Office as "a hopeless place": Revelle, Roger, "Oceanography, Population Resources and the World: Oral History Transcript/Roger Randall Dougan Revelle," interviewed by Sarah L. Sharp, Regional Oral History Office, the Bancroft Library, University of California, Berkeley, 1986, 5–6.

55   "You can have *her*,": Sears Interview, Weir, 1992, CD.

55   "I was 'palmed off' on him": Sears, Mary, "Beginnings," 13.

CHAPTER 5: HYDRO FIGHTS A WAR

57   to ensure the safe navigation of the oceans: Pinsel, Marc I., *150 Years of Service on the Seas: A Pictorial History of the U.S. Naval Oceanographic Office from 1830 to 1980*, vol. 1 (1830–1946), Dept. of the Navy, Oceanographic Office, 1981, 19. States that the Hydrographic Office was reorganized in 1871 and the title of Hydrographer was created with a list of duties to include maintaining archives, charts, and instruments.

58   In the Pacific alone, the troops needed hundreds of charts: Mundy, Liza, *Code Girls: The Untold Story of the American Women Code Breakers of World War II* (New York: Hachette Books, 2017), 118.

58   the war brought new threats to the safety of navigation: Pinsel, 14.

58   the agency broadcast urgent updates: *History of the Hydrographic Office During the Second World War, 1939–1945*, Department of the Navy, Office of Naval History, 1948, 96.

58   twenty-five years old and obsolete: Pinsel, 56.

59   demands for charts of strategic areas: *History of the Hydrographic Office*, 85.

59   "an unprecedented demand for charts.": *History of the Hydrographic Office*, xiv.

59   distribution to naval and commercial vessels: *History of the Hydrographic Office*, xiii.

59   "the leading chart producing agency": Bryan, George S., Admiral, U.S.N., "The Oceanographic Work of the Hydrographic Office During the Past Year," August 2, 1942, National Archives, Washington, D.C., R637, Entry 49, Box 125.

60   "pursuit of an impossible perfection.'" Bryan, R637, Entry 49, Box 125.

60   the agency advertised in the *New York Times*: "Hydrographic Positions Open," *New York Times*, April 3, 1942, accessed October 27, 2019.

60   "older persons and the physically handicapped": *History of the Hydrographic Office*, 23–24.

61   Technicians would photograph the smooth sheets: *History of the Hydrographic Office*, 23.

61   eighteen successive runs were sometimes necessary: *History of the Hydrographic Office*, xiii.

61   Women had already proven themselves: "The Auxiliary Territorial Service in the Second World War," Imperial War Museum, https://www.iwm.org.uk/collections/item /object/1500013553, accessed October 27, 2019.

61   sixty-five thousand British women were serving in the armed forces: "Focus on . . . Women in Uniform" The National Archives, https://www.nationalarchives .gov.uk/womeninuniform/wwii_intro.htm, accessed December 19, 2021.

62   Women were also serving in the Russian Army: Shaw, Anthony, *World War II Day by Day* (New York, NY: Chartwell Books, 2000), 58, 74.

62   fourteen hundred women had shown up to apply: Mundy, *Code Girls*, 160.

62   the navy but they strenuously resisted any efforts to allow women in their ranks: Hancock, Joy Bright, *Lady in the Navy: A Personal Reminiscence* (Annapolis, MD: Bluejacket Books, 1972), 52.

62   "dogs or ducks or monkeys": Hancock, *Lady in the Navy*, 49.

62   Department of Aeronautics drafted a comprehensive plan: Hancock, 28.

63   employed civilian women in technical roles: Mundy, *Code Girls*, 160.

63   "there are no billets . . . which might be filled": Hancock, *Lady in the Navy*, 51.

63   "Their lack of enthusiasm stemmed,": Hancock, 51.

64   their femininity and futures as "good mothers.": Hancock, 55.

64   "They have begun to realize that the 'man power' of the country": "From 'Gobettes' to WAVES (and SPARS): Laying the Groundwork," HomefrontHeroines.com, https://www.homefrontheroines.com/exhibits/from-gobettes-to-waves-and-spars/, accessed July 12, 2021.

64   "I think women can stand up under that type of living": Roosevelt, Eleanor, "My Day," October 15, 1943, United Feature Syndicate, Inc., https://www2.gwu.edu/~erpapers /myday/displaydoc.cfm?_y=1943&_f=md056620, accessed July 12, 2021.

64   "I showed your letter": Hancock, *Lady in the Navy*, 56.

65   these caps gradually fell away: Williams, Kathleen Broome, "Women Ashore: The Contribution of WAVES to US Naval Science and Technology in World War II," *Northern Mariner/Le Marin du Nord*, VIII, no. 2 (April 1998), 4.

65   Initial estimates provided for approximately 10,000 WAVES: Hancock, *Lady in the Navy*, 61.

65   WAVES even instructed male pilots: Williams, Kathleen Broome, "Women Ashore," 9.

65–66   "The major reason for increased chart production": Administrative History of the Hydrographic Office, Department of the Navy, Office of Naval History, xiv.

66   The women proved themselves capable: Pinsel, *150 Years of Service*, 59–63.

67   the total labor force at Hydro had ballooned: *History of the Hydrographic Office*, 216.

67   she saw vivid recruiting posters: Huntsberger, Karen Berkey, *I'll Be Seeing You: Letters Home from a Navy Girl* (Eugene, OR: Luminare Press, 2018), 40.

68   started giving her high-priority jobs: Huntsberger, 120.

68   "had ferried the Hydrographer from the train": Mary Sears and Dean Bumpus Interview by Victoria Kaharal, for the "Woods Hole Oceanographic Institution History Colloquy," July 15, 1991, WHOI Archives.

69   "Miss Sears is a professional oceanographer": Bryan, George S., memo, "Miss Mary Sears—Request for Assignment to Hydrographic Office," January 4, 1943, National Archives, Washington, D.C., RG 37, Entry 49, Box 198.

71   She was instructed to bring the waiver: Hartenstein, Paul B., "Waiver of physical defect for enlistment in the U.S. Naval Reserve," memo from the Chief of Naval Personnel to Mary Sears, January 16, 1943, Denton Papers, Woods Hole, MA.

72   She learned the traditions and customs of the navy: Woodruff, Cpt. J. L., "Wave Training," *U.S. Naval Institute Proceedings*, February 1945, 151–55.

73   one of the leading fashion designers in the world came to design the WAVES uniform: "Uniform Identity," *Homefront Heroines: The WAVES of World War II*, https://www.homefrontheroines.com/exhibits/uniform-identity/, accessed July 15, 2021.

73   "I thought of comfort, freedom and, of course, the lines of a woman's body.": Vincent, Katherine, "The Waves' Uniforms: 'Womanly, Workmanlike,' *New York Herald Tribune*, August 29, 1942, 1, 6. Courtesy of the New-York Historical Society Library, https://wams.nyhistory.org/wp-content/uploads/print/15915_image_1.pdf, accessed July 14, 2021.

73   "they do not have to look like men,": Vincent, 1, 6.

73   gold buttons for officers and navy-blue plastic buttons for enlisted women: "Women's Reserve of the U.S. Naval Reserve (WAVES): Insignia, Jacket Devices," https://www .history.navy.mil/research/library/online-reading-room/title-list-alphabetically/u /womens-reserve-1943.html, accessed October 27, 2020.

74   "I don't look that great in khaki or green": "Uniform Identity."

74   "it had two pockets just inside where you could put Kleenex.": "Uniform Identity."

75   to substantiate her claim: Sears Interview, Smith, 1982, I-25.

75–76   received her sailing orders: "500 Waves Receive Their Sailing Orders," *The Boston Globe*, Boston, MA, April 7, 1943, 17.

CHAPTER 6: THE WAR BENEATH THE SEA

77   One such project, the development of the bathythermograph: Bryan, George S., memo, "Miss Mary Sears—Request for Assignment to Hydrographic Office," January 4, 1943, National Archives, Washington, D.C., RG 37, Entry 49, Box 198, 1–2.

78   Still, German U-boats: Padfield, Peter, *War Beneath the Sea* (New York, NY: John Wiley & Sons, 1995), 8–9.

78   Even though the Treaty of Versailles: Padfield, 40.

78   With Karl Donitz: Padfield, 44.

79   In 1936 he handed the project off: Spilhaus, Athelstan, F., "A Bathythermograph," *Journal of Marine Research* 1, 1938, 95–100.

80   Spilhouse initially used: Spilhaus, Athelstan, F., "On Reaching 50: An Early History of the Bathythermograph, *Sea Technology*, Nov. 1987, 22–23.

80   Allyn Vine, a trained physicist: Weir, Gary, *An Ocean in Common* (College Station, TX, Texas A&M University Press, 2001), 128.

80   The BT had become: Spilhaus, "On Reaching 50," 27.

81   Weiant excelled at operating the instrument: Weiant, Carl A., Jr., "News Release Form for the Bureau of Navigation," completed August 26, 1941, from the military personnel record of Carl Andrew Weiant, National Personnel Records Center, the National Archives, St. Louis, Missouri.

82   The badly injured Weiant: Claes, Johnny, "SS Otho," https://www.wrecksite.eu/wreck .aspx?22482, accessed March 21, 2020, Death Certificate of Carl A. Weiant, from the military personnel record of Carl Andrew Weiant, National Personnel Records Center, the National Archives, St. Louis, Missouri.

82   Their raft floated in the Atlantic: "Weiant, Carl A., Jr., Ensign, U.S.N.R., File No. 101143(deceased) Request information re:," Memorandum to the Chief of the Bureau of Personnel from the Hydrographer, August 20, 1943, National Archives, Washington, D.C. RG 37, Entry 48, Box 124, 1.

82–83   "When we learned that the late Ensign Weiant": Iselin, C. O., letter to Lt. Comdr. B. E. Dodson, August 31, 1943, from the military personnel record of Carl Andrew

Weiant, National Personnel Records Center, the National Archives, St. Louis, Missouri.

83   The real time identification: Schlee, *The Edge of an Unfamiliar World*, 293.

83   If time permitted before: Blair, Clay, *Silent Victory: The United States Submarine War against Japan* (Philadelphia, PA: Lippincott, 1975), 458–59.

83   "The bathythermograph inspires feeling": Schlee, *The Edge of an Unfamiliar* World, 294.

84   "Thank God for Allyn Vine,": WHOI Colloquy, July 15, 1991, transcript 13.

84   Weiant's were only the first of over 60,000 bathythermograph slides: Schlee, Susan, p. 294.

CHAPTER 7: A SEAT AT THE TABLE

86   Without them there was no way: Weir, Gary, *An Ocean in Common* (College Station, TX: Texas A&M University Press, 2001), 148.

86   *"Speed is essential"*: "Minutes of the Joint Meteorological Committee Subcommittee on Oceanography," January 27, 1943, National Archives, Washington, D.C., RG 218, Entry 1, Boxes 206–207, 1–2.

86   As Seiwell attempted to keep up: "Minutes of the Joint Meteorological Committee Subcommittee on Oceanography," January 28, 1943, National Archives, Washington, D.C., RG 218, Entry 1, Boxes 206–207, 3.

87   there were only a handful of oceanographers: Bates, Charles C., and Richard H. Fleming, "Oceanography in the Hydrographic Office," *Military Engineer*, August 1947, 341.

87   While the population of the capital city: "District, Measured: Posts from the District of Columbia's Office of Revenue Analysis", https://districtmeasured.com/2018/03/22/2017-marks-the-third-time-in-70-years-dc-has-had-694000-residents/, accessed October 30, 2020.

87   The overcrowding was so bad: *Life*, January 1943, 47.

88   The government took over basketball arenas: Brinkley, David, *Washington Goes to War: The Extraordinary Story of the Transformation of a City and a Nation* (New York, NY: Alfred A. Knopf, 1988), 120.

88   The former owner, Colonel Samuel Taylor Suit: "Suitland Federal Center," United States Census Bureau, https://www.census.gov/history/www/census_then_now/suitdland_md/suitland_federal_center.html, accessed May 15, 2020.

89   was the first to occupy the new Suitland Federal Center: Pinsel, *150 Years of Service*, 59.

89   developers had added a modern shopping center, a fourteen-acre victory garden, and a daycare center: "Suitland Federal Center," United States Census Bureau, accessed May 15, 2020.

90   or try her hand at painting in the hobby corner stocked with art materials: "Waves Play Big Part in Navy Hydrographic Program," *Palm Beach Post*, May 14, 1944, 24.

91 Amphibious assaults were not unheard of before World War II: Isely, Jeter A., and Philip A. Crowl, *The U.S. Marines and Amphibious War: Its Theory, and Its Practice in the Pacific* (Princeton, NJ: Princeton University Press, 1951), 17–20.

91 He drew up Operations Plan 712H: Isely and Crowl, *The U.S. Marines and Amphibious War*, 25–27.

92 "Chaos reigned,": Marine Brigadier General Eli Cole wrote in his after-action report: Alexander, Joseph H., *Storm Landings: Epic Amphibious Battles in the Central Pacific* (Annapolis, MD: Naval Institute Press, 1997),13.

93 how to speed up the process of collecting information for urgent reports for the military: "Minutes of the Joint Meteorological Committee Subcommittee on Oceanography," January 27, 1943, National Archives, Washington, DC., RG 218, Entry 1, Boxes 206–207. 1.

94 had made the decision to centralize oceanographic intelligence: "Minutes of the Joint Meteorological Committee Subcommittee on Oceanography," May 13, 1943, National Archives, Washington, D.C., RG 218, Entry 1, Boxes 206–207, 1–2.

94 Seiwell was being deployed to the European theater: Bates, Charles C., *"Hydro" to "Navoceano": 175 Years of Ocean Survey and Prediction by the U.S. Navy*, (Rockton, IL: Corn Field Press, 2005), 70.

95 the AAF oceanographic unit had completed an impressive thirty-nine studies for army and navy commanders: Minutes of the Joint Meteorological Committee Subcommittee on Oceanography, May 13, 1943, National Archives, Washington, D.C., RG 218, Entry 1, Boxes 206–207. 1–2.

CHAPTER 8: THE VAST PACIFIC OCEAN

96 "places that are now the battleground for civilization.": Goodwin, Doris Kearns, *No Ordinary Time: Franklin and Eleanor Roosevelt: The Home Front in World War II* (New York, NY: Simon and Schuster, 1994), 319.

96 "as our protection from attack have become endless battlefields.": Goodwin, *No Ordinary Time*, 320.

97 the sixty-four-million-square-mile Pacific Ocean: https://www.gdrc.org/oceans/world-oceans.html, accessed January 5, 2022.

98 navy floatplanes rescued the rest of the survivors: Rea, Billy A., "Eddie Rickenbacker and Six Other People Survive a B-17 Crash and Three Weeks Lost in the Pacific Ocean," HistoryNet, https://www.historynet.com/eddie-rickenbacker-and-six-other-people-survive-a-b-17-crash-and-three-weeks-lost-in-the-pacific-ocean.htm, accessed Dec. 31, 2021.

98 they died because they hadn't been found in time: "Watermanship," FM21–22 *War Department Basic Field Manual*, April 25, 1944, https://archive.org/details/FM21–22, accessed February 5, 2020.

98 One portion was found off the coast of Portland, Maine: Bates, Charles C., and Richard H. Fleming, "Oceanography in the Hydrographic Office," *Military Engineer*, August 1947, 342.

99   "I'd like to know if you have any information": Letter from Mary Rimmele to Mary Sears, January 7, 1974, Folder labeled "Correspondence," Sears Papers, WHOI Archives.

100   "just three or four days before he died.": Letter from Mary Sears to Mary Rimmele, January 11, 1974, Folder labeled "Correspondence," Sears Papers, WHOI Archives.

100   "The convenience of a cumulative oceanographic card index": Sears, Mary, *Oceanographic Index: Cumulation 1946–1973: Marine Organisms, Chiefly Planktonic, Volume 1 Zooplankton-Copepods (Exumella)* (Boston, MA: G.K. Hall & Co. 1974), iii. A copy of an advertisement obtained from Woods Hole Archives, Sears Papers, issued by G.K. Hall & Co. lists fifteen total volumes published through 1974.

100   "from several hundred file drawers in Mary's Bigelow office to about two feet of bookshelf space.": "G.K. Hall Publishes 'Reader's Guide to Oceanography' by Mary Sears," *WHOI Newsletter*, August 22, 1973, documents twelve volumes with more planned in the future, https://darchive.mblwhoilibrary.org/bitstream/handle/1912/9829/v14n11_1973–08–22.pdf?sequence=1&isAllowed=y, accessed December 27, 2021, 1–2.

101   how leeway, the sideways drift of an object such as a rubber life raft, affected its overall direction: "Minutes of the Joint Meteorological Committee Subcommittee on Oceanography," January 27, 1943, National Archives, Washington, D.C., RG 218, Entry 1, Boxes 206–207, 1–2.

101   They endorsed Sears's conclusions: "Minutes of the Joint Meteorological Committee Subcommittee on Oceanography," May 27, 1943, National Archives, Washington, D.C., RG 218, Entry 1, Boxes 206–207, 1–2.

101   Sears got the exciting news: "Centralization of Oceanographic Activities," Memo from Vice Chief of Naval Operations to the Hydrographer re. oceanographic staff for the Hydrographic Office, June 16, 1943, National Archives, Washington, D.C., RG 37, Entry 49, Box 16.

102   Chace even left detailed instructions: "Annual Report of the Director of the Museum of Comparative Zoology at Harvard College to the President of Harvard College for 1941–1942," Cambridge, MA, 1942, 37–39.

102   The MCZ had been founded: "Museum of Comparative Zoology, Harvard: History," https://mcz.harvard.edu/invertebrate-zoology-history, accessed December 1, 2019.

102   came into the orbit of Dr. Henry Bryant Bigelow and discovered his life's work: Chace, Fenner A., Jr., "Oral History Interview with Fenner A. Chace, Jr., by Pamela M. Henson, Interview" on October 6, 1977, Smithsonian Institution Archives, 1.

102   Chace spent his first year as a graduate student working long hours in the darkest corners of the basement: Chace, Fenner, "A Biographical Thanks," in the "Spotlight" column of *No Bones About It: Newsletter of the Department of Invertebrate Zoology, Smithsonian Museum*, November 1996, 6.

103   he took the Northwestern School of Taxidermy correspondence course: "Northwestern School of Taxidermy," https://history.nebraska.gov/collections/northwestern-school-taxidermy-omaha-neb-rg5451am, accessed December 1, 2019. The Northwestern School of Taxidermy of Omaha, NE, was in existence from 1903 to the 1980s and sold taxidermy supplies and materials for a correspondence course in removing and treating hides and in preserving and mounting animal specimens.

103   "I have to draw things in order to see them.": Chace, "Oral History," 24.

103   there were "field men,": Chace, 32.

104   His wife, well acquainted with his florid hemophobia: Lemaitre, Rafael, "Remarks on the Life and Works of Fenner A. Chace, Jr. (1908–2004), with a List of His Taxa and Complete Bibliography," *Crustaceana* 78, no. 5 (May 2005), 625.

104   "an individual who shuns controversy": Chace, Fenner A., Jr., "Waldo L. Schmitt, 25 June 1887–5 August 1977," *Crustaceana* 34, 1978, 85.

105   where he lived for a dollar a day in a hotel with maid service: Chace: "Oral History," 9.

105   known as "silk handkerchiefs," for aviators: Chace, "Oral History," 1.

106   The British had allegedly hijacked a shipment of the exotic paper: Giaimo, Cara, "How Millions of Secret Silk Maps Helped POWs Escape Their Captors in WW II," *Atlas Obscura*, December 20, 2016, https://www.atlasobscura.com/articles/how-millions-of -secret-silk-maps-helped-pows-escape-their-captors-in-wwii, accessed July 10, 2020.

106   a small compass and a metal file: Garber, Megan, "How Monopoly Games Helped Allied POWs Escape During World War II," TheAtlantic.com, January 9, 2013, https:// www.theatlantic.com/technology/archive/2013/01/how-monopoly-games-helped -allied-pows-escape-during-world-war-ii/266996/accessed June 19, 2020.

106   worked with American companies: "MIS-X: The U.S. Escape and Evasion Experts," National Museum of the United States Air Force, May 1, 2015, accessed June 20, 2020. See also: https://spyscape.com/article/top-10-cia-mi9-escape-and-evasion-gadgets for photos of escape devices.

107   Different samples of cloth were put to the test: Stanley, Albert A., "Cloth Maps and Charts," *Military Engineer* 39, March 1947, 126.

107   Additional shaded arrows were added to the chart: Day, Deborah, "Cloth Survival Charts, Also Called 'Waterproof Handkerchiefs,'" Cloth Map Instructions, Scripps Institution of Oceanography Archives, October 10, 1996, https://library.ucsd.edu/scilib /hist/day_survival_charts_hankerchiefs.pdf, accessed June 19, 2020.

108   Harald Sverdrup at Scripps Oceanographic Institution had designed: Day, "Cloth Survival Charts."

108   an escape to Australia on a twenty-foot fishing boat: Dickey, Christopher, "The Great Escape," *New York Times*, January 23, 2000, 25, accessed July 10, 2020. See also for further details, Gause, Damon L., *The War Journal of Major Damon "Rocky" Gause* (New York, NY: Hyperion, 2000).

109   improved the chances a pilot would survive being stranded at sea: Doll, John G., *Cloth Maps, Charts and Blood Chits of World War II* (Hoosick Falls, NY: Merriam Press, 1988), 27.

109   credited the "intelligent use" of them with their safe return: "Cloth Charts Bring Survivors Back," *Air Sea Rescue Bulletin* 2 (September 1945), 6.

109   The maps she had helped develop: Sears Interview, Smith, 1982, 2–43.

CHAPTER 9: OCEANOGRAPHERS TO THE RESCUE

110 Admiral Bryan had experienced an epiphany: *Hydrographic WAVES*, a yearbook compiled by the WAVES staff of the Hydrographic Office, published by the Hydrographic Office, July 1944, 8.

110 "I recall that there were many misgivings": *Hydrographic WAVES*, 1.

111 "the girls don coveralls": *Hydrographic WAVES*, 16.

112 Patrician Hollingsworth from Denver, Colorado: *Hydrographic WAVES*, 43.

113–114 "We knew that most of the WAVES weren't engineers": *Hydrographic WAVES*, 6.

114 The Hydro WAVES were even filmed for *Report to Judy*: *Hydrographic WAVES*, 49–50.

115 "From the moment we arrived they truly 'welcomed' us": *Hydrographic WAVES*, 9.

115 "suitable oceanographic staff": Newton, J. H., "Centralization of Oceanographic Activities," June 9, 1943, 1. National Archives and Records Administration (NARA), Washington, D.C., RG 37, Entry 19, Box, 16.

116 Dora Henry, a civilian oceanographer: "Justification for filling vacancy in absolutely essential position," Memo from the Chief of Naval Operations to the Assistant Secretary of the Navy, Navy Department, July 8, 1943, RG 37, Entry 48, Box 124.

116 She packed up her three children: McLaughlin, P. A., Anita Whitney, Arnold Ross, Alan J. Southward, William A. Newman, "Dora Priaulx Henry: 24 May 1904–16 June 1999," *Journal of Crustacean Biology* 20, no. 1, 2000, 199–200.

117 only at the level of research associate: McLaughlin, 199–200.

117 Dr. Thompson, the department chairman: Redfield, Alfred C., Clifford A. Barnes, and Francis A. Richards, "Thomas Gordon Thompson, 1888–1961," The National Academy of Sciences, Washington D.C., 1973, http://www.nasonline.org/publications /biographical-memoirs/memoir-pdfs/thompson-thomas.pdf, accessed December 1, 2019, 240.

119 "has added considerably to our knowledge of the barnacles of the Gulf of California": Henry, Dora Priaulx, "Notes on Some Barnacles from the Gulf of California," *Proceedings of the United States National Museum* 93 (Washington D.C., 1943), 367.

119 She could also measure the circular barnacle footprint: Shih, Ivy, "Barnacles Are a Clock for the Dead," *Hakai Magazine*, November 13, 2019, accessed April 8, 2021.

119 "They're on everything,": Communication between author and Anita Whitney, April 2, 2021.

119 Chace also guided Henry: Chace, Fenner A., Jr., Letter to Dr. Dora Priaulx Henry, June 9, 1941, Archives of the Museum of Comparative Zoology.

120 many of these women made discoveries that exceeded: McLaughlin, P. A., and S. Gilbert, "Women's Contributions to Carcinology," in *History of Carcinology*, ed. Frank Truesdale (Rotterdam: A. A. Balkema, 1993), 191.

120 "Two other women scientists who might have mentored me": Colwell, Rita, and Sharon Bertsch McGrayne, *A Lab of One's Own: One Woman's Personal Journey Through Sexism in Science* (New York, NY: Simon & Schuster, 2020), 20–21.

121 "One, she was a woman": McLaughlin and Gilbert, "Women's Contribution to Carcinology," 191; Steinbeck, John, *The Log from the Sea of Cortez* (New York, NY: Viking Penguin, Inc., 1941), lxxii–lxiii. This episode was recalled by marine biologist Ed Ricketts, who was friends with both Dora Henry and John Steinbeck.

122   The navy was not going to take advice from someone in a skirt: Steinbeck, lxxiii.

122   Bernard was commissioned in 1942 as a major: *Preventative Medicine in World War II*, ed. Robert S. Anderson, Office of the Surgeon General, Dept. of the Army, Washington, D.C., 1969, 842–43.

123   for her "helpful criticisms": Grier, Mary C., *Oceanography of the North Pacific Ocean, Bering Sea and Bering Strait: A Contribution Toward a Bibliography* (Seattle, WA: University of Washington Publications Library Series, 1941), vii.

CHAPTER 10: CLOSING THE INTELLIGENCE GAP

131   "We were caught so utterly unprepared.": "Topographic Intelligence," undated document from Freedom of Information Act (FOIA) Electronic Reading Room-Central Intelligence Agency (hereafter CIA FOIA website), https://www.cia.gov/readingroom /docs/CIA-RDP79-01147A000100010021-4.pdf, 1, accessed December 30, 2021.

131   To help remedy the intelligence gap: Bramell, James A, "History of the National Intelligence Survey Program," The Directorate of Intelligence Historical Series, September 1969, 2.

132   "Who even thought we should be required to know": "Topographic Intelligence," undated document from CIA FOIA Electronic Reading Room, https://www.cia .gov/readingroom/docs/CIA-RDP79-01147A000100010021-4.pdf, 1, accessed December 30, 2021.

132   the British had the edge in strategic planning: Reardon, Steven L., *Council of War* (Washington, D.C.: National Defense University Press, 2012), 1.

132   Roosevelt formed his own Joint Chiefs of Staff: "Origin of the Joint Chiefs of Staff," Washington, D.C., https://www.jcs.mil/About/Origin-of-Joint-Concepts/, accessed August 15, 2021.

133   the British had prepared a detailed analysis: Reardon, *Council of War*, 13.

133   "They had us on the defensive practically all the time.": Reardon, 13.

133   formed the Interservices Topographical Department: Rose, Edward and J. C. Clatworthy, "Specialist Maps of the Geological Section, Inter-Service Topographical Department: Aids to British Military Planning During World War II", *Cartographic Journal* 44 (February 2007), abstract, https://www.researchgate.net/publication /233612768_Specialist_Maps_of_the_Geological_Section_Inter-Service_Topo graphical_Department_Aids_to_British_Military_Planning_During_World_War_II, accessed January 2, 2022.

134   "To make available one publication containing all the necessary detailed information": "Joint Intelligence Committee Basic Directive for the Joint Intelligence Study Publishing Board, Annex 'B' to Appendix 'A'" April 27, 1943, https://www.cia.gov/read ingroom/docs/CIA-RDP79-01147A000100070007-4.pdf, accessed August 20, 2021, 6.

134   to improve the quality of the reports: "History of JANIS (for G-2)", September 1945,

CIA FOIA website, https://www.cia.gov/library/readingroom/docs/CIA-RDP79-01147 A000100010024-1.pdf, accessed, June 15, 2019.

134   thirteen-chapter outline: "Appendix 'B' Draft: Basic Directive: Joint Intelligence Study Publishing Board (J.I.S.P.B.)," undated, CIA FOIA website, https://www.cia.gov/reading room/docs/CIA-RDP79-01147A000200030014-9.pdf, accessed July 1, 2021, 5. Later in the war the outline would expand to fifteen chapters.

136   "can best be compiled by the Oceanographic Unit": Train, H. C., "Request for Compilation by Hydrographic Office and Oceanographic Information for Joint Army and Navy Intelligence Studies," July 15, 1943, National Archives, Washington, D.C., RG 37, Entry 49, Box 16.

137   the landings at Gavutu and Tanambogo: Alexander, Joseph H., *Storm Landings* (Annapolis, MD: Naval Institute Press, 1997), 2.

138   oceanographic intelligence on tides, reefs, surf zones, and beach gradient: Alexander, 29.

139   the major conduit between military and governmental agencies and the White House: Rigby, David, *Allied Master Strategists: The Combined Chiefs of Staff in World War II* (Annapolis, MD: Naval Institute Press, 2012), 57.

140   the structures looked like gap-toothed combs: Williams, Paul K., *Images of America: Washington, D.C.: The World War II Years* (Charleston, SC: Arcadia Publishing, 2004), 100.

140   "I didn't think I would ever be let into the Gates of Heaven": "'Temporary' War Department Buildings," U.S. National Park Service, https://www.nps.gov/articles /temporary-war-department-buildings.htm, accessed November 16, 2020.

140   Munitions Building and Main Navy lasted more than five decades: Williams, *Images of America*, 95.

140   from social hubs to stenographer pools: Williams, 101.

142   issued an amended priority list: Bailey, Vaughn, George H. Kountz, and Kirk H. Stone, "JANIS Memorandum #13," September 9, 1943, https://www.cia.gov /readingroom/docs/CIA-RDP79-01147A000300040038-1.pdf, accessed January 17, 2020.

143   She also learned to expect a change in JANIS priorities: Sears interview, Kaharl, 1989, 10.

143   reports by trained geographers for combat missions: Foott, Bronwyn, and Barbara Wojtkowski, "Preserving History: Digitisation of Allied Geographical Section, South-West Pacific Area, Terrain Study Collection, Monash, University Library, http://map pingsciences.org.au/wp-content/uploads/2015/06/BrowynFoottBarbaraWojtkowski -PreservingHistory.pdf, accessed May 21, 2020.

143   "More could be added on tides": "Minutes of the Planning Meeting for JANIS 157 (Western New Guinea)," The Joint Intelligence Study Publishing Board, Washington, D.C., November 23, 1943, https://www.cia.gov/readingroom/docs/CIA-RDP79 -01147A000100030134-7.pdf, accessed January 5, 2022.

145   "Please thank Miss Sears": Burwell, Lt. Charles L., written correspondence to Lt.

Comdr. B. E. Dodson, July 31, 1943, National Archives, and Records Administration, Washington, D.C., RG 37, Entry 48, Box 124.

145   more of the Oceanographic Unit's research into operational plans: Gurliacci, David, "Former Darien Selectman Charles Burwell's Role in the D-Day Invasion," Darienite .com, June 5, 2019, accessed April 20, 2020.

CHAPTER 11: TARAWA

147   The navy would soften enemy positions before the landing: Cox, Samuel J., "H-025–1: Operation Galvanic—Tarawa and Makin Islands, November 1943," Naval History and Heritage Command, January 31, 2019, accessed June 10, 2020.

147   this kind of large-scale overpowering attack: Alexander, *Storm Landings*, xiii. Naval historian Joseph Alexander referred to these as "storm landings" defined as "risky, long-range, large-scale, self-sustaining assaults executed against strong opposition and within the protective umbrella of fast carrier task forces."

147   "There are no amphibious cakewalks,": Alexander, xiii.

148   "Higgins boats," barge-like vessels: "Higgins Boats," Naval History and Heritage Command, https://www.history.navy.mil/browse-by-topic/exploration-and-innovation /higgins-boats.html, accessed January 2, 2022.

149   the navy adopted the Higgins boat as their standard landing craft: Isely, Jeter A., and Philip A. Crowl, *The U.S. Marines and Amphibious War: Its Theory, and Its Practice in the Pacific* (Princeton, NJ: Princeton University Press, 1951), 68.

149   The daily tidal cycle when the sea rises and falls varies: "What Are Spring and Neap Tides?" https://oceanservice.noaa.gov/facts/springtide.html, accessed December 21, 2021.

150   "The use of the amphibian tractor": Alexander, *Storm Landings*, 46.

150   not nearly enough to transport even half the troops to shore: Isely and Crowl, *U.S. Marines and Amphibious War*, 208.

151   prompting Sherrod to unclasp his watch: Sherrod, Robert, *Tarawa: The Story of a Battle, Fortieth Anniversary Edition* (New York, NY: Bantam Books, 1983), 61.

151   "as soon as I can get an amphtrack for you": Sherrod, 62.

152   "We'd watch these lines of marines climb out of the Higgins boats": Pase, Charles, "Oral History Interview," April 12, 2001, by Floyd Cox, The National Museum of the Pacific War, Center for Pacific War Studies, Fredericksburg, Texas, 12.

152   "It's hell in there,": Sherrod, *Tarawa*, 63.

153   "I could have reached out and touched a hundred bullets,": Sherrod, 64.

153   minimum four feet they needed to clear the reef: Olson, Donald W., "The Tide at Tarawa," *Sky and Telescope Magazine*, November 1987, 526–28.

153   The landing devolved into chaos: Winters, Harold A., *Battling the Elements: Weather and Terrain in the Conduct of the War* (Baltimore, MD: Johns Hopkins University

Press, 1998), 224. Of the 125 amphibious tractors employed at Tarawa, 90 were destroyed.

154   now the fate of the entire mission was in jeopardy: Alexander, *Storm Landings*, 49–50.

154   "We steered our way through them": Pase, Charles, "Oral History Interview," 17–18.

154   by the morning of the third day: Alexander, Joseph H., "Across the Reef: The Assault on Betio," *Naval History Magazine* 22, no. 6 (December 2008). https://www.usni.org/magazines/naval-history-magazine/2008/december/across-reef-assault-betio, accessed December 21, 2021.

155   1,027 were killed and 2,100 were wounded: Alexander, "Across the Reef," https://www.usni.org/magazines/naval-history-magazine/2008/december/across-reef-assault-betio, accessed December 21, 2021.

155   planners were simply guessing at tide variations: Winters, 221.

155   the tides at Tarawa were fully explained: Email to author, November 8, 2019, from Donald W. Olson, Texas State University, explaining that after Tarawa was secured by the marines, the navy stationed a small ship in the lagoon to monitor tide levels with a tide gauge. From this data, Tarawa harmonic constants, necessary for precise tide calculations, were derived.

156   the water level stayed within six inches of its mean level of 3.3 feet: Olson, "The Tide at Tarawa," 526–28.

156   "There had to be a Tarawa,": Alexander, "Across the Reef," https://www.usni.org/magazines/naval-history-magazine/2008/december/across-reef-assault-betio, accessed December 21, 2021.

156   "There were no foxholes offshore": "Vandegrift Backs Method at Tarawa," *The New York Times*, December 18, 1943, 3.

CHAPTER 12: REVERSING THE MANDATE

158   "You killed my son on Tarawa,": Potter, E. B., *Nimitz* (Annapolis, MD: Naval Institute Press, 1976), 264.

159   Each one was its own story: Alexander, *Storm Landings*, 4–5.

159   caused landing craft to be stranded on the coral reef: "Knox Upholds Plan of Tarawa Action," *New York Times*, December 1, 1943.

159   targets in the Philippines: "Agenda for Planning Meeting of JANIS 155," December 7, 1943, https://www.cia.gov/readingroom/docs/CIA-RDP79-01147A000100030132-9.pdf, accessed December 23, 2021.

160   demanded strict adherence to deadlines: Bicknell, George W., "Memoradum to Members of the Board, JISPB," March 30, 1944, https://www.cia.gov/readingroom/docs/CIA-RDP79-01147A000100030094-2.pdf, accessed Dec. 23, 2021.

160   "To obtain positions": "Campaign Plan Granite," January 15, 1944, Commander in Chief, Pacific Ocean Areas, https://archive.org/details/DTIC_ADA606368, December 23, 2021, 1.

162 handed over to Japan under a mandate: "Advanced Base Operations in Micronesia," Dept. of the Navy, Headquarters, United States Marine Corps, Washington, D.C., August 21, 1992, https://www.ibiblio.org/hyperwar/USMC/ref/AdvBaseOps/index.html, accessed February 24, 2020.

162 The Philippines would be cut off from American protection: Campbell, Earnest G., "Japan's Mandate in the Southwestern Pacific," United States Naval Institute Proceedings 68 (June 1942), 829–31.

162 Japan restricted shipping: Wilds, Thomas, "How Japan Fortified the Mandated Islands," *United States Naval Institute Proc.* 81 (April 1955), 401.

162 there were already eight fully outfitted bases: Wilds, 407.

162 Japan's Absolute Defense Sphere: "The Japanese Revise Their Strategy," https://www.ibiblio.org/hyperwar/USA/USA-P-Strategy/Strategy-27.html.

163 The Marianas were a long way from friendly shores: "D-Day," History.com, June 5, 2019, accessed June 10, 2020.

163 Allied hopes in Europe rested on the success of this massive invasion: "D-Day," History.com, June 5, 2019, accessed June 10, 2020.

163 the Germans were at work constructing the Atlantic Wall: Parker, Bruce, *The Power of the Sea* (New York, NY: Palgrave Macmillan, 2010), 43.

164 they would have to predict when low tide: Parker, Bruce, "The Tide Predictions for D-Day," *Physics Today* 64 (September 2011), 39.

164 Doodson used two large tide-predicting machines: Parker, *The Power of the Sea*, 44.

164 Doodson kept them running from early morning to late at night, seven days a week: "The Tide Predictions for D-Day," 45.

165 a location so secret: Parker, "The Tide Predictions for D-Day," 46.

165 Based on Doodson's analysis: Parker, 37–38.

165 the tide predictions proved to be accurate: Parker, "The Tide Predictions for D-Day," 40.

166 Carruthers, Sears's British counterpart: Robinson, Samuel A., *Ocean Science and the British Cold War* (New York, NY: Springer International, 2018), 40–42.

166 D-Day was especially somber at the Hydrographic Office: Huntsberger, 149.

167 The *Mansyu* was a workhorse of her time: "Report on Oceanic Survey in the Western Part of the North Pacific Carried Out by HIJMS *Mansyu* from April 1925 to March 1928," Japanese Hydrographic Department, Tokyo, 1932.

168 the voyage of HMS *Challenger*: Bishop, Tina, P. Tuddenham, M. Ryan, et al., "Then and Now: The HMS *Challenger* Expedition and the 'Mountains in the Sea' Expedition,'" National Oceanic and Atmospheric Administration, https://oceanexplorer.noaa.gov/explorations/03mountains/background/challenger/challenger.html, accessed April 23, 2021.

169 steep-sided volcanic peaks with narrow shelves: "Joint Army Navy Intelligence Study of Marianas Islands," Joint Intelligence Publishing Board, April 1944, III-14, JANIS studies available at the National Archives at College Park, MD, RG 263, Entry A1 47-A, A1 47-B.

170   the offshore coral reef and underwater rock formation lurked offshore: Isley and Crowl, *U.S. Marines and Amphibious* War, 316–17.

170   the marines hoped to escape these dangers: Alexander, *Storm Landings*, 82–85.

170   Operation Forager would be led by: Alexander, *Storm Landings*, 67.

170   "We don't want another blunder like the one at Tarawa,": Blassingame, Wyatt, *U.S. Frogmen of World War II* (New York, NY: Random House, 1964), 5.

171   Turner was asking Kauffman to expose his team to unnecessary risk: Blassingame, 9.

173   plunging waves caught the stern: Alexander, *Storm Landings*, 62–63.

173   The marines had no answer: Alexander, 62–63.

173   "I ran around out there trying to find some way to get in over the reef.": Graves, John, oral history interview by Kep Johnson on December 14, 2003, National Museum of the Pacific War, Center for Pacific War Studies Fredericksburg, Texas, 6.

174   "helpless on the coral reef,": Dana, James D., *Corals and Coral Islands* (London: Sampson Low, Marston & Company, 1875), 102–3.

174   American losses came to sixteen thousand: Alexander, *Storm Landings*, 73.

174   the most horrific and lasting memory of Saipan: Alexander, 72.

175   Knox mandated that Black service members be accepted for general service: Nalty, Bernard C., *The Right to Fight: African-American Marines in World War II*, 1995, https://www.nps.gov/parkhistory/online_books/npswapa/extcontent/usmc/pcn-190 –003132–00/sec14.htm, accessed July 29, 2020.

175   "It was unreal, absolutely unreal. Like a bad dream,": Montford Point Marines: Loyalty and Service in the Face of Prejudice and Discrimination, Randall Library, University of North Carolina, Wilmington, Steven Robinson Interview, June 29, 2005, https://library.uncw.edu/web/montford/transcripts/Robinson_Steven.html, accessed August 7, 2020.

175   "We were fighting the war against the bigotry at home": Montford Point Marines, Steven Robinson Interview, 2005.

176   "The Negro Marines are no longer on trial": Nalty, *The Right to Fight*.

176   The Montford Marines went on to serve at all three invasions: Altman, Alex, "Were African-Americans at Iwo Jima?" *Time.com*, June 10, 2008, accessed July 30, 2020.

176   Segregation in the military would continue: "America's First Black Marines: The Montford Pointers," *ShareAmerica.com*, June 19, 2020, accessed July 30, 2020.

177   "mostly rough and broken": "Joint Army Navy Intelligence Study of Marianas Islands," Joint Intelligence Publishing Board, April 1944, III-11.

177   a model amphibious assault: "Joint Army Navy Intelligence Study of Marianas Islands," III-14; Alexander, *Storm Landings*, 82–85; Isley and Crowl, *U.S. Marines and Amphibious War*, 391. The air force base on Tinian would be the takeoff point for the *Enola Gay*, equipped with an atomic bomb destined for Hiroshima.

CHAPTER 13: THE OCEANOGRAPHIC UNIT DIGS IN

179   *"Scuttlebutt* extends its deepest sympathies": *Scuttlebutt,* Hydrographic Office, Suitland, MD, June 15, 1945, 2.

179   "killed last week in an aeroplane crash.": *Scuttlebutt,* June 19, 1944, 8.

179   "killed in action off the Philippines": *Scuttlebutt,* January 27, 1945, 7.

180   "Best of luck, Chief.": *Scuttlebutt,* April 13, 1945, 4.

180   The *Sumner* was the first ship in the vicinity: "USS *Sumner,* Report of Pearl Harbor Attack," https://www.history.navy.mil/research/archives/digital-exhibits-highlights /action-reports/wwii-pearl-harbor-attack/ships-s-z/uss-sumner-ag-32-action-report .html, accessed on February 4, 2020, quoting from USS *Sumner* (AG-32) Action Report, December 11, 1941.

181   narrowly escaped crippling damage to its rudder: Bates, Charles C., *"Hydro" to "Navoceano": 175 Years of Ocean Survey and Prediction by the U.S. Navy, 1830–2005* (Rockton, IL: Corn Field Press, 2005), 75–78.

182   "I stayed up all last night": Sears Interview, Smith, 1982, 2–36.

183   "It went off into the blue and you never knew.": Sears Interview, Smith, 1982, 2–143.

183   "military necessity does not wait for explorers and scientists": Sears, Mary, "Expansion of Oceanographic Work in the U.S. Navy Hydrographic Office During and Following World War II," 23, undated document, Sears Papers, WHOI Archives.

185   They were able to find a wide range of references: Peiss, Kathy, "Why the U.S. Sent Librarians Undercover to Gather Intelligence During World War II," *Time.com,* January 3, 2020, accessed June 30, 2020.

185   she didn't know where they would have found all the oceanographic publications: Sears Interview, Smith, 1982, 2–31.

186   The bibliography included articles like: Grier, *Oceanography of the North Pacific Ocean,* 65.

186   With his marine biology background, Emperor Hirohito: "Emperor Hirohito: The Marine Biologist Who Ruled Japan," *History of Oceanography,* https://oceanscience history.com/2015/08/15/emperor-hirohito-the-marine-biologist-who-ruled-japan/, accessed April 25, 2021.

187   The enlisted WAVES had found a cornucopia: JANIS 103, Chapter III: "Joint Army-Navy Intelligence Study of Palau Islands, Oceanography, Coasts and Landing Places," April 1944, Joint Intelligence Study Publishing Board, United States Government, III-52.

188   Operation Stalemate to capture the Palau Islands: Isely and Crowl, *U.S. Marines and Amphibious War,* 392.

188   "this is going to be a short one, a quickie.": Isely and Crowl, 396.

190   *Submarine Supplements to the Sailing Directions*: "Summer Supplement to Hydrographic Office Publications No. 122, 123, and 124, The Japanese Empire Area: June, July, and August," Hydrographic Office, United States Navy Department, May, 1944, 1.

190   observations from submarine patrols: "Summer Supplement," 45, 57.

191   background noise levels: JANIS 103, Chapter III, III-12.

192   bioluminescence in the region: JANIS 103, Chapter III, III-13.

192   Joint Pacific Intelligence Center, Pacific Ocean Areas (JICPOA): Moore, Jeff M., "JICPOA: Joint Intelligence During WW II," *Military Intelligence Professional Bulletin*, July–September, 1995, 35–39.

193   spotty aerial reconnaissance: Peto, George, and Peter Margaritis, *Twenty-two on Peleliu, Four Pacific Campaigns with the Corps: The Memoirs of an Old Breed Marine* (Havertown, PA: Casemate Publishers, 2017), 181.

193   Peto climbed down a ladder inside the LST: Peto and Margaritis, *Twenty-two on Peleliu*, 187.

193   LVTs started to grind over the limestone surface: Alexander, *Storm Landings*, 110–11.

194   The marines were pinned down: Peto and Margaritis, *Twenty-two on Peleliu*, 191–92.

194   "Back on the reef I saw burning amtracs and struggling marines": Alexander, *Storm Landings*, 117.

195   "It was a terrible, terrible landing.": Brehmer, Oris A., oral history interview by Richard Minsenhimer, September 27, 2013, The National Museum of the Pacific War, Center for Pacific War Studies, Fredericksburg, Texas, 16.

195   "a young marine on the side of me that got hit": McCoy, Giles Gilbert, oral history interview by Mike Zambrano, August 21, 2007, The National Museum of the Pacific War, Center for Pacific War Studies, Fredericksburg, Texas, 14.

195   The vicious, bloody fight to take Peleliu lasted ten weeks: Alexander, *Storm Landings*, 124.

197   Nimitz's chief strategist, Admiral Forrest P. Sherman: Memo from Adm. Forrest P. Sherman, Dep. Chief of Staff, CINCPAC to Cpt. C. G. Moore, Chair JTS, December 18, 1944, https://www.cia.gov/readingroom/docs/CIA-RDP79-01147A000100010012-4.pdf, accessed January 4, 2022, 1–2.

CHAPTER 14: NARROWING THE PATH TO VICTORY

199   wide lapels and cuffed trousers gave way: Milbank, Caroline Rennolds, "How the War Wore on Us," *Chicago Tribune*, December 1, 1991, https://www.chicagotribune.com/news/ct-xpm-1991-12-01-9104180592-story.html, accessed May 7, 2021.

199   Gasoline rationing followed tire rationing: Goodwin, *No Ordinary Time*, 357.

199   The carpooling boom caught on: *Scuttlebutt*, October 21, 1944, 6.

200   "gloomy in winter and hot in the summer": Goodwin, *No Ordinary Time*, 98.

200   "Mrs. Roosevelt shook hands with each of us": Huntsberger, *I'll Be Seeing You*, 136.

201   Bicknell turned up the heat on the contributors: "Memorandum # 30," The Joint Intelligence Publishing Board, March 15, 1944, https://www.cia.gov/readingroom/docs/CIA-RDP79-01147A000300020012-1.pdf, accessed December 25, 2021; and "Minutes of the 56ᵗʰ Meeting: Planning Meeting for JANIS 87," The Joint Intelligence

Publishing Board, March 15, 1944, https://www.cia.gov/readingroom/docs/CIA-RD P79-01147A000100030102-2.pdf, accessed December 25, 2021.

202   Formosa was an enticing target: JANIS 87, "Joint Army-Navy Intelligence Study of Formosa (Taiwan)," Joint Intelligence Study Publishing Board, June, 1944, I-3.

203   she worried about the accuracy of her calculations: Sears, Mary, "Beginnings," 15.

203   steering clear of any mention of the exact location: Sears Interview, Smith, 1982, 2–31.

204   Others were not so careful: Sears Interview, Smith, 1982, 2–31.

204   "handsome box . . . faced with white Georgia marble,": Robins, Rae, "Public Soon to Have Use of White Marble Annex to Nation's Great Library," Sunday Star, Washington, D.C., November 13, 1938—Part Two, accessed May 10, 2021.

205   library placed special emphasis: MacLeish, Archibald, "Annual Reports of the Librarian of Congress," 1941/1942–1943/1944, Washington, D.C., U.S. Government Printing Office, 1941–1945.

206   about her alleged Communist Party activities: Memo regarding "Mary Catherine Grier," from C. E. Owens to Louis J. Russell, Chief Investigator (HUAC), dated February 26, 1953, National Archives and Records Administration, Washington, D.C., RG 233, Box 22, 6.

206   "I went to the library to hunt for what they might need.": "Hearings Before the Committee on Un-American Activities, House of Representatives," Eighty-Third Congress, First Session, February 25, 26, 27, 1953, 1604.

207   "I never discussed it with anyone outside of the office,": "Hearings Before the Committee on Un-American Activities," 1598.

208   seventeen major textual sources: JANIS 87, "Joint Army-Navy Intelligence Study of Formosa (Taiwan)," Joint Intelligence Study Publishing Board, June, 1944, introductory memorandum dated June 30, 1944.

209   oceanographers had highlighted several major areas of concern: JANIS 87, Chapter III, III–16.

209   whether American forces should take Formosa: Frank, Bennis M., and Henry I. Shaw, Jr., "Volume V, Victory and Occupation," History of the U.S. Marine Corps Operations in World War II, Historical Branch, G-3, Headquarters, United States Marine Corp., https://www.ibiblio.org/hyperwar/USMC/V/USMC-V-I-1.html.

209   Formosa was the more desirable target: "Operation Causeway: the Invasion That Never Was," https://sites.google.com/site/operationcauseway/, accessed December 25, 2021.

211   The JANIS report on the Philippines: JANIS 154, Chapter III, "Joint Army-Navy Intelligence Study of Philippines (Except Mindanao) Oceanography," July 1944 154, III-12 to III-21.

211   Sears was able to make general prognostications: Sears, Mary "Expansion of Oceanographic Work in the U.S. Navy Hydrographic Office during and following World War II," undated, ten-page page document, WHOI Archives, Sears Papers, 5.

212   to identify safe alternative landing sites: Smith, Robert Ross, The War in the Pacific:

Triumph in the Philippines, Center of Military History, United States Army, Washington, D.C., 1993, 31.

212 carried the sarcasm to a new level: *Scuttlebutt,* February 17, 1945, 10.

213 "Christmas Mary": Private communication between the author and Leslie Sears Karpp, October 13, 2020.

213 on doorsteps for neighborhood children: Private communication between the author and Wendy Nies, October 14, 2020.

213–214 "We hope to be able to celebrate the next year in the States.": *Scuttlebutt,* November, 25, 1944, 5.

214 "Men working, fighting and dying": *Scuttlebutt,* December 22, 1944, 2.

214 As Sears had predicted, gentle swells: Smith, *The War in the Pacific,* 73–77.

CHAPTER 15: FLYING BLIND IN IWO JIMA

215 Iwo Jima might have been an ugly duckling: Alexander, *Storm Landings,* 127–31.

216 limited reports on Iwo Jima: Untitled, undated document from CIA FOIA website listing oceanographic publications generated by the Hydrographic Offfice during World War II, https://www.cia.gov/readingroom/docs/CIA-RDP79-01147A000200050073-2 .pdf, accessed December 24, 2021.

217 frank warnings of "sheer and forbidding cliffs": *Sailing Directions for Nanpo Shoto,* H.O. Pub. No. 1232, United States Navy Department, Hydrographic Office, January 1945, 2–3.

217 "*With a swell, landing is impossible.*": *ONI 60, Geographic Monograph of Formosa, Nansei Shoto (Southwestern Islands) and Nanpo Shoto (Islands South of Honshu), Part 1, Nanpo Shoto,* Office of Chief of Naval Operations, Division of Naval Intelligence, September 13, 1942, 24, 157.

217 American military commanders were feeling confident: "Amphibious Operations: Capture of Iwo Jima 16 February to 16 March 1945," Chapter IV, Intelligence, 4–1, https://www.ibiblio.org/hyperwar/USN/rep/Iwo/Cominch/Iwo-4.html, accessed December 24, 2021.

218 advised the use of Marston mats: "Iwo Jima: First Supplement to Nanpo Shoto Information Bulletin No. 122–44, October 10, 1944," CINCPAC-CINCPOA Bulletin No. 9–45, United States Pacific Fleet and Pacific Ocean Areas, January 10, 1945, 12–13.

218 The steel sections were perforated: Mola, Roger, "These Portable Runways Helped Win the War in the Pacific," AirSpaceMag.com, April 29, 2014, https://www.airspace mag.com/multimedia/these-portable-runways-helped-win-war-pacific-180951234/, accessed June 6, 2020, stating that two million tons of temporary runway were produced in World War II and that it has been used in every war since.

218 "I told our skipper that was the wrong beach for us to be going in on,": Anderson, Art G., oral history interview by Leon R. Smith and Ross Smith, August 1, 1986, The National Museum of the Pacific War, Center for Pacific War Studies, Fredericksburg, Texas, 2.

219   the marines sent in frogmen to assess the beaches: Blassingame, *U.S. Frogmen of World War II*, 119. States that the UDTs made a mistake because a few feet beyond the waterline the sand was "powder fine." Art Anderson's version conflicts with that of Joseph Alexander's (*Storm Landings*, 136) where Alexander states that planners knew in advance that Iwo's steep beach and loose volcanic sand would "complicate the movement of vehicles" and that they "worked furiously to improve beach trafficability."

219   "We did more crawling than anything else.": Nardecchia, Bud, oral history interview by Steve Whitson, February 18, 2005, The National Museum of the Pacific War, Center for Pacific War Studies, Fredericksburg, Texas, 14.

219   Exhausted marines crawled on all fours: Isely and Crowl, *The U.S. Marines and Amphibious War*, 478–79.

220   the marines were unable to flee or dig foxholes: Cox, Samuel J., "H-042–1: 'Nightmare in Hell'—The Battle for Iwo Jima, February–March 1945," Naval History and Heritage Command, February 2020, https://www.history.navy.mil/content/history/nhhc/about-us/leadership/director/directors-corner/h-grams/h-gram-042/h-042–1.html, accessed December 24, 2021.

220   "you'd go up and you'd slide back,": Talmage, Arthur, oral history interview by Charlie Simmons, October 19, 2012, The National Museum of the Pacific War, Center for Pacific War Studies, Fredericksburg, Texas, 25.

220   "Nowhere in the Pacific War had I seen such badly mangled bodies.": Alexander, *Storm Landings*, 142.

220   "just throw it up on the beach like kindling wood": Anderson, Art G., The National Museum of the Pacific War, Center for Pacific War Studies, 2.

221   The beach looked like a salvage yard: Alexander, Joseph, "The Battle of Iwo Jima: A 36-Day Bloody Slog on a Sulfuric Island," *World War II Magazine*, February 2000, https://www.militarytimes.com/news/2018/02/17/the-battle-of-iwo-jima-a-36-day-bloody-slog-on-a-sulfuric-island/, accessed May 12, 2021.

221   In his after-action report: "Amphibious Operations: Capture of Iwo Jima 16 February to 16 March 1945," Chapter I, Narrative, 1–7, https://www.history.navy.mil/research/library/online-reading-room/title-list-alphabetically/a/amphibious-operations-capture-iwo-jima.html, accessed April 7, 2020.

221   The preliminary observations of the underwater demolition team: "Amphibious Operations: Capture of Iwo Jima 16 February to 16 March 1945," Chapter IV, Intelligence, 4–3, https://www.history.navy.mil/research/library/online-reading-room/title-list-alphabetically/a/amphibious-operations-capture-iwo-jima.html, accessed April 7, 2020.

223   they sent in their best civil engineers to design a web of hillside caves: Alexander, *Storm Landings*, 131–32.

223   the only major Pacific battle where American forces sustained more casualties than the Japanese: Isely and Crowl, *The U.S. Marines and Amphibious War*, 529.

223   "I hope that I will not get too many letters cursing me": Potter, *Nimitz*, 367.

224   They participated in a war bond drive: Cox, "H-042–1: 'Nightmare in Hell'—The Battle for Iwo Jima, February–March 1945." Despite the success of the fundraising drive, questions were later raised about the identities of the men credited with

raising the flag, see Dwyer, Colin, "Marines Confirm Decades-Old Case of Mistaken Identity in Iwo Jima Photo," NPR.org, June 23, 2016, https://www.npr.org/sections /thetwo-way/2016/06/23/483235411/marines-confirm-decades-old-case-of-mistaken -identity-in-iwo-jima-photo, accessed December 24, 2021. See also, "Joe Rosenthal and the Flag- Raising on Iwo Jima, https://www.pulitzer.org/article/joe-rosenthal-and-flag -raising-iwo-jima, noting that the photo helped raise $26 billion.

CHAPTER 16: PENETRATING THE ZONE OF SAFETY

225   "Spring brings new hope to the world,": *Scuttlebutt*, April 13, 1945, 8.

226   Spring also brought the revival of outdoor sports: *Scuttlebutt*, March 17, 1945, 2.

226   The WAVES had "scooped the spring season for hats": *Scuttlebutt*, January 20, 1945, 3.

226   *The Fighting Lady*, a documentary: *The Fighting Lady*, Twentieth Century-Fox, Hollywood, California, 1944.

228   "The efficiency and promptness with which the Hydrographic Office": Hydro Administrative History, 259.

228   Okinawa's capture would afford access to air bases: Appleman, Roy, James M. Burns, Russell A. Gugeler, and John Stevens: *Okinawa: The Last Battle*, (Washington D.C.: The Center for Military History, the United States Army, 1948), 40.

229   American planners expected to encounter defenses in depth: Floyd, Dale E., "Cave Warfare on Okinawa," in *Builders and Fighters: U.S. Army Engineers in World War II*, ed. Barry W. Fowle (Honolulu, Hawaii: University Press of the Pacific, 2005), 393–402.

229   American forces had captured sixty Japanese charts: Hydro Administrative History, 240.

230   three hundred and thirty-three available beaches: "JANIS 86: Revised Estimate of Nansei-Shoto," Joint Intelligence Publishing Board, Washington, D.C., August 1, 1944, 3.

230   Naval commanders favored landing on the beaches of Hagushi: Dyer, George Carroll, and Ernest McNeill Eller, *The Amphibians Came to Conquer: The Story of Admiral Richmond Kelly Turner*, United States Department of the Navy, Washington, D.C., 1972, 1076.

230   "each was fringed with a coral reef": Dyer and Eller, 1077.

231   Roosevelt expanded the armed forces: Goodwin, *No Ordinary Time*, 608.

232   Admiral Nimitz was taking no chances with the pivotal Okinawa offensive: Alexander, *Storm Landings*, 150.

232   the battle for Okinawa exceeded all others in the numbers of men and tonnage shipped: Appleman and Burns, *Okinawa: The Last Battle*, appendix C, tables 4 and 5.

233   On the night before Love-Day of the Battle of Okinawa: Dyer and Eller, *The Amphibians Came to Conquer*, 1080.

233   "We would take Okinawa,": Pyle, Ernie, *Last Chapter* (New York, NY: Henry Holt and Co., 1946), 74.

234 A press boat sailed by with Ernie Pyle: Wellman, William F., Oral History interview by Richard Misenhimer on October 19, 2007, The National Museum of the Pacific War, Center for Pacific War Studies, Fredericksburg, Texas, 17.

234 the largest convoy of marines and soldiers launched in the Pacific: Isley and Crowl, *The U.S. Marines and Amphibious War*, 557.

235 observing the flight patterns of seabirds: Blanchard, Duncan C., "The Life and Science of Alfred H. Woodcock," *Bulletin American Meteorological Society* 65, May 1984, 458–59.

235 smoke generated by fog-oil generators behaved similar to the birds: Blanchard, 458–59.

236 "People lived in it, slept in it.": "Oceanographic Smoke Screen Covers Anchorage at Assault on Okinawa," undated article from the *Falmouth Enterprise*.

236 "Smoke was made at sunset, and every morning and evening": Memo from Commanding Officer (USS LST 227) to Commander-in-Chief, U.S. Fleet, "War Diary for April 1945," USS LST 227, April 1, 1945, 2, Naval History and Heritage Command.

236 there was no way to hide from all the kamikazes: Isely and Crowl, *The U.S. Marines and Amphibious War*, 558.

236 The Japanese also deployed suicide boats: Dyer and Eller, *The Amphibians Came to Conquer*, 1088.

236 He saw no dead bodies, no wounded, not even the wreckage: Pyle, *Last Chapter*, 82.

237 "It was a bad day for us. He was one of us,": Wellman, Oral History, 29.

237 a strong front moved in on April 4: Dyer and Eller, *The Amphibians Came to Conquer*, 1095.

238 Okinawa would be remembered as one of the bloodiest battles of the war: Dyer and Eller, 1104.

CHAPTER 17: CLOSING IN ON VICTORY

239 "I have a terrific pain in the back of my head,": Michaelis, David, *Eleanor* (New York, NY: Simon & Schuster, 2020), 428.

239 The president had succumbed: Brinkley, *Washington Goes to War*, 272.

239 "Is there anything *we* can do for *you*? For you're the one in trouble now.": Michaelis, *Eleanor*, 430.

240 Truman felt like he had been "struck by a bolt of lightning.": Walsh, Kenneth T., "The First 100 Days: Harry Truman Showed Decisiveness and Intelligence," U.S. News & World Report, February 26, 2009, https://www.usnews.com/news/history /articles/2009/02/26/the-first-100-days-harry-truman-showed-decisiveness-and -intelligence?context=amp, accessed December 25, 2021.

240 "All of Washington is so upset over the president's death": Huntsberger, *I'll Be Seeing You*, 194.

240 "the whole world has lost and mourns a great man.": *Scuttlebutt*, United States Hydrographic Office, April 13, 1945, 2.

241   The Germans surrendered: Brinkley, *Washington Goes to War*, 275.

241   "We must work to finish the war.": Brinkley, 275.

241   The Joint Chiefs estimated casualties of 250,000 to 1,000,000 American troops: Alexander, *Storm Landings*, 173–74. See also, Robert H. Ferrell, *Harry S. Truman and the Bomb: A Documentary History* (Worland, WY: High Plains Publishing, 1996,) 106.

242   "I don't want to conduct another Okinawa": Alexander, *Storm Landings*, 174.

242   The board had issued a new priority schedule for the Japanese Islands: Kountze, George H., "Janis Memorandum #41," The Joint Intelligence Study Publishing Board, May 16, 1944, https://www.cia.gov/readingroom/docs/CIA-RDP79-01147A000300040005-7.pdf, accessed December 25, 2021.

244   "Let's give 'em out there that extra push to hasten victory,": *Scuttlebutt*, United States Hydrographic Office, June 2, 1945, 2.

244   "the Hydrographic Office is the center for all oceanographic research of the Army and Navy": *Scuttlebutt*, July 14, 1945, 3.

244   "the Silent Service" in the Pacific: "War in the Pacific: The Pacific Offensive," *A Guide to the War in the Pacific*, https://www.nps.gov/parkhistory/online_books/npswapa/extContent/wapa/guides/offensive/sec3.htm, accessed August 5, 2021.

245   Larger trucks and tanks, though, would have no chance: JANIS 84, Chapter I, "Joint Army-Navy Intelligence Study of Southwest Japan: Kyushu, Shikoku, and Southwestern Honshu, Brief," Joint Intelligence Study Publishing Board, August 1944, I-6.

246   strong local currents that could affect small boats: JANIS 84, Chapter III, III-1.

246   "the sound of screws,": Schlee, *The Edge of an Unfamiliar World*, 300–301.

246   the Americans assembled troops, ships, and equipment for Operation Olympic: Alexander, *Storm Landings*, 183–84.

247   "The test was successful": Groves, Leslie R., to Henry Stimson, "Memorandum for the Secretary of War, July 18, 1945," The Harry S. Truman Library and Museum, Independence, Missouri, The Decision to Drop the Atomic Bomb Collection, 1, https://www.trumanlibrary.gov/library/research-files/leslie-r-groves-henry-stimson?documentid=NA&pagenumber=1, accessed April 18, 2020.

247   The United States would warn Japan: Ferrell, *Harry S. Truman and the Bomb*, 31.

248   The declaration went unanswered: Ferrell, 37–39.

248   "The force from which the sun draws its power": Ferrell, 48.

248   "Cheers from crowds": *Daily News*, August 15, 1945, 10.

248   "This capital city . . . relaxed its worn nerves": "Celebration of V-J Day, 08/14/1945," The National Archives, https://unwritten-record.blogs.archives.gov/2013/08/13/celebration-of-v-j-day-08141945/, accessed December 20, 2021.

248   "We knelt in the sand and cried.": Alexander, *Storm Landings*, 192.

EPILOGUE

248   overt military hostilities ended: "Japan Surrenders!" https://www.history.com/this
-day-in-history/japan-surrenders, accessed July 15, 2020, stating that the Japanese
agreed to surrender on this date, although the official surrender declaration would be
signed on September 2, 1945.

249   locate prisoners of war and to air-drop food: *Basic Outline Plan for Blacklist Operations to Occupy Japan Proper and Korea After Surrender or Collapse*, Annex 5 f,
"Evacuation of Allied Prisoners of War and Civilian Internees," 1–8, General Headquarters, United States Army Forces, Pacific, August 8, 1945, Archive.org. accessed
April 27, 2020.

250   Ridge's high praise of JANIS 84: Ridge, T. L., Lt. Col., in memo to Chief of Naval
Operations re: "Joint Army and Navy Intelligence Studies (JANIS), Comments and
Recommendations Thereon," October 29, 1945, 1.

252   "Your performance of all these duties was at all times exceptional, and beyond the
high standard normally expected.": Nimitz, C. W. to Lt. Commander Mary Sears, (W),
USNR. re. "Commendation," May 20, 1946, from Sears military records, Denton Papers, Woods Hole, MA.

253   "Commander Mary Sears, USNR (W) (1905–1997) established a small oceanographic
unit in the Hydrographic Office during World War II": Danzig, Richard, memo re.
"Assignment of a Name to a Surveying Ship," (SECNAV Notice 5050) October 7, 1999,
Department of the Navy, Washington, D.C.

254   "She was the conscience of oceanography": Revelle, Roger, "The Oceanographic and
How it Grew," presented at the Third International Congress on the History of Oceanography: September 22–26, 1980, WHOI, Woods Hole, MA.

254   "She has done as much for the advancement of oceanography": Iselin, Columbus O.,
"Iselin Personal History," Woods Hole Oceanographic Institution Archive, Columbus
O'Donnell Iselin Papers, undated.

255   "one of the most influential carcinologists of the twentieth century,": Lemaitre, Rafael, "Remarks on the Life and Works of Fenner A. Chace, Jr. (1908–2004), with a List
of His Taxa and Compete Bibliography," *Crustaceana* 78, 2005, 622.

255   Henry described eleven new species of barnacles: McLaughlin, Patsy A., Anita Whitney, Arnold Ross, Alan J. Southward, and William A. Newman, "Dora Priaulx Henry:
24 May 1904–16 June 1999," *The Journal of Crustacean Biology*, 20, no. 1, 2000, 199–
203.

256   selected Dora Henry to christen: McLaughlin, P. A., and S. Gilchrist, "Women's Contributions to Carcinology," 165–207.

256   chief analyst on the project staff of the Arctic Institute of North America: *Arctic Bibliography*, The United States Department of Defense, Washington, D.C., 1953, 1.

256   put her bibliography skills to good use once again: Eckel, Edwin B., "The Geological
Society of American: Life History of a Learned Society" (Boulder, CO: Geological Society of America, 1982), 92.

256   Revelle posited that carbon dioxide from fossil fuels: Munk, Walter H., "Tribute to
Roger Revelle and His Contribution to Studies of Carbon Dioxide and Climate

Change," *Proceedings of the National Academy of Sciences* 94, https://www.pnas.org
/content/94/16/8275 , accessed December 25, 2021, 8275–8279.

257   "Because the Federal Government has very little memory": Revelle, Roger, "How Mary
      Sears Changed the United States Navy," *Deep-Sea Research* 32(7A), 753–754, Revelle
      credited Sears, even though he was also an oceanographer in the navy because she
      held the formal title first, when the position was created after the war.

257   "There is still so much we don't know.": "Welcome to the Naval Oceanographic Of-
      fice," United States Navy, https://www.cnmoc.usff.navy.mil/navoceano/, accessed
      June 18, 2020.

257   "the most widely used intelligence document": "National Intelligence Survey Pro-
      gram 1948–1968," The Directorate of Intelligence Historical Series, CIA Historical
      Staff of the Central Intelligence Agency, September 1969, https://archive.org/details
      /NationalIntelligenceSurveyProgram1948-1968/C01421957/page/n0/mode/2up, ac-
      cessed on April 25, 2020.

Photo Insert Credits

Index